The New Torchlight List

ALSO BY JAMES R. (JIM) FLYNN

THE MODERN WORLD
The Torchlight List: Around the world in 200 books
How to Improve Your Mind: Twenty keys to unlock the modern world
Senza alibi: Il cambiamento climatico—impedire la catastrophe
(English title: *No place to hide:*
Spend an evening to learn about climate change)

PHILOSOPHY
Fate and Philosophy: A journey through life's great questions
Humanism and Ideology: An Aristotelian view
How to Defend Humane Ideals: Substitutes for objectivity

INTELLIGENCE
What Is Intelligence? Beyond the Flynn Effect
Are We Getting Smarter? Rising IQ in the twenty-first century
Intelligence and Human Progress:
The story of what was hidden in our genes
Does Your Family Make You Smarter?:
Nature, nurture, and human autonomy
Race, IQ, and Jensen
Asian Americans: Achievement beyond IQ

AMERICAN POLITICS
American Politics: A radical view
Where Have All the Liberals Gone? Race, class, and ideals in America
Beyond Patriotism: From Truman to Obama

POETRY
O God Who has a Russian Soul:
Poems about New Zealand and its people

The New Torchlight List

IN SEARCH OF THE
BEST MODERN AUTHORS

JIM FLYNN

AWA PRESS

First edition published in 2016 by Awa Press,
Unit 1, Level 3, 11 Vivian Street, Wellington 6011, New Zealand.

ISBN 978-1-927249-44-4

Ebook formats
Epub 978-1-927249-45-1
Mobi 978-1-927249-46-8

A catalogue record for this book is available from the
National Library of New Zealand.

Cover photograph by Maxim Chuvashov, Getty Images
Book design by Keely O'Shannessy
Typesetting by Tina Delceg
This book is typeset in Minion Pro

Printed by 1010 Printing Group Ltd, China

Discover more great books and authors at awapress.com.

Produced with the assistance of

ARTS COUNCIL OF NEW ZEALAND TOI AOTEAROA

To my mother

Mae Flynn (née Fanny Mae Scott)

(1891–1983)

[The artist] speaks to our capacity for delight and wonder, to the sense of mystery surrounding our lives; to our sense of pity, and beauty, and pain ... to the subtle but invincible conviction of solidarity that knits together the loneliness of innumerable hearts ... which binds together all humanity—the dead to the living and the living to the unborn.
JOSEPH CONRAD, 1897

When I say it is a pure piece of fiction, it is because the story speaks for itself: The writer does not come between his story and the reader.
V.S. NAIPAUL, 1980

I think always people will be reading [novels] but it will be a small group of people. Maybe more people than now read Latin poetry, but somewhere in that range. ... To read a novel requires a certain amount of concentration, focus, devotion to the reading.
PHILIP ROTH, 2009

CONTENTS

LITERATURE AND ITS USES

A young man recently helped me check out a book at the library. I asked him if he had ever read the author. He replied, "Actually, I haven't read a book since I finished my English major." This young man is not alone. Thanks to the National Endowment for the Arts, we have data on reading patterns in the United States from 1984 to 2004. Among seventeen year olds, the percentage who rarely or never read for pleasure increased in these two decades from nine to nineteen. The percentage who read almost every day fell from thirty-one to twenty-two.

You might think a university education would provide an antidote. It is actually counterproductive. Of the high school seniors circa 2001, forty-nine percent read little—less than one hour a week—or nothing for pleasure; for university seniors of 2005 the NEA figure was sixty-three percent.

As might be expected, the very ability of these young people to read prose is eroding. Those who earned a bachelor's degree and could read with reasonable proficiency declined over the decade between 1992 and 2003 from forty percent to thirty-one.

Despite the spread of tertiary education, I believe we are rearing a generation which has too little knowledge of history. This is unfortunate. People who live only in the bubble of the present can be too easily manipulated by their governments and media. They can become cynical but lack the depth of knowledge and awareness needed to be a critic. George Orwell thought a manipulative state would have to rewrite history. He was mistaken: if people know no history they are already captive minds.

In compiling my 2010 book *The Torchlight List* I had the advantage of knowing which books are considered classics—books that have appealed to readers decade after decade, or generation after generation. After I finished that book I decided it might be interesting to try to find some modern classics. I spent a few hours almost every evening for six years reading a total of over 400 books by writers who are still active, or have been until recently, or have been translated into English in the last few years.

Here you have my picks. I recommend 207 books, almost all by contemporary authors. They include seventeen that were covered in *The Torchlight List* because without them the contribution of these authors could not be evaluated. They also include a few books of longer standing, which are so good no one would want to miss them. Some contemporary authors have written only one good book, while others, more rarely, are artists so outstanding that almost everything they write is superb. I have sometimes provided historical background on nations that will help you put the books into context.

I have been pleased with the reception of *The Torchlight List*. Most of those for whom it was intended liked it, including many teachers and librarians desperate to get young people to read. In New Zealand some schools have introduced a "Torchlight Certificate", which they give to students when they read a certain number of books from the list. They believe this enhances the "wide reading requirement" that high school students must fulfill in years twelve and thirteen.

Those who criticized the book tended to be people who wanted their own favorite books listed, or wanted books to be included purely on the basis of literary merit. They should each write their own list. Others showed a complete lack of awareness of what would turn off a new reader. They wanted me to tell them to read Thucydides, Herodotus, Dante, Don Quixote, and so forth. Appreciating books like these comes after you learn to love reading.

Others have asked me if I read mainly to become historically and politically informed. Of course not: like anyone else I read mainly for pleasure. But I welcome becoming better informed as a bonus. They also asked whether I regretted having omitted certain books and if I had read new books that, had I been aware of them at the time, I would have included. The answer to both questions is yes.

So you have in front of you a few second thoughts but mainly the best of my reading since 2010. Like its predecessor, this book is intended for two sorts of people: those who read little but are willing to try and read more, and those who love reading and want to spread their wings a bit—for example, to sample books in translation from countries with which they are not familiar.

I claim no credentials as a literary critic: for me a book just needs to have an interesting plot, convincing characters, and a coherent style. I have a repugnance for new-age stuff, sophomoric philosophizing, the showing off of erudition, and the latest linguistic and stylistic gimmicks. In other words I prefer novelists who write for readers rather than for other novelists. Sample a few books I recommend and a few I do not, and decide for yourself. At a minimum, you should find some good writers of whose existence you were unaware. And I doubt very much that anyone would enjoy all of the novels I felt were a waste of my time. You might find at least some were a waste of your time as well.

I classify authors primarily by their nation of origin but there are exceptions. Some have written novels set in several countries and I had to decide where it was most appropriate to list them. Travel writers almost always range across nations and continents and I sometimes placed them according to their subject matter. Within sections, authors are placed in order of birth.

A final note: I give a book a star if I think it a worthwhile read; at times I qualify this by adding an R to indicate it may appeal only to a restricted readership. I award two stars when I am confident a book will become a classic. Only time will tell if I am right.

NORTH AMERICA

Patricia Highsmith (1921–1995)
Some critics hail Highsmith as part of a tradition that began with Dostoevsky. Setting Dostoevsky aside, she does not quite capture either a time or a person who epitomizes a time in a way that rivals F. Scott Fitzgerald in *The Great Gatsby* or C.P. Snow (no apologies for citing him even though he is out of fashion).

The Talented Mr. Ripley ★ (1955) is not a great novel but it is a minor tour de force. It portrays the inner life of a man who has a moral deficiency but is more interesting than a mere sociopath. Ripley is not without any morals. He is capable of a peculiar kind of pity, but this is overridden by a sense of righteousness when he kills out of self-interest, particularly anyone he finds unsympathetic. The realization of how peculiar he is comes slowly and is well crafted. Chapter Five is outstanding: the core of the man's character is captured by his attitudes toward his "friends" and his being reduced to tears by an unexpected gift. There are, however, too many introspective passages pondering whether or not his crimes will escape detection.

Truman Capote (1924–1984)
Capote's style reached maturity in 1958 with his novella *Breakfast at Tiffany's* ★. The writing in this is excellent, and

the central character, a young woman in New York trying to get a rich husband and have fun along the way, has touching moments of self-knowledge. His 1966 novel *In Cold Blood*★★ is riveting. I have no sympathy with the mass media's steady diet of lurid images of people being killed, but Capote elevated the story of the 1959 murder of a Kansas farm family to high art. Nothing I say can adequately convey how clothed in beauty is the prose concerning the inevitable destruction of decent people, particularly the sixteen-year old daughter.

It's a pity Capote never completed another novel: after his death only a novel written when he was a juvenile and an unfinished novel appeared; neither were particularly good.

Capote was also a screenwriter. Along with John Huston, he wrote the script for the terrific comic film *Beat the Devil*, which starred Humphrey Bogart, Jennifer Jones, Gina Lollobrigida, Robert Morley, Peter Lorre, Ivor Barnard, who is perfect as a demented fascist, and Manuel Serrano. Serrano is truly great as an Arab official who longs for Paris. When he asks if it would be more chic to drive a Rolls-Royce or a Bentley, Bogart tells him that a man of his standing would of course have both.

I now turn to new books, and often new authors, I have read over the last five years.

Russell Hoban (1925–2011)

Russell Hoban left the United States for London at the age of forty-four. He wrote sixteen adult novels and won a cult following partially based on their supernatural elements.

The two novels I admire are set in London, although the second has an American as one of its two major characters. Both are devoid of the supernatural.

Turtle Diary (1975) is a good but not outstanding novel about two lonely people who have given up on life and cooperate to liberate three giant turtles from a zoo's aquarium. This enterprise shows how desolate they are. Unfortunately, the first half of the book has lots of meditations on this and that: "permutations are not unlimited. Only a certain number of things can happen and whatever can happen *will* happen" is an example. Then there are fifty effective pages about the movie *King Kong* and the transport of the turtles, and the last scenes develop some of the minor characters.

The Bat Tattoo (2002) reads like a superior wise-guy crime novel with much musing about life and God and guilt:

"Speak to me as the son of God. Tell me something."

"I have nothing to say," said Christ. "This is all there is."

Also: "Being alone is a lonely thing, but that's all there is …"

Also: "Life is a process of one goneness after another."

Hoban is one of those writers who uses every character to offer witty comments, without regard to whether the comments are at odds with the character in question.

Mother and child:

"There is a Balm in Gilead."

"Where's Gilead?"

"I'll let you know when I find it."

Doctor and patient:

"A lot of accidents are not accidental."

"If I had my notebook with me I'd write that down."

"Maybe you can remember it."

"I'll try."

There are some art appreciation lectures (usually quite interesting) and love talk (pretty bad).

E.L. Doctorow (1931–2015)

Doctorow links the last generation of writers with the present. His first novel, *Welcome to Hard Times*★ (1960), describes what life was really like in the old West: grim and no points for being a hero. (They die young.) The only real accomplishment is survival, and a brothel can be the growth industry that makes a town economically viable. The Robert Altman film *McCabe & Mrs. Miller* is recommended to complete the picture.

The Book of Daniel (1971)★ is based on the lives, trial, and execution (for treason) of Ethel and Julius Rosenberg in 1953, with significant alterations. The children's visit to their parents in prison, prior to the parents' deaths, is almost unbearable.

In *Ragtime*★★ (1975) Doctorow uses a middle-class family who live in New Rochelle, New York, to weave a panorama of what mattered in and to America from 1902 to 1914. Many characters are historical figures, including Harry Houdini, J.P. Morgan, Henry Ford, Emma Goldman (the anarchist), Booker T. Washington, Emiliano Zapata (the

Mexican revolutionary), Sigmund Freud, Carl Jung, and Archduke Franz Ferdinand, whose assassination in Sarajevo triggered the First World War. It sounds awful but is done wonderfully well. There is a black man named Coalhouse Walker whose crusade for justice attains success the moment before, probably at his own invitation, the police shoot him. Exhausted, he had no will left to live or fight.

World's Fair★ (1985) gives a child's view of New York in the 1930s, the Depression years but also a time when life in that city was almost normal, what with the existence of the extended family, with its solidarity and tragedies, and the relative safety of city streets. This culminated in the New York World's Fair of 1939 to 1940, with the slogan "The Dawn of a New Day". The Second World War had begun and the post-war world of consumer fraud is foreshadowed in the book's rhetoric.

The 1930s was also the heyday of organized crime in America. For more on this, read *Billy Bathgate*★ (1989). The protagonist's life is interrupted when he becomes a minor player in the gang of mobster Dutch Schultz. Even Schultz emerges as a convincing character.

Recently I read three novels by Doctorow published over the last decade. *The March* (2005) makes you feel you were there to experience the bloodshed of the American Civil War during General William Sherman's scorched-earth march through the heart of the south. One soldier found a horror greater than anything he had known since he was in the third grade under Sister Agnes Angeline. Sherman and his officers are well depicted but two common soldiers strike a false note in their banter. However, the worst flaw is that Doctorow's sympathy for the freed slaves spills over into his writing. The virtues, sensibilities, and musings about the true nature of freedom by one of these slaves, Pearl, are an embarrassment. A morality play spoils what has always been Doctorow's greatest skill: the creation of striking characters made plausible.

Homer and Langley★R (2009) is about two brothers, the older deranged by being gassed during the First World War, the other dependent on him because of his blindness. The older brother eventually severs all ties with the outside world and so gradually squeezes the younger's life dry. Their home becomes a nightmare, crammed with hoarded useless junk. On one occasion gangsters force entry at gunpoint. When they discover a Model T Ford in the living room, they begin to panic—they realize they are in a madhouse. The style of this book is always elegant and sometimes moves you to tears. However, to read it you must want either a dissection of abnormal psychology or an example of the utter cruelty of fate.

Andrew's Brain (2014) reports conversations between a man and his analyst, and includes some entries from the patient's notebook. He is a sociopath with no normal feelings of guilt or regret, but happens not to want to harm others. He refers to himself in the third person, talks about a fictitious friend named Andrew, and believes Andrew is unavoidably accident-prone—that is, he harms those near him without intending to. For example, he kills his infant daughter by administering a lethal "medicine" that a pharmacist has mistakenly given him. There are some exceptional moments, such as the description of the tragedy of 9/11 and the Twin Towers, but I found Andrew less interesting than most of Doctorow's characters.

Clearly, in my opinion, Doctorow's later work began to slip, but how many other authors have written at least six great or near great novels?

Toni Morrison (born 1931)
Before I discuss the merits of this author I will say something about how her novels educated me. They refer to blacks being expelled by force from American towns in the post Civil War period, the 1860s, and until relatively recently. This rang a bell because I had heard that Corbin, a city in south-eastern Kentucky, had expelled its black citizens in 1954 after the Supreme Court's decision to ban segregation in education.

As someone who is probably among the one percent of Americans who have much in-depth knowledge of black history, I also knew segregationist sentiment was present even in "liberal" northern states. At one stage in the 1950s, for example, a mob threatened to drive blacks out of a public housing project in Milwaukee, leading Frank Zeidler, its great socialist mayor, to sleep there for a week: if the mob were going to do violence to blacks they would have go through him first.

I also knew that many affluent suburban neighborhoods even in the north had once had restrictive covenants that banned blacks, and also others such as Jews and Catholics, and that de facto racial segregation in housing is still the norm in most cities.

Then I read James W. Loewen's *Sundown Towns* (2005). I was stunned to find that before 1964 a majority of towns and cities in Illinois, 474 out of 671, were "sundown towns". As recently as 1970 a city called Anna posted signs saying: "Nigger, Don't Let the Sun Go Down on You." The town's very name was taken from the slogan "Ain't No Niggers Allowed".

Cities as large as Appleton, Wisconsin (population 57,000) were sundown towns. Some of these places even used "white" in their names to advertise their racial character. I may have unknowingly resided in one: Whitewater, Wisconsin had no black residents in 1960. I learned I had been misinformed about Corbin driving out blacks in 1954: no blacks had been allowed to live in the city since a race riot in 1919. A sole black was tolerated because he was regarded as the village idiot. Many sundown towns persisted until the 1980s.

Morrison's most acclaimed book *Beloved*★ (1987) has as its main characters Sethe, a former slave, Baby Suggs, the mother of Sethe's husband Halle, who has descended into madness, and Sethe's lover Paul D. It is one thing to know how horrible conditions were under slavery and how blacks were brutalized all over the south right after the south's defeat in 1865. It is another to be taken into the minds of characters who experienced these things.

Ties of love were futile. Baby Suggs had to eradicate her tendency to love even her newborn child: "Anyone Baby Suggs knew, let alone loved, who hadn't run off or been hanged, got rented out, loaned out, bought up, bought back, stored up, mortgaged, won, stolen or seized." She had six fathers for her eight children. Women were lent to an adjoining plantation to be impregnated by an unknown male slave. Men had steel bits fitted into their mouths like horses as punishment.

Blacks looked at whites and asked: "What are these people? You tell me Jesus. What are they?" Whites knew what blacks were like: "Whatever the manners, under every dark skin was a jungle … screaming baboons, sleeping snakes, red gums ready for their sweet white blood."

Morrison's second novel *Sula*★ (1973) features two women raised in a black town on the outskirts of a white town in Ohio. Sula is a near sociopath: "Hers was an experimental life"; "she might say, 'Why do you chew with your mouth open?' not because the answer interested her but because she wanted to see the person's face change rapidly." However, I found her less interesting than the town itself, which existed between 1865 and about 1965. The style is usually immaculate.

Song of Solomon★ (1977) takes place in a black community in Michigan between 1931 and 1963. Once again the depiction of the town is wonderful. The fact a black was murdered simply because he owned a service station is an appropriate introduction to the history of lynching: in real life a black was once killed because he owned a flash car that poor whites could not afford. The "Aunt Jemima" act—pretending to be a witless clown in order to disarm police—is one I have witnessed.

The main character in this book, Milkman, initially lacks compassion for others but he finds it as he discovers his family's history. For me he was less convincing than some of the other members of his family—for example, his older sister threatened by spinsterhood, who is brilliantly portrayed.

Morrison's recent novels have not attracted the critical acclaim of those published before 1990. I read *Home**, published in 2012. Her style had become straightforward rather than poetic but that was no sin in my eyes. A man treated as an equal in the army during the Korean War comes home to the racist America of the 1950s. He and his kin face what blacks faced at that time: being run out of town; being shaken down and robbed by police; realizing it was absurd to call the police when mugged; finding houses were not for sale to blacks. However, the emphasis is on the soldier's recovery from the trauma of his dehumanization in Korea. The fact the racial theme is a backdrop makes the book all the more impressive.

Aside from *Beloved*, which gives a universal image of the reality of slavery, Morrison will appeal to all those who want to understand the full history of what it has been like to be black in America. Other writers such as Doctorow and Robert Stone have given snapshots of American blacks at certain times and places, which supplement that story.

Philip Roth (born 1933)
Here is another great writer who, like Doctorow, links the last generation to the present. Roth has written twenty-two novels, all of them alive and kicking. *The Anatomy Lesson*★ (1983) is a good comic novel. One character makes pornographic films but has principles: he will not film sex between people and animals out of concern for the animals. *Operation Shylock: A Confession*★ (1993) will convince you that all Jewish-Americans are not Israeli chauvinists. Roth finds that someone who looks like him is pretending to be him and has gone to Israel. This impersonator has aroused great enthusiasm among Roth's Palestinian friends. He wishes to persuade the European nations from which Jews have come to Israel to welcome them back. The subliminal text is, of course, that the very presence of Israel has created a dilemma, making justice for both Israelis and Palestinians impossible.

American Pastoral★★ (1997) is a great novel about a virtuous man, Swede Levov, and the purgatory he endures after his daughter becomes a terrorist during the late '60s. She goes underground, and when he finds her she has discovered a new way of destroying herself: she has become a Jainist and is starving herself to death because it is wrong to kill and eat living things. His entire world falls apart, including his marriage. *I Married a Communist*★ (1998) reminds us just how hysterical the Cold War anti-communist witch-hunt became: "Momma, Momma … those men up in his study are speaking Russian."

I decided to read three of Roth's most recent novels. *The Plot Against America*★R (2004) is about anti-Semitism and how it has affected Jews, from everyday life to education and career aspirations. The celebration of how the people he writes about imbued their lives with modest significance is compelling. He explores what might have happened if Charles Lindbergh, the famous aviator, had become United States president in 1940 on a wave of "Keep us out of the war" sentiment. Lindbergh was an anti-Semite, although not of the most rabid kind.

The events that follow mix the likely with the improbable. The role of the latter, I presume, is to show how lethal anti-Semitism can be. The theme of the book is such that it may appeal mainly to those who have a special curiosity about Jewish Americans. There is some humor: a man who has lost his lower leg shouts, "Shark! Shark!" whenever he emerges from swimming in the ocean.

Exit Ghost★ (2007) is the last of Roth's Zuckerman novels. Nathan Zuckerman lives in rural New England, hiding from the modern world. A friend gives him two kittens to lighten his isolation and asks him what he will call them. "A and B," he replies. He briefly returns to New York, where he meets a young woman who utterly captivates him. He knows that even successful seduction would simply torture him because he is now impotent, and that he has abandoned all sanity. He writes a play about imaginary conversations with the woman. There is nothing to lose: he would have these fantasies anyway, and at least he gains the satisfaction of artistic expression.

He flinches from a test of wills with a man set on writing a biography that would demean a deceased author. He learns his dead mentor supposedly said, "Reading/writing people, we are finished. We are ghosts witnessing the end of the literary era." The book is not perfect. However, it's the best account I know of the desperation of a passionate man whose body has begun to betray him.

Roth has said that *Nemesis*★ (2010) may be his last novel. In this book a man cannot accept that the world is blind to human suffering and thus irresponsible. He turns against God, citing the deaths of innocent children, and against himself because he has abandoned young people he was supervising during a polio epidemic. He escapes to a summer camp, brings polio with him (he thinks), and is partially crippled by it. He salvages some shred of his self-esteem by sparing his fiancée the burden of being tied to him.

The portrayal of the Jewish community of Newark, its flavor, its hysteria—the cause of polio was unknown and so everything was suspect, from hot dogs to the Jews themselves—and its alienation from other ethnic communities, particularly the Italians, is perfect. I well remember the reign of polio and how it afflicted one of my university friends as late as 1953.

Cormac McCarthy (born 1933)

This author is rightly praised for a spare style that arouses emotion through understatement. In the first book of his Border trilogy, *All the Pretty Horses*★ (1993), there is a scene in which John Grady Cole, testifying in court, shows the bullet holes in his leg. The judge asks him how he avoided gangrene: "'I burnt em out with a hot pistol barrel.' There is absolute silence." This is a man they can respect and believe.

He travels to Mexico. The evocation of Mexican history and the people who once lived the harsh life of ranchers in south-west Texas are excellent. Cole visits the wife of a preacher who cures over the radio: the preacher himself is modest enough to grant that he cannot raise the dead. He realizes that time itself cares nothing for the living or the dead, "Nothing for their struggles, nothing for their names". Cole's day has gone: "Passed and paled into the darkening land, the world to come"—a world in which all he loves and hates will be forgotten.

In the second volume of the trilogy, *The Crossing* (1994), the style is still there but understatement has ended and pretentious prose begun to intrude. There is endless analysis of the human predicament. A hermit tells us "everything is necessary"; "all tales are one"; "Life is a memory, and then it is nothing. All law is writ in a seed." There are pages of this: "Such as it was. Such as it had become. Such as it would be." All we need is the biblical "And thus it came to pass."

Then comes a philosophical opera singer: "The shape of the road is the road". Then a blind man: "what can be touched falls into the dust." Then a Takui Indian: "the world cannot be lost." Finally a gypsy: "the truth was darker yet as truth is wont to be."

Giving up on the trilogy, I read *No Country for Old Men* (2005). It is about Anton Chigurh, a relentless psychopath. He does have a moral balance sheet: he has no pity but keeps whatever bargain he makes with potential victims. The style of this book is somewhat better. There is a discussion of how Vietnam divided America between the generations. The younger generation went to fight without patriotic support (hippies spat on them) and without God. The older generation was not prepared for hippies—"people on the streets of our Texas towns with green hair and bones in their noses speakin a language they couldn't even understand." There is a clear preference for the good old world, where men were men and women knew their place. Police are shattered as respect for the law gives way to sadists who murder each other over drugs, and men like Chigurh who murder without compunction.

Larry McMurtry (born 1936)
An outstanding film of the same title was based on Larry McMurty's third novel *The Last Picture Show*★ (1966), which captures the utter godforsakenness of two boys, Sonny and Duane, being raised in the 1950s in a small isolated windswept Texas town. There is nothing beyond sex, boredom, and awful films. At eighteen, Duane's girlfriend Jacy is a total product of the environment, and sports a

Mortimer Snerd doll in her bedroom. She is pretty with no ambition beyond being in the fast set, being the subject of town gossip, and the hope of an eventual movie-star marriage. Her completely sane mother takes pleasure where she can, fully aware of the barrenness of the landscape. The bond between the two boys is well depicted. Their parting, when one goes off to fight in Korea, is moving.

Terms of Endearment (1975) inspired an Oscar-winning film. It revolves around an attractive woman approaching fifty who fears old age and half wants a man who will anticipate (or rebuff, or something) her every mood. Despite the author's art, the woman's omniscience about her own motives and everyone else's is hard to take. There are a few amusing touches but too often her behavior is ridiculous rather than funny: she is just a bad vehicle for a comic novel. There is some slapstick that probably filmed well. In the epilogue the author abandons the mother for the daughter. This is by far the best part of the book.

Lonesome Dove★★R (1985) won the Pulitzer Prize. It is so good that everyone should read it. The second star gives it classic status but that must be qualified: it is a classic for anyone who wants to know about a fascinating period of American history: the "winning of the West" between the Civil War of 1861–1865 and about 1885.

Two aging men once led the Texas Rangers, who kept Mexicans from controlling land north of the border, the Rio Grande, and broke the military power of the Indian tribes in the area. The men have become bored because their locale has been pacified. One laments the spread of European civilization: he admires the untamed world that is disappearing. The other takes the notion of a "civilizing mission" for granted and is proud of his role in its success: a duty honorably performed.

The men embark on a trek with a herd of cattle to distant Montana to recapture the romance of their past. Today there is much sympathy for the losers, the American Indians, whose military subjugation was inevitable. Either huge tracts of land had to be closed to white settlement or the Plains tribes had to be pacified, which is to say their culture destroyed. The tribes the men encounter on their trek are beaten into submission or destitute or hate whites. Blue Dick, an Indian notorious for cruelty, is untamed: "I raped women and stole children and burned houses and shot men and run off horses and killed cattle and robbed who I pleased … I despise all you fine-haired sons of bitches." Any Plains Indian with a horse and gun and a lust for freedom participated in a zero-sum game of kill or be killed.

Frontier society was tragic for many whites. There were a lot of prostitutes and few "respectable" women. The former were at the mercy of brutal customers. The latter often died in childbirth, lost most of their children, went mad, or committed suicide—"Can't stand listening to this wind no more." Viable spouses were few. Many men never spoke to a woman until maturity and had no conception of their needs. As a result they became hopeless romantics and fell in love with the first attractive prostitute they met. Even men of more substance were unsuitable as husbands: some offered their wives docility but no conversation; others could at least talk but were restless and unreliable.

McMurty's characters and style are superb. The death scenes, and there are many of these, are moving. Even the sudden demise of two debonair pigs is moving. The ending is a masterstroke. I will read more of this author's novels.

Don DeLillo (born 1936)
DeLillo's novel *Underworld* (1997) has received extravagant praise as a successor "to the Russian masterpieces of Dostoyevsky and Tolstoy" (Philip Gerard) that has "raised literary standards to new highs" (Gay Talese). Well, it is ambitious—over 800 pages—and catches something of what the United States was like from 1950 to 1990. There is the pervasiveness of the Cold War, Italian life in the Bronx, and the brutal discipline in Catholic schools. Sister Edgar could be the Sister Medea who terrorized my first-grade class in Washington D. C. in 1941. My classmates the Fitzpatrick twins got sick every morning when they arrived at school: being lifted off the floor by your sideburns is very painful. When Sister Medea died, we were told that as a sign of her sanctity the stigmata, the wounds Christ suffered on the cross, appeared on her corpse.

There are some funny passages in *Underworld*. When Father Paulus is told the Pope has been witnessing supernatural events, he says, "If you'd been drinking dago red until three in the morning, you'd have visions too." However, none of the characters except one—Albert Bronzini, a high school teacher and chess mentor—held my interest. The book is worth reading for its historical portraits of the time only if you are already fairly knowledgeable: it assumes considerable familiarity with events and people.

As for its literary merits, DeLillo just does not have a first-rate style. It is kind of Hemingway spoiled by sure signs of a writer striving for effect—namely, extravagant adjectives and adverbs: slouchy funk of hormones, nits and tater voice, suits arrayed like executives in hell. After I read the book, I found DeLillo had said Hemingway was indeed his model. There are long passages that are rather empty—for example, the "insight" that everything depends on the balance of terror between the United States and Russia is called "an amazing thing to say". The book ends badly with Sister Edgar merging with J. Edgar Hoover, the loathsome head of the FBI. This is to show that "everything is connected in the end". The word that unifies all is, of course, "peace".

It is hard to write the great American novel when you are trying to write the great American novel. DeLillo himself has said certain parts of *Underworld* are extravagant and overindulgent. I decided to give him a second chance and read a book whose theme promised less and therefore might amount to more.

Point Omega (2010) is his latest. It borders on passive aggression. A man, his daughter, and a film-maker gather in a desert house. The daughter disappears into the desert without explanation. The style creaks with the strain of seeking to impress: "He looked at Jessie and then smiled, seeming to remember in his grogginess that there was something he wanted to do. He wanted to smile." The man acts as a guru: his astonishingly empty sayings are treated with great reverence. He always "bites the skin off the edge of his thumbnail, always the right thumb, still do it, loose piece of dead skin, that's how I know who I am"; "Matter wants to lose its self-consciousness ... We want to be the dead matter we used to be"; "Whoever was there? That's who was there."

Give this book a miss. I will have to be persuaded to read more of DeLillo.

Robert Stone (1937–2015)

Stone's first novel *A Hall of Mirrors*★ (1964) is a must read. The first third is inferior to the rest and there are long passages about the hallucinations and rambling conversations of alcoholics and drug addicts, but the portrayal of New Orleans and the lives of the down-and-out before the civil rights revolution is powerful. The lives of black Americans in the south become real in a way social statistics can never convey. The style and black humor are extraordinary: interviews with black welfare recipients, descriptions of the way people earn their living—for example, gutting catfish—and the state of mind of "social conservatives" stay with you.

The mock speech that disk jockey Rheinhardt gives to a racist and xenophobic audience is a masterpiece. Those present are extolled as not being "perverts with rotten brains" (like the English), "a sordid little turd" (the French) or "nuts like the Kraut". They are the sort who perceive the menace of "a gigantic leering coon with a monstrously distended member [who is] waiting [to rape] in a watermelon patch". If blacks prevail "it's gonna rain bearded men. The Great Lakes will turn to little brown people. Our boys in uniform all over the world will turn queer and toss up their hair in sequins."

Foley, a preacher, describes his early life of sin: his lovely children died one by one because of drink. A social worker is described as a "a man who's ready to walk on water for the Negro race". A political opportunist who wants to rid the welfare rolls of blacks "glided about the room as though seeking flies for his breakfast". Will a little golden-headed girl "have to sit in the same classroom with all those eight-foot spade kids with their teeth filed to points?"

Stone's *Dog Soldiers*★ (1973) is well worth reading but very grim. Many of the characters supply heroin and are beyond the limits of normality in their nihilism. Indeed, the least horrifying are those who are merely alcoholics, or just people who have lost their moral compass. The Vietnam War, which is vividly described, destroyed any illusions these people had about right and wrong. After a company went to see Bob Hope in a film without permission, they were sent on a dangerous patrol. The punishment worked: virtually everyone who saw the film died. A battalion is mistakenly cut to ribbons by fragmentation bombs in friendly fire. These weapons were also used in Iraq, yet we are supposed to take objections to chemical weapons seriously. Every teenager encountered has no purpose beyond self-destruction.

The black humor is funny: "May the poetry of your love never turn to prose." A strip club has a sign over the bar— "Today is the First Day of the Rest of Your Life". Headlines in a scandal sheet include "Skydiver Devoured by Starving Birds!" and "Mad Dentist Yanks Girl's Tongue". The principle being defended by fighting in Vietnam: "I don't know what I'm doing or why I do it."

A Flag for Sunrise★(1977) is a yarn about intrigue in a fictitious Central American nation. It is more than that thanks to Stone's ability to create characters who speak and joke in accord with their psychology (sometimes we get more than enough of their psychology). The revolutionaries are dedicated. Virtually everyone else is, as usual, utterly disillusioned—appropriate given America's role in Latin America—although some retain a remnant of humanity. Stone uses arresting images to convey places and people's desolate lives. An elegant bench is "covered with parakeet shit, and mongrel dogs lay asleep beneath it". The local zoo is famous for its three-legged cow. A boy receives a dollar tip and flees two older boys who mean to kill him for it. Children amuse themselves by trying to stone to death a cow that is entangled in wire. A leper wears a "kiss me" T-shirt.

In *Damascus Gate* (1998), Stone follows a group of religious fanatics in Jerusalem. He tries to give them depth but pays the price: some seem far too intelligent and sensible to be fanatics. The protagonist ponders far too much about his agony of soul. The fanatics state their religious "views" at great length and you have to be knowledgeable about religious literature to make sense of them. You also have to be politically sophisticated to understand the ideologies and behavior of the numerous sects and ethnicities in Israel.

Bay of Souls (2003) is like *A Flag for Sunrise* but the characters are weaker still. A modern educated woman is supposed to believe that her soul has been stolen. *Death of the Black-Haired Girl* (2013) is a university novel with some good characters, such as a former nun. However, the characters and style lack the electricity of Tom Wolfe's *I Am Charlotte Simmons*★ (2004), perhaps the best recent university novel. Nonetheless, I enjoyed the passages about the police and the urban poor: "Grandma weighs ninety pounds, she's on crack, mom's a slave or turning tricks at interstate rest areas, adolescent dad's working on his prison tats or wearing curlers for his roomie." In sum, prior to 1980 Stone did a brilliant job of dramatizing America's darker side. His recent work is less interesting.

Marilynne Robinson (born 1943)

This Idaho-born writer has published four novels. *Housekeeping* (1980) was her first. Two girls are raised by a series of foster parents in a small isolated town in the American west. The book has convincing characters and a lyrical style. However, it is spoiled by a temptation to go beyond using language to advance the development of character, plot or theme and to employ it simply for its elegance. Almost all of chapter eight—thirty-three pages—is self-indulgent writing. The theme that life is an aimless drift in an unsubstantial world is hammered to death with talk about "it is better to have nothing" and "I wore her cloak like beatitude".

Twenty-four years later in *Gilead*★ (2004) Robinson realized her true potential. The story has similarities with the novel *Plumb* by New Zealand writer Maurice Gee. John Ames, an elderly minister near death, looks back over his life. The book captures how some people can bask in the peace of mind that faith confers. Too much repetition of this theme is relieved by excellent background on the town of Gilead: "A stranger might ask why there is a town here at all. … It was just a dogged little outpost in the sand hills … that John Brown and Jim Lane could fall back on when they needed to heal and rest … set up in the heat of an old urgency that is all forgotten now."

Ames' grandfather fought in the struggle, and later became estranged from his son, a pacifist. As an old man he is portrayed as a fierce and adamant Christian: he kept giving away anything and everything to the poor.

Home (2008) covers the same time and place by portraying the semi-tragic lives of a neighboring minister's son and daughter, and the sorrow the son caused his father. Their spiritual agony is described over and over with too many tears on too many people's cheeks. However, the book is almost redeemed by a brilliant last eighty-seven pages that are deeply moving.

Lila (2015) also takes place in Gilead. It consists of the thoughts of Lila, a young woman who married John Ames, the elderly minister in *Gilead*, after a nomadic life that made her barely literate. The book is highly repetitive, with much about Lila's insecurity, whether anyone deserves hell, whether she and John can ever know one another, and on and on and on. It would have been worth about a chapter in the original *Gilead* novel to flesh out John Ames' story.

Michael Ondaatje (born 1943)
Ondaatje left Sri Lanka, formerly Ceylon, at the age of four and lives in Toronto. He was a joint winner with Barry Unsworth of the Booker Prize for *The English Patient* in 1992. His first novel, *Coming Through Slaughter* (1979) tries to get into the mind of Buddy Bolden, a jazz musician who lived surrounded by the violence of black New Orleans. The music of jazz musicians is usually more interesting than they are. I recall an interview with Big Bill Broonzy:

"When you interpret Chicago jazz, Big Bill, how different is it from New Orleans jazz?"

"It's all how you blows it."

Buddy Bolden is no exception and neither are his fans and friends. Songs and snippets interrupt the text ("Passing wet chicory that lies in the fields like the sky"). When swimming, people inevitably swim "towards the sound of madness". Everyone is exhausted much of the time.

However, *In the Skin of a Lion*★ (1987) portrays interesting people, the visionaries who planned modern Toronto and the workers whose labor ranged from the dangerous to the utterly exhausting to the soul-destroying. Men arrive before dawn and work until six p.m. at a leather factory. They stun cattle with sledgehammers, leap into pools of dye and stomp the skins of recently slaughtered animals until the dye takes, stand ankle-deep in salt squeezing out shit and waste from animal intestines—the salts and acids bestowing a terrible odor no one can get rid of, and eventually suffer tuberculosis, arthritis, and rheumatism. The hunting down and murder of unionists in the timber fields was identical to what occurred in the United States at the time. If you want to understand why radicals idealized the working class and why workers became anarchists, this book will teach you. There are boring sex scenes and love letters but the narrative redeems all.

The English Patient (1992) was much acclaimed. When not analyzing the human condition the style was captivating, but very little happened that excited my interest. There is much about the mystique of the desert. There is a love affair, and one of the parties, Kip, an Indian who is a bomb-disposal expert, takes on depth. His gratitude and loyalty to the few English who treat him as human are moving, but he is spoiled at the end by melodrama. It is not clear, by the way, that the Allies would "never have dropped an atom bomb on a white nation". The fire bombs dropped on Dresden in Germany killed 25,000 people. There is interesting detail about how the retreating Germans left behind thousands and thousands of land mines in Italy and the heroism of those who had to deal with them.

Anil's Ghost (2000) portrays the recent civil war in Sri Lanka in all its savagery. The central character, a young Sri Lankan returning home to document crimes against humanity (murder, torture) manages to get her local friend and collaborator tortured and murdered. What did she expect? Her lack of awareness about the probable consequences of her words and deeds borders on the imbecilic.

The book has some sketches of how doctors found their lives turned into a nightmare. There are too many "profound" passages that are silly: Asanga the Wise and his followers lived in solitude and after they died there was "no song of sweeping"; "I don't think clarity is necessarily truth." The latter is offered in defense of a revered archeologist who faked evidence because he knew what had to be true.

In *Divisadero* (2007)—the word is Spanish for division—three young people in California are split asunder by a violent act of their father. Because of the trauma the boy goes away to become a gambler and one daughter becomes an archivist working in France on a literary figure, Lucien Segura. The other daughter remains at home. Why they remain incommunicado rather than anxious to reunite is unanswered, although the stay-at-home woman does want to reunite with her brother. With over a hundred pages to go, these characters are abandoned in favor of a biography of Segura and a couple close to him. The only rationale is that tales of isolation happen everywhere. The book betters the average novel but not by much.

In Ondaatje's most recent novel *The Cat's Table*★ (2011) the style is excellent, a free-flowing stream of gentle prose. In the early 1950s three boys aged about eleven take an ocean trip from Ceylon to London. Their experiences on board and fate in later life are presented as a memoir about Ondaatje but the story is described as fictitious: it is very odd to write a fictitious memoir about yourself. What the boys do and what they learn about the larger world on the voyage is fresh and interesting. I found the drama of a criminal being transported on the ship was more of a distraction than an enhancement. The psychoanalysis of how the boys' mature personalities could be traced to their eleven-year-old traits varies between the convincing and the contrived.

Jane Smiley (born 1949)

While a professor of English at Iowa State University, Jane Smiley received the Pulitzer Prize for *A Thousand Acres*★ (1991). The story is based on Shakespeare's *King Lear*. The narrator, Ginny Cook, is one of three daughters of Larry Cook. This aging father has built up a model thousand-acre farm, which he passes on to two of his three daughters, Ginny and Rose. Idle, he takes to drink and tries to regain control. A bitter court dispute divides the family. Rose reawakens Ginny's repressed memories of their father sleeping with both of them after his wife's death. The characters, the family's interaction, and the sex abuse seem very real, the latter being handled with rare detachment.

Two of Smiley's more recent novels, while reasonably

enjoyable, were less interesting. I looked forward to *Moo* (1995) because I like comic novels set in universities. There are some funny parts. The university is driven by fundraising. A professor who has always wanted a museum devoted to the history of the pig industry is told a donor has been found, but the donor wants the museum to be about chickens.

In any comic novel the problem is now to make the characters comic without making them paper thin. Some of Smiley's characters do not make the grade. If you expect something like Professor Welch in Kingsley Amis's *Lucky Jim* you will be disappointed. There is a lot of boring stuff about a fanatical free-marketer, and maudlin stuff about the inability of a black girl to survive being the target of one racial epithet on one occasion. Her older sister is, like me, unimpressed.

Good Faith (2003) has main characters that work well enough. But the long passages about real estate, the brave new world of financial opportunity, and even the sex scenes tend to interrupt the flow of the plot.

Rebecca Goldstein (born 1950)
Goldstein's first novel, *The Mind-Body Problem*★ (1983), based on her experiences as a graduate student at Princeton University, captures her as a young woman in a style that is lively and unmannered. *The Dark Sister* (1993), written ten years later, imitates the style of Henry James. I do not like his style and some passages indicate that Goldstein does not like it much either. She certainly does a good job of capturing

its flavor, using the Latin "socius" for "companion", using cancerous shades for ash grey, calling Fifth Avenue "the great longitudinal thoroughfare". *Mazel* (1995) has some excellent content, such as the description of the religious festivals of the shtetl, the small villages in which Eastern European Jews once lived, and of a contemporary Orthodox wedding seen through the eyes of the non-Orthodox father of the bride.

Goldstein is a talented biographer. *Incompleteness: The Proof and Paradox of Kurt Gödel*[★R] (2005) gives a picture of the great logician and his contribution to mathematics. He destroyed the dream that mathematics can be made into a self-sufficient, logical system, within which all true propositions are provable given certain axioms and the rules of logic. He showed that in arithmetic there will always be propositions that are "arithmetically sound", proceed naturally from arithmetic procedures, and yet cannot be proved from the axioms posited. You can posit additional axioms to cover them, but then the enlarged system yields new sound but unproven propositions. As to difficulty, I already knew something of Gödel and still had to read and reread very carefully. That is not a criticism: to accommodate the general reader the author would have had to parody Gödel's work.

Erik Larson (born 1954)
Erik Larson has become a great popular historian in the mold of Barbara Tuchman, Cecil Woodham-Smith, and Bruce Catton. The earliest of his histories, *Isaac's Storm* (1999), shows his promise rather than his mature talent.

On September 1, 1900 a hurricane hit Galveston, Texas, killing 8,000 people. Larson describes the false optimism that preceded the disaster, which included that of Isaac, the local meteorologist. When the storm struck, Isaac was confident his home would survive. It did not. His wife and thirty-two people who took shelter there perished. Isaac's personal history offers a contrast between childhood then and today. To get pocket money, he set animal traps and rose early to check them, so he would be ready to start his farm chores at four a.m. He was six years old. This was not the result of penury: the farm was one of the richest in the district.

Larson's next book *The Devil in the White City*★★ (2003) is perhaps his best. The 1893 World's Fair was held in Chicago. The geniuses behind it were Daniel Burnham, an architect, and Fredrick Law Olmsted, a landscape architect who designed its surroundings; he had created Central Park in New York in 1858. The fair's exhibits paved the way for the twentieth century, although they did include a 22,000-pound cheese. A serial killer called H.H. Holmes added a tragic touch: he built a "World's Fair Hotel" nearby, specially designed to slowly kill pleading victims in a room that doubled as a gas chamber. The book goes well beyond sensationalism: Larson uses the perfect city of the World's Fair as a counterpoint to the reality of life outside.

Thunderstruck★ (2006) links Guglielmo Marconi and Dr Crippen. After endless trial and error, Marconi perfected the wireless telegraph, even though the scientists told him he was wasting his time. After his wife's suspicious death, Dr Crippen and his lover fled by ship. The captain used the wireless to alert the police, and created a sensation with daily bulletins about how the couple were behaving while unaware their arrest was imminent.

Larson captures the flavor of Edwardian England in the first decade of the twentieth century. Darwin's theory of evolution caused a plague of séances as people sought new evidence for life after death. Once the First World War began, thousands of parents took solace in "contacting" their deceased sons. The period was saturated with sex but so proper that a woman was successfully sued for stating that another woman dyed her hair. Facts about poverty stunned even the upper classes, but did not prevent Nellie Melba and her guests from enlivening a party by throwing peaches out the windows on to the heads of passers-by.

In the Garden of Beasts★ (2011) is excellent. It traces Hitler from his tenure as chancellor, when it was still possible he could be overthrown, to the massacre of his rival Ernst Röhm and other opponents in July 1934, when he achieved absolute power. Margaret Dodd, daughter of the American ambassador to Berlin, goes from admiration of the vibrant new Germany to awareness of Hitler's plans for war and extermination of the Jews, particularly after she has to save one of her numerous lovers from execution. Her evolving state of mind is a brilliant device for making clear why Americans could not perceive, or could not face, what Nazi Germany was like until it was far too late.

Dodd became so alienated that Stalin's Russia saw her as a potential spy. After her father returned to America in 1938 he was virtually alone among ambassadors in trying to educate Americans about the world war that was coming. Perhaps the most extraordinary example of Nazi fanaticism was that telephone operators were forbidden to say, "D as in David," David being a Jewish name. They had to say, "D as in Dora."

John Grisham (born 1955)
Critics do not usually take this author seriously and it's easy to see why. His novels do not aim very high. They are money-spinners that hold the reader's interest and provide a bit of entertainment. The frustrating thing is that he could do so much better. In virtually every book there is a bit of dialogue or description that catches a character beautifully. Sadly the quality is never sustained.

An example is *The Testament* (1999). The depictions of the dysfunctional Phelan family and the infinite greed of professional America is striking. There is a well done potted history of Brazil. But then the major character is spoiled by careless dialogue and cheap wisecracks, and the novel spoiled when the ghost of a newly dead missionary solves all his problems by teaching him the power of prayer. (Just ask God's forgiveness and all will be well.) Really. Grisham must have millions in the bank by now. Why does he not set out to write an outstanding novel?

Lionel Shriver (born 1957)

Born in North Carolina, this author lives in London and writes novels set in both the US and UK. The three I read all dealt with people on the very edge of normality. The best is *We Need to Talk About Kevin*★ (2003), about a family raising a sociopath, a manipulative boy with sadistic tendencies and no conscience. The boy is plausible and so are his parents, estranged by the fact his mother sees him as he is while his father is convinced of his normality and thus believes the boy's mother is irrationally hostile.

The Post-Birthday World (2007) is about a woman who cannot sexually desire a man without loving him, and whose current love transforms love for any other into complete indifference. This may be a trait more common of women than men. The novel contrasts two possible futures, one of which follows from a kiss consummated and the other from the same kiss resisted. There is an irritating reversal of who is doing what on the two story levels. Much of the writing is fluent but too much of the behavior of the husband, wife, and new lover seem contrived to fit the plot.

The same is true of *Big Brother* (2013), whose narrator is so fixated by love of a sibling that she is willing to sacrifice anything to help him lose weight and reclaim his life. There is a literary device towards the end—a revelation that what the reader was led to believe was fact was really fiction—that seems to be there only so the novel can have such a literary device. Someone seems to have told the author that a modern novel ought to work on several levels.

Ben Fountain (born 1958)
Billy Lynn's Long Halftime Walk★ (2012) is Ben Fountain's first novel. It came late in his life—he was fifty-four when he wrote it—but keep an eye on this author. Eight "heroes" who fought in Iraq are taken on a tour of the United States to drum up support for the war. One, Billy, is nineteen. His view of the war—dying to no purpose—is contrasted with that of most Americans—fight terrorists there rather than here. A hero responds to a grateful patriot: "You don't need to thank us … they're killers, they're having the time of their lives" and "this is the most murdering bunch of psychopaths you'll ever see." Someone asks if the cold weather might freeze a soldier who has passed out. The answer is "He's fine. He's happy. He's like a cockroach, you can't kill him!" The insanity of the Dallas Cowboys, a football team that stocks 50,000 pieces of chewing gum, makes Billy wonder what sort of way of life he is defending. He and a beautiful cheerleader fall in love and for the first time he feels important. Billy tells her he is twenty-one. He goes back to the war with every chance of dying. The farewell scene with his family is very affecting.

James Lasdun (born 1958)
The Horned Man★★ (2002) uses a touch of magic realism that is entirely appropriate. Towards the end the main character grows the horn of a unicorn, or at least thinks he does, as a symbol of evil hidden within. The transition from someone whose account of events seems plausible to someone who

may be guilty of a series of murders, with ambiguity as to how guilty he is, if at all, is accomplished by one unsettling "event" after another, rather like tamed Kafka. The style, a spare prose, suits a man trying to think his way to an explanation of bizarre experiences. There are other nice things: how the code of an American university turns every encounter with a woman into a minefield; the viciousness behind the mannered courtesy of the English upper class; his relationship with his ex-wife; being turned away from a club in favor of a woman leading an older man on a dog leash.

Lasdun's second novel *Seven Lies* (2005), although certainly better than competent, is less interesting. The main character is an East German who lives with his beloved wife near his beloved New York. After the fall of the communist regime in 1989 the files of the Stasi, the secret police, are being made public, and these will reveal that he was an informer and targeted his wife's previous lover. He feels his world has collapsed and pays a blackmailer to be silent and eventually kill him: he wants to leave his wife with the life insurance money and there will be no money if he commits suicide. I felt the wife's character was not fully developed. It isn't clear why she is already semi-alienated and why she refuses US citizenship. The ostensible reason is that she is appalled by the plight of America's underclass, but why she feels America is worse than other nations, particularly communist East Germany, is not explained.

I look forward to Lasdun's next book because of his facility with style: a boy becomes his family's "poet-intellectual" despite the fact he has "never written a poem and … never read a book unless I had to for class"; "One can imagine Stalin's state of mind as he sat on [the] stage receiving these tributes—the absolute disbelief in the sincerity of a single word being uttered; the compulsive need to hear them none the less"; "[the United States'] unappreciated attempt to spread the gift of itself to the rest of the world"; "standing guard for the hour and a half it took [the Peoples Own Washer] to heat up"; foodstuffs on sale in New York were "to us as startling as if a New Yorker should walk into a shop and find delicacies from Jupiter and Venus casually on display."

Jonathan Franzen (born 1959)
The third novel of this writer, *The Corrections*★ (2001), and the fourth, *Freedom*★ (2010), are worthy of praise. Both show the American family under stress because of things that are perennial, such as incompatibility, loss of identity, decay with age, and sexual desire. Franzen puts these into modern context and paints some strong characters. The mother in *The Corrections* and the "errant" wife in *Freedom* hold your interest. But too many of Franzen's views on what the novel should be affect his prose. The books are well short of classics, but I do want to read more from this author. He believes America is almost a rogue state. (So do I.)

Douglas Coupland (born 1961)
Coupland is Canadian. His *Generation X* (1991) appeals to many young people. Older readers may find the book

congenial if they sympathize with youths who want to perpetuate early adolescence as long as possible. Coupland makes desperate efforts to make these young people sound interesting: "Dag says that he's a lesbian trapped inside a man's body. Figure *that* out." But really they do not do anything much or know enough to analyze anything. They just pose, pose, pose endlessly.

Coupland probably does catch how these youths think about themselves, which means many chapters close with homilies that sink to unfathomed depths of goo, particularly in the last chapter. It's clear why the book is popular with youth wary of adulthood: they can feel superior by admiring this way of life without actually having to live it. It offers them a fantasy of thinking and speaking in an impressive way they cannot actually mimic because they lack the education and vocabulary of the author.

All Families are Psychotic* (2002) is a sort of bestiary that portrays a family plumbing the depths of what the modern world can do to people. A son with AIDS gives it to his father's new trophy wife. His mother gets AIDS when the father shoots the son and wounds her accidentally with the same bullet, the son's blood being conveyed to her wound. Another son is suicidal and alcoholic. The daughter is a thalidomide child who has one hand and has grown up to be an astronaut. Both she and her husband are having affairs with her boss and his wife. You get the idea.

Coupland now has his style under much better control, despite the occasional lapse. It would be easy to make the characters caricatures but he succeeds in making them plausible, and the writing is often very funny. An urbane European commiserates with someone living in Kansas City. If only he had known, he would have brightened his friend's life with "tickets for regional dinner theater, paintings of weeping clowns", etc. He uses dolphins for cancer trials but has no regrets. They are "nasty little beasts. They'd mug you, and rape you, and take your handbag within three seconds if they thought they could."

Eleanor Rigby (2004) is not divided into chapters, a minor irritant. It has a serious theme—the dark side of loneliness—and interesting twists. The main character is recognizably human. The same cannot be said for her son: he crawls along a highway to show he is humble and yearns for a tornado with a halo. *All Families are Psychotic* is a better book.

JPod (2006) is about "geeks" who invent computer games. To be interested in their conversation you have to be obsessed with fashion: what is hip in terms of cars, clothes, films, pop music, and so forth. As for its style, here are some samples: "It is not so much a backward step as a step sideways on to an escalator that takes you to a place where you find out your mother is a lesbian before you know what a lesbian is"; "Bree is the best of the geeks. She is made out of cheese but cheese shot full of tasty M&Ms." And so on, for 450 pages. The worst thing is that Coupland himself appears as a character. This is a sure sign of a writer in decline, as witness *Galápagos* by Kurt

Vonnegut. There are sixty-five pages of dollar signs, random numbers, and the first 10,000 digits of pi. At least they make the book go faster.

David Foster Wallace (1962–2008)

Wallace committed suicide at the age of forty-six after years of depression. His magnum opus was *Infinite Jest* (1996). Initially, two wonderful scenes impressed me. The first was an interview with a tennis player for a university athletic scholarship. The player remained mute until he began to make sounds like "a drowning goat" and writhed uncontrollably to the floor. The second was an addict planning a four-day pot orgy that was to be his last—this despite innumerable previous "last" orgies. The detail is incredible. For example, he needs the right food, soft drink, bread, sandwich meat, mayonnaise, tomatoes, M&Ms, cookies, Oreos, cake, ice cream, and four cans of chocolate frosting to be eaten with a large spoon.

This was the only book I did not read to the end. After 120 pages I realized I was in for paragraph after paragraph of detail about trivia: "The organopsychedelic muscimole, an isoxazole-alkaloid derived from *Aminita muscaria*, a.k.a. the fly agaric mushroom—by no means … to be confused with *phalloides* or *verna* or certain other kill-you-dead species of North America's *Amanita* genus … [and] goes by the structural moniker 5-aminomethyl-3-isoxazolol". Such passages include descriptions of premises, furnishings, gadgets, organizations, and events. Every twenty pages or so there is a funny remark: a man was "the size of a young dinosaur, with a massive and almost perfectly square head he used to amuse his friends when drunk by letting them open and close elevator doors on"; "[a coach] was asked to resign … because of a really unfortunate incident involving a riding crop"; a man's appearance [disguised as a woman] was "not merely unattractive but inducing something like sexual despair"; "The noise of the herd is tornadic, locomotival. The expressions on the hamsters' whiskered faces is businesslike and implacable." In addition, if you want to know what it is really like to endure endless, all-consuming anxiety, you will find it here.

This should be enough to judge whether you would like to try *Infinite Jest*. I cannot assess Wallace's other two novels because I did not read them. Wallace said *The Broom of the System* (1987) was like a dialogue between Wittgenstein and Derrida. That was enough for me. *The Pale King* (2011) is an unfinished novel published posthumously. It is described as ranging from dialogues between co-workers about civics and cartography to snippets of the 1985 Illinois tax code.

Chuck Palahniuk (born 1962)
Fight Club★ (1996) by Chuck Palahniuk does something I would have thought impossible. TV has conditioned a whole generation by drastically limiting their attention span. They are accustomed to a dramatic event (murder, rape, car chase) every few minutes. Most of us who love reading reject such media in favor of writers who deliver

what a novel has always had to offer: gradual development of character, scene, and plot. What Palahniuk has done is write a novel that assumes a ten-second attention span and delivers a visceral punch every page. No TV drama can match this book for shock after shock. The author can actually beat the media at their own game.

Naturally, this limits the scope of the novel to darkness and its style to minimalism. His characters inflict wounds on themselves and each other as they spiral down to destruction. But he does it with style. "I really wanted to put a bullet between the eyes of every endangered panda that wouldn't screw to save its species," he writes. And "Don't think of this as rejection. Think of it as downsizing." And "Recycling and speed limits are bullshit ... They're like someone who quits smoking on his deathbed."

A few pages earlier a waiter has confronted a hotel manager whom he is blackmailing by threatening to reveal what goes on in the kitchen—urinating in the soup, etc. The manager objects to his appearance. The waiter flattens his own nose, bleeds all over the office, grabs the manager and bleeds all over him, giggling, pleading, "Please don't hit me again, and please give me the money, you have so much and I have so little." The manager begins to scream.

I suspect you will not want a steady diet of this kind of novel. Palahniuk is by no means a great writer. Compare him to his closest relative in "conventional" literature, Kurt Vonnegut, for example. But if you want to sample the genre this is the best one I have read. He has written eleven more.

I tried *Lullaby* (2002). Either the novelty of his style had worn off or he had lost some of his verbal punch.

Palahniuk has had a life that encouraged bleakness. His father began an affair with a woman whose imprisoned ex-boyfriend swore revenge. After his release, he shot them both and set fire to her home. Palahniuk does readings of his short story "Guts". He reports that a total of seventy-three people have fainted during these, one a man who was trying to escape but fainted before he reached the door. He is not without compassion: he volunteered to work at a hospice, taking terminally ill people to support-group meetings. I assume he was not just gathering material.

Sebastian Junger (born 1962)
Junger writes very good non-fiction reportage. *The Perfect Storm*★ (1997) is a sensitive account of six men who were killed on a commercial fishing vessel, the *Andrea Gail*, which sailed out of Gloucester, Massachusetts and sank in the North Atlantic in October 1991. The description of the alcoholic and desperate culture of the men who risk their lives in swordfish hunting is a vivid addition to the literature about those in the modern world who still do soul-destroying work, although in this case the men take pride in what they do.

Ann Patchett (born 1963)
Patchett's best novel is *Bel Canto*★ (2001), which is based on the Lima crisis of 1996, during which fourteen members of the Túpac Amaru Revolutionary Movement took hostages at

a party at the official residence of the Japanese ambassador. Patchett's portrayal of their leader—"Why anyone would want a long life escaped him"—makes their psychology powerfully clear. The captors and captives develop relationships that humanize them and make you wish there were some alternative to a tragic outcome. For example, a hostage opera star discovers that a young terrorist is a wonderful natural talent and begins tutoring him.

The plots of this writer's subsequent novels do not serve her as well. *Run* (2007) is about an Irish Catholic family in Boston that includes two adopted black boys, now young adults. Thanks to an accident, they discover their birth mother and a girl of eleven who thinks she is their sister. (She is actually not the birth mother's daughter but the child of a friend.) Some of the scenes and characters ring true with my own Irish-American background, particularly the Catholic funeral at which the departed is congratulated on her luck: she is being reunited with God sooner than those in attendance. But there are too many touches that strain for the sentimental. Some work but some do not. An older son—who of course is white—is overdone as a black sheep with a heart of gold. The tenor of the girl's inner life is uneven. She laments that if she had been put out for adoption, her (pseudo) mother "would be all alone now". Well yes.

In *State of Wonder* (2011) two scenes of bereavement make a promising start, but the main character's psychology is shallow and the story ends in melodrama. I backtracked to an early novel by Ann Patchett that had been praised. The main characters in *The Magician's Assistant* (1997) are a recently deceased magician (Parsifal), his previously deceased male lover (Phan), and his surviving assistant (Sabine) who loved Parsifal. Sabine gets messages from these two men through dreams. Phan tells her he killed Parsifal so Parsifal would not suffer from a terminal illness, thinking this was what Sabine wanted. She accuses him of murder. In the next dream, Phan apologizes but Sabine reassures him she regrets her accusation. He takes her to his home in Vietnam, and she reflects that she had better be on his good side or how will she find her way back to Los Angeles. Parsifal wants her to comfort his family, from whom he was alienated when he left them at the age of eighteen to live his life as a gay man. (He is "visiting" them from the hereafter but they do not know this.) They all forge bonds of love. There is some good writing here but too much raw sentiment for my taste.

Donna Tartt (born 1963)
Donna Tartt's first novel about students of classics at an American university—*The Secret History*★★ (1992)—was wonderful. The students, who end up murdering one of their number, are too special to be representative of American undergraduates, but every character rings true and the rhythm of the prose is perfect. Unfortunately, this author now seems to suffer from Joseph Heller syndrome: Heller's first novel was so good he felt empowered to publish his later ones without judicious editing.

Her second novel, *The Little Friend*⋆ (2002), is undisciplined. It took ten years to write and her model was *War and Peace*. This is a pity. It contains far too much about the mental world of Danny Ratliff, a criminal meth addict, local screwballs, and scenes such as dropping snakes off a bridge on drivers below. But I feel there is just enough worthwhile writing to make it worth reading: Harriet, the young girl who is the main character, and Ida Rew, her beloved black housekeeper, work well together. Some parts are affecting, such as Harriet's reactions when Ida relates the indignities she suffers because of her race, and the scene when Ida departs from the household.

After another eleven years Tartt published *The Goldfinch* (2013). It is just a big bad book. The first fifty pages remind us she can still write. After that there are only a few well-done scenes—for example, the first encounter between Theo (the hero or anti-hero) and his true love. Almost everything is overwritten: Theo's grieving about his mother's death; the glories of a painting (of a goldfinch) that comes to symbolize all that is good and beautiful; the agonies of withdrawal symptoms; a cast of criminals impossible to assimilate; and Boris, Theo's dreadful best friend. Every time you think you are rid of Boris he keeps popping up to bore anew (no pun intended). There are tedious passages about "death" and the book ends with a silly philosophy of "life". Compare the section on "love" with the few moving words at the end of Thornton Wilder's *The Bridge of San Luis Rey*⋆⋆ (1927).

Let us hope this talented writer resolves to resist the temptation that has destroyed so many others—namely trying to write great novels—and settles for writing well.

Jonathan Lethem (born 1964)
I cannot quite give a star to Jonathan Lethem's novel *The Fortress of Solitude* (2003) but he too bears watching. The central character is a white boy whose politically correct Puerto Rican mother and white father put out him out on the streets for companionship; they also send him to a school that is overwhelmingly black. He goes through hell as he grows up; muggings are an everyday occurrence. I liked some things that resonated with my childhood, such as playing stoop ball, but you have to think that pop music and avant-garde art are the most fascinating things in the world to live through a lot of the pages. You must also share the ethos of "tagging", welcome a lot of self-analysis, and love Brooklyn, New York. Perhaps if you are a New Yorker you fit the bill. There are several really strong characters, including Heather Windle and Mingus. The ending is accomplished nostalgia.

I decided to read Lethem's recent books to see if his talent could be less demanding on his reader's psychology. *You Don't Love Me Yet*⋆ (2007) is a diagnosis of what keeps a woman about to turn thirty from despair. Lucinda is totally immersed in the pop music scene of Los Angeles. Life beyond music consists of sex, delicatessen food, drink, and vomit. However, she pines for love and falls madly "in love" with people who have nothing to offer except sex or their "talent". She almost disintegrates when her latest lover immediately leaves her for another, despite being aware this kind of behavior is endemic in everyone she knows. Her band has fallen apart but the juvenile fantasy that sustains her comes to her rescue. Success and a true love—actually a lover from her past—are on the horizon. Somehow Lucinda knows they will be famous. You feel saddened by anticipating what her morale will be like at forty.

Chronic City (2009) is about Perkus, a recluse who views the world of Manhattan culture (art, film, literature, music) through the eyes of Marlon Brando and makes inspiring remarks. Like all sages he has little interesting to say. All language seems "a monstrous compendium of embedded histories I'm helpless to understand"; "rock critics are like little animals that live in holes"; "time has a way of getting its bills paid".

He helps his circle experience something close to an introverted mystical experience, losing their sense of self by contemplating a chaldron, a supposedly magical vase. The book builds up to this revelation: "The world was ersatz and actual, forged and faked, by ourselves and unseen others." This book is strictly for those who want to understand the closet world of the Manhattan self-styled élite.

In *Dissident Gardens* (2013), a scene between a daughter of seventeen and her hysterically childish mother is perhaps the worse piece of writing I have read by a serious author: the mother sticks her head and then the daughter's into an oven. The mother is just too infantile to be taken seriously.

The rest of the book is about the radical activities of this woman, her daughter, their husbands, and various relatives, with the addition of a gay black man who trades on his minority status and has a pretentious self-image. Some passages read well (the black police lieutenant, the Quakers) and some really badly (the Lenny chapter, Rose's last "affair"). As a left-wing chronicle, *Dissident Gardens* does not live up to Michael Ondaatje's *In the Skin of a Lion* or Lessing's *The Good Terrorist.* Lethem can write but has no awareness of when he is at his best.

Candice Millard (born 1968)

Candice Millard's *Destiny of the Republic*★ (2011) is a worthy addition to the historical literature on America. James Garfield was shot on July 2, 1881, only a few months into his presidency, and has tended to drop out of history. Millard's book rescues from oblivion a man whose qualities put him up there with Thomas Jefferson and Abraham Lincoln. He was intelligent and principled—too principled to have sought the office—and blessed with a rare eloquence. His assassination stirred the public as much as Lincoln's had sixteen years earlier, although it did not bring out the best in human nature. It was suggested his killer be thrown to wild dogs or forced to devour himself, starting with his toes.

The portrait of America is fleshed out with an account of the politics of the day. Republican Party politician Roscoe Conkling and the spoils system dominated who was appointed to public office: the party that won was expected to reward its supporters. It was considered an intolerable affront to democracy if anyone could not just walk off the street into the White House, see the president during his "office hours", and present their credentials, including party loyalty, for office. The incumbent spent at least half his day on such matters and found it difficult to devote himself to affairs of state. The assassination of Garfield by a disappointed office-seeker led to the first steps toward reforming the civil service with a merit system.

The nineteenth century was the era of the self-made man. It included an ideal of what a learned person should be: someone who, without the aid of much formal education, worked incredible hours to improve himself. Garfield and Lincoln were both examples. With Alexander Graham Bell this dedication extended to efforts to improve the lives of others. Bell not only invented the telephone but tirelessly devoted himself to the deaf. (His wife had lost her hearing when she was five.) He tried to save Garfield by perfecting a device to locate bullets in the body but did not reach the president in time. Garfield's doctors finished him off with their crude efforts to find and remove the bullets.

Gillian Flynn (born 1971)
Flynn's first three novels are all mystery stories in which a non-detective comes up with the solution. They are page-turners and her style improves with each book. She conveys the hopelessness of depressed small towns in midwestern

United States. It is hard to tell which are the more moving, the middle-class teenagers, the poor, or the down and out. Lacking anything to focus their existence on except sex, booze, drugs, and random acts of cruelty, they are beyond hopelessness.

Try reading one novel, see if you appreciate her very appropriate bleak style, and go on to the others if you do. *Sharp Objects* (2006) has some tough-guy language, which fades, and too much melodrama. However, the description of working at the local pig factory-farm foreshadows better things to come: "The constant screams—frantic metallic squeals—drive most of the workers to wear earplugs, and they spend their days in a soundless rage. At night they drink and play music, loud. The local bar, Heelah's, serves nothing pork-related …"

In *Dark Places* (2009) I thought the narrator's limitations would forbid depth, but as I read I felt more at home with her and was moved by the characters portrayed. The passages about the homeless living in an arsenic-poisoned dump are brilliant. As for the poor, an isolated young woman describes her life: "I wished I'd met an accountant or something like that. I never know where to go to meet nice men. In my whole life. I mean, where do you go?"

Gone Girl★ (2012) is better still. It shows a wider mastery of style, particularly the "diary" of Amy. Amy herself has to be taken as a given: you cannot ask whether anyone could really be like her. The other characters are well done, especially the "good cop" and people from Amy's past.

Tom Rachman (born 1974)

Rachman was born in London but brought up in Vancouver. *The New York Times* and other critics hailed his first novel *The Imperfectionists*★ (2010) for its portrayal of character. The story concerns the staff of an English-language newspaper in Rome. Lloyd Burko, a Paris correspondent whose career declines as he ages, and his ex-wife and son all take on reality as his story is told. Herman Cohen and his ambition for a dear friend is a heartbreaker. Oliver Ott, who is as unhappy as only a sensitive man can be unhappy, is forced to be the villain who kills the paper. The writing style varies from good to passable; the author spoils some character vignettes with punchlines that are both melodramatic and unnecessary.

The Rise and Fall of Great Powers (2014) is a step down. Because her mother is irresponsible, when Tooly is a child her father cares for her. From age ten, friends take over her upbringing. At age twenty she strikes out on her own, financially supported by her one true friend. At every age—she is thirty-two in the present—she is nomadic. She and most of the other characters are supposed to be exotic but the majority just have colorful life histories, some boring, a few not. The political analyses of the post-war world are cynical but whose would not be? The depiction of college life is convincing except for the prolonged sex scenes. The attempts at humor generally fall flat, except for an excellent spoof of post-modernism, which "offered hope to those seeking gainful employment without communicating a single clear thought". Something better is needed if we are to enjoy further novels from this author.

Hanya Yanagihara (born 1975)

Hanya Yanagihara was raised in Hawai'i and Texas and lives in New York. She worked on her first novel, *The People in the Trees* (2013), for twenty years. Paul Theroux hailed it as impressive. It details the career of a Nobel Prize winner who adopted more than forty children from his visits to a Polynesian island tribe and is convicted of sodomy. She writes well when describing this man's first trip to the islands, his interaction with two other scientists, the culture of the native people, and the steps that led to his great discovery. There are some subtleties. He confesses to sadism—enjoyment at incinerating ants and killing laboratory rats—without self-awareness. However, as so often in a first novel, the book offers far more detail than the movement of the plot requires. This may be because it is loosely based on a real case.

Yanagihara's second novel *A Little Life* (2015) is about four young artists who are friends and live in New York. The initial depiction of the four is very effective. However, one character, Jude, becomes the centerpiece. Jude was abused as a child and considers himself unworthy. We are told this over and over and over again for hundreds of pages: "Caleb had reminded him how inhuman he was, how deficient, how disgusting"; "He had fantasies of emptying a container of gasoline over himself and then striking a match"; "He sometimes had an image of himself surrendering to [the beasts], and they would cover him with their claws and beaks and talons and peck and pinch and pluck away at him until he was nothing, and he would let them."

It is a hard to draw a line between pathos and bathos but I believe Jude crosses it. His initial abuser actually teaches him to mutilate himself; another runs him down with a car. A sadist beats him; Jude, of course, feels he is merely getting what he deserves. His "happy days" are a gay relationship with Willem (one of the four) in which the sex makes him feel surrounded by howling hyenas. There is some humor. Poetry on the New York subway: "Their relationship consisted / In discussing if it existed." Below this someone wrote: "Dont worry man I cant get no pussy either." Jude describes a sculpture's work as "of the puerile and obvious sort, like a Barbie doll's legs glued to the bottom of a can of tuna fish".

The book raises the question of whether or not Yanagihara has the personal depth to write a great novel, but the style is so good and the art of characterization sometimes so deft we ought to wait and see. There are two beautifully written chapters towards the end, followed by the 200th description of Jude's sense of worthlessness.

Kevin Powers (born 1981)
Powers served in Iraq during the first two of the four years—2004 to 2007—when sectarian violence and US losses were at their height. The narrative passages of *The Yellow Birds*★ (2012) convey the utter despair and disillusion of Americans

unfortunate enough to fight in Iraq. Some passages are very effective, particularly those where Iraqi civilians are killed when no one really wants to kill them. The title is taken from a US army cadence that soldiers chant when marching:

> A yellow bird with a yellow bill
> Was perched upon my windowsill
> I lured him in with a piece of bread
> And then I smashed his fucking head

Writers such as Ann Patchett ("inexplicably beautiful") and Tom Wolfe ("like *All Quiet on the Western Front*") have given it accolades, but as a work of art it does not come close to the best war novels, such as *Birdsong*, *A Time to Love and a Time to Die*, *A Different Man*, or indeed *All Quiet on the Western Front*. Someone, perhaps Powers' editors, convinced him he had to say profound things about death, the arbitrariness of life, and the senselessness of existence. These passages are long, repetitive, and shallow. Read it for the narrative. I hope this author's next novel will be better, but his lead poem in the collection *Letter Composed During a Lull in the Fighting* does not impress.

Looking Back

Marion Starkey (1901–1991)

An earlier book I want to mention is *The Devil in Massachusetts*★★ (1969) by Marion Starkey. It concerns the witch trials that took place in Salem, Massachusetts in 1692 and '93. Despite some minor factual errors this is an almost perfect book. Every character—the hysterical girls who were "possessed", the so-called "witches", the ministers who had them killed—comes to life. The mindset that made all this seem sensible migrated to colonial America from Europe. The mix of sexual sensation, child "testimony", fear, and professionals corrupted by their own ideology emerges as a potentially potent stew wherever human beings live. Although this book was written nearly fifty years ago it is uncanny in its relevance at a time when we have surrounded child sexual abuse, which is real, with myths, persecutions, and experts who act like defenders of the faith.

SOUTH AMERICA

Gabriel García Márquez (1927–2014)
Before reading this author you will profit from some background to the politics of Colombia. Soon after the country took its present shape in 1830, two parties emerged. The Conservatives allied themselves with the Catholic Church and favored strong central government dominated by the business and landed classes. The liberals wanted a secular society, decentralized government, and popular control. They hated one another so much that the closest analogy is a clan feud. Violence became endemic.

Two major civil wars were fought but minor conflicts were almost continuous. The war of 1899 to 1902 killed 100,000 people and that from 1948 to 1958, sparked by the assassination of the Liberal candidate for president, killed 300,000.

There were 200 assassinations between 1946 and 1966. Between 1958 and 1974, a National Front government was created by an agreement that the parties occupy the presidency in turn, and that all other offices and the civil service would be divided equally. Since then the presidency has been genuinely contested. However, from 1964 to the present a new civil war has pitted both of the old parties against FARC (Revolutionary Armed Forces of Columbia) and the ELN (National Liberation Army), which hold these old parties are nothing more than two faces of an oligarchy. This conflict has killed over 200,000 people. The ELN has been in decline since 2000 and peace talks are underway with both groups, interrupted by outbreaks of violence.

In Evil Hour★★—the 1968 edition, translated in 1979, replaced the censored 1962 edition—makes real, as no narrative history can, how Colombia's divisions poisoned life even when full-scale civil war was in abeyance. The mayor is a liberal. He has an abscessed tooth that causes unendurable pain but the only dentist is a conservative. He forces the dentist to operate at gunpoint. He remarks that he may come back for some fillings. The dentist says, "Come whenever you want, to see if my wish to have you die in my house comes true."

The mayor makes strenuous efforts to convince the conservatives that the new liberal government intends to rule fairly. A police killing destroys his credibility and the dentist (who had guns hidden under the floor) goes to join the guerrilas. There is a brilliant image of what Colombia has become. Márquez describes a bloody dog fight—the howls, the bared teeth, and the crippled dogs. He originally intended to call the novel *This Town of Shit*.

Márquez also gives civil war a prominent place in his much admired *One Hundred Years of Solitude* (1967, translated 1970). This book is well written although I found the magic realism off-putting. Ghosts keep appearing. A gypsy visits Earth after his death because he cannot bear the solitude of death, and then dies again. The gypsies perform miracles. All of this is supposed to convince you that reality has limits, whatever that may mean.

Chronicle of a Death Foretold (1981, translation 1982) is good, although not essential reading. It shows how the code of family honor can turn men into murderers even when they do not want to kill. In *Love in the Time of Cholera**, loosely based on the life of Márquez's parents, the action takes place between 1880 and 1930. This story will convince you that what we Anglo-Saxons call romantic love pales beside the passions of Latin Americans.

The General in His Labyrinth (1989, translated 1990) is an attempt to analyze the mind and dreams of Simón Bolívar, the "Great Liberator" who led the successful struggle to abolish Spanish rule from most of that country's South American colonies. The detail will be confusing unless you already know the history. Bolívar was not equally appreciative of all Latin Americans. On Mexican cuisine he wrote: "They eat everything that moves." His list included "red maguey worms, armadillos, river worms, mosquito eggs, grasshoppers, the larvae of black ants, wildcats, water beetles in honey, corn wasps, cultivated iguanas, rattlesnakes, all kinds of birds, midget dogs, and a strain of beans that jumped without stopping".

Simón Bolívar said something quite remarkable about the United States, which in 1830 was a feeble fledgling nation filled, it believed, with republican virtue: "And don't go with your family to the United States. It is omnipotent and terrible, and its tale of liberty will end in a plague of miseries for us all." How could he have foreseen so well the history of US policy in Latin America?

Of Love and Other Demons (1994, translated 1995) shows how concepts such as demonic possession and illness can blind people to the nature of behavior—behavior that may be unusual but is actually neither dangerous nor sick.

Márquez's worst book is *The Autumn of the Patriarch* (1975, translated 1976). Although largely based on Juan Vicente Gómez of Venezuela, it tries to capture the essence of all South American dictators. It is written as one long paragraph and is simply unreadable.

Mario Vargas Llosa (born 1936)

Vargas Llosa's first novel *The Time of the Hero* (1962, translated 1966) was a courageous exposé of what life was really like for military cadets in Peru. However, I found this author's habit of stringing together the thoughts and words of many characters was tedious, and prevented any particular character from commanding attention. These faults were exacerbated in his second novel *The Green House* (1965, translated 1968), although the character of the harp player takes on some substance. Just as I was about to give up, I found that some of Vargas Llosa's later novels were good. They have to do not with his native Peru but with two other Latin American nations, Brazil and the Dominican Republic.

In *Aunt Julia and the Scriptwriter*★ (1977, translated 1982), the main character is Marito, an eighteen-year old who works for a radio station and has an affair with his aunt. The station specializes in soap operas: it used to buy the scripts in bulk from Cuba but has now hired a Bolivian scriptwriter. This man, Pedro, writes excitingly. He gives a priest and a Jehovah's Witness identical names, suggesting they are much the same. (Peru is a Catholic country in which the Jehovah's Witnesses are unwelcome.)

There are many demeaning references to Argentines. Two approach Pedro about an episode in which he says that Argentine women enjoy eating the lice they pick out of their children's hair. He dismisses them abruptly: "Go sing tangos and wash your ears!"

The War at the End of the World★ (1981, translated 1984) is impressive. It recounts the history of a cult founded in late nineteenth-century Brazil by the Counselor, a man as pure and inspiring as his politics are insane. He creates an "ideal" community. As his influence grows, the government convinces itself he threatens their efforts to gain control over the provinces. They plant evidence that he is in league with a (fictitious) British plot to subjugate Brazil and send military expeditions to crush him. Thanks to his converted former bandits, who are masters of tactics, and his fanatical followers he routs the first two expeditions and it takes virtually the whole Brazilian army to defeat him.

There are many wonderful characters, for example the Counselor himself, the colonel who is killed leading the second expedition, and the Counselor's élite cadre. There are some apt touches. My favorite is the legend of Robert the Devil, held up as evidence that even the worst soul can be saved. He killed damsels and holy hermits just for the fun of it. After his conversion, he did penance by going down on all fours, barking like a dog, and sleeping with the animals. He went about begging the kin of his victims to torture him. He later married the queen of Brazil.

A close second: once the cult is liquidated, the army holds interrogations to find out what happened to one of the ex-bandits. An old woman has the answer. "Archangels took him up to heaven," she says, clacking her tongue. "I saw them."

Aside from being a pleasant read, the book captures many themes of Latin American history. There is a rigid hierarchy of color, and whiteness is considered the quintessence of beauty. Nonetheless, Latin American passion refuses to respect race. Portuguese, Indians, and blacks mate with one another, producing every shade of color.

The war between the Counselor and the government is really the war between old and new: religious fervor and rural traditional culture versus rationalism and modernity. The idealists in the military are convinced that only they have the moral purity to abolish the civilian government, which is divisive, venal, and without discipline or purpose. This attitude has been the curse of Latin America, with its many military coups. Usually when the generals take over, they find that they are out of their depth. Trujillo, as we shall see, was an exception.

Vargas Llosa's books are not consistently good. *In Praise of the Stepmother* (1988, translated 1990) must be the most boring erotic novel ever written, unless you are titillated by a seven-year old seducing his stepmother and trying it out on his nursemaid, or by men plucking the hairs of their nose.

However, one of his recent books is well worth reading. First a bit of background. The island of Hispaniola in the Caribbean is split between the nations of Haiti and the Dominican Republic. Between independence in 1844 and the debt crisis of 1900 to 1904 the Dominican Republic was ruled badly and plagued by civil wars and repeated invasions from Haiti. America took effective control of its revenue in 1905, and occupied the country from 1916 to 1924. In 1930, ending six years of relatively good government, General Trujillo seized power in a so-called "election" after he had violently suppressed all opposition. He ruled until his assassination in 1961.

Vargas Llosa's account of Trujillo, *The Feast of the Goat** (2000, translated 2001) is not a great work of art: one of the main characters, a woman who as a fourteen-year old was violated by Trujillo, is too melodramatic. But it holds your attention and its analysis of the soul of a Latin American tyrant makes it required reading. Aside from his sexual appetites, Trujillo is the best possible kind of tyrant. He is not personally venal. His family are allowed to live in luxury, but they are not allowed to send millions abroad and he himself has no interest in money. Most of the state-owned enterprises are in his name but he provides a rationale for this: none of his officials would dare steal from him personally but they would steal the state blind.

A fanatic patriot, Trujillo wanted to make his country into a progressive and strong state. He built hospitals, roads, and schools, and introduced pensions. He alone got the nation out of debt and thereby rid it of the humiliation of American control of its finances. America supported him despite his excesses, turning against him only after a series of embarrassments culminating in a failed attempted to assassinate the president of Venezuela. Some of the dialogue between Trujillo and his chief lieutenants, such as his puppet president Joaquín Balaguer, is masterful.

Trujillo made peace with Haiti early on and slaughtered thousands of Haitians on his side of the border. This was not unpopular because the Haitians created many social and economic problems and, being former black slaves from Africa, led to fears the republic would lose its Spanish heritage. In fact, only sixteen percent of today's population of the Dominican Republic is white. Seventy-three percent is mixed and those more white than black (Trujillo himself was part black) call themselves white. Currently, President Danilo Medina has resurrected the race issue and targeted 450,000 unregistered Haitians for expulsion.

The story of Trujillo may prompt you to ask what is so bad about a "benevolent" tyrant. Plato answered this question in *Republic*: a tyrant is like a man on an island surrounded by his slaves. Trujillo coopted a few slaves who were both competent and cruel to help him run his government and secret police. He played them off against one another, demoralized them, and killed anyone who was critical. This reign of terror meant that everyone of substance (who was not killed) became a half-person, someone who had lost the will to think, feel, or live for himself.

After Trujillo was killed, the United States invaded to depose a democratically elected left-leaning president, Juan Bosch, and put Joaquín Balaguer, the man who had been Trujillo's puppet, back in power. This led to twelve more years of repression. Balaguer, by the way, was also a murderer and a swine in his personal life.

After 1978 things got better. Antonio Guzmán Fernández and his opposition party were in power until 1986, after which Balaguer served two more terms as an elected president but no longer dared use violence against the opposition. He spent two hundred million US dollars on a huge lighthouse that beamed the image of a cross into the night sky, visible for miles.

There is a passage in *The Feast of the Goat* on the ideal Latin American wife, whose submission to her husband is total: "quiet, obliging, long-suffering … put up with his drunkenness, his affairs with women, his fighting … and always welcomed him with a smile … willing to believe his excuses when he bothered to give any".

Junot Díaz (born 1968)
Junot Díaz left the Dominican Republic at the age of six and was raised in the United States. He won a Pulitzer Prize for his book *The Brief Wondrous Life of Oscar Wao*★R (2008). I didn't like the slang style but appreciated some passages and

characters. He describes the hero's school as "Like being put in the stocks and forced to endure the peltings and outrages of a mob of deranged half-wits". The hero is asked: "Hey, Oscar, are there faggots on Mars?" The sister and mother are real enough, although the above-mentioned slang gets in the way of the mother. The book is mainly about the protagonist's experiences in America, but if you want to know what life was like under Trujillo and Balaguer the footnotes are priceless.

John Charles Chasteen (born 1955)
If you feel ready to get a feel for South America as a whole, read Chasteen's *Born in Blood and Fire: A Concise History of Latin America*★ (2001). It is clearly written and does a good job of balancing what is common with how diverse the various nations are in terms of culture and ethnicity. Chasteen notes that things have improved since 1980. Democracy is now dominant and dictatorship rare.

LOOKING BACK

If you are interested in Mexico, you must read Graham Greene's *The Power and the Glory*★★ (1940). This novel, definitely a classic, is about the attempt to suppress the Catholic church in the Mexican province of Tabasco in the 1930s. The dialogue between the priest, alcoholic but courageous, and the lieutenant, ruthless but principled, who executes him is particularly good. Both men are fully human and much better than most of us, yet their ideals are irreconcilable.

UNITED KINGDOM

Roald Dahl (1916–1990)

Roald Dahl was not only a great exponent of children's fiction but also wrote autobiographies, short stories and two adult novels. All his books are stylistically perfect but I am not a fan of his short stories. The few I have read are heavily dependent on shock effect, and fall well short of those of Honoré de Balzac, O. Henry, and James Joyce.

The novels are lightweight: *Some Time Never: A Fable for Supermen* (1948) is a *Gulliver's Travels*-type story that uses gremlins to satirize the follies of humans bent on self-destruction. It is memorable only because of its depiction of the visceral agony of the British people and pilots who had to contend with the Battle of Britain, the attempt by the Germans to bomb them into subjugation from July to October 1940.

My Uncle Oswald (1979) is an odd waste of talent. It anticipates the invention of the sperm bank. Oswald uses a female collaborator to get kings, artists, writers, and geniuses to donate. There are some asides that seem amusing in context ("Hawaiian women … had prehensile toes and in almost any situation you cared to mention, they used their feet rather than their hands") but the sex theme begins to bore the author as much as the reader. The ending is both flat and abrupt: Dahl clearly wanted to put the book out of its misery.

The autobiographies are a different matter. Each was written for the age that matched Dahl's age at the time the action takes place and they tend to be brief. Nonetheless they tell what it was to be English, or at least an affluent English male, throughout the twentieth century.

Despite his older sister and father dying when he was three, Dahl's childhood was happy until he became subjected to the barbarism of the English public school. *Boy: Tales of Childhood*★ (1984) has more about pranks and candies than I needed to hear, but it conveys the despair of an unhappy child who cannot complain to his mother because the school censors all letters. At his primary school the headmaster enjoys sadistic caning; each stroke lacerates the skin and the wounds take three weeks to heal. The school gives short rations of food to save money. At secondary school, the headmaster, Dr Geoffrey Fisher, is even more sadistic, and it tells us something of the times that he was later considered suitable to become Archbishop of Canterbury. Student prefects also torment and cane the younger boys. After such barbaric treatment at the hands of their own countrymen, it is no wonder that graduates of British public schools became communist spies. The book ends with Dahl leaving for Africa to work for Shell Oil in 1936.

Going Solo★ (1986) corrects the date to 1938. This volume has some telling anecdotes about the overseas English who ran the empire: formal dress for dinner, the sacredness of polo, having one's "boy" cut one's toenails.

At twenty-three Dahl joined the Royal Air Force; he was

a fighter pilot from late 1939 until June 1941. His flying experience revealed much that was new to me. I knew something about the men who defeated the German pilots in the Battle of Britain: the average age was twenty-two and average life expectancy four weeks. I did not know that the odds were little better in Africa and the Middle East.

Fortified by the blind courage of youth, Dahl seems impervious to personal danger as fellow pilots die all around him. When he arrives in Greece, a corporal tells him he will not last a week. He demurs—"Don't say that"—as if chastising someone for a discourtesy. He is sent into battle on virtual suicide missions in a plane he has not learned to fly. His squadron leader barely acknowledges his presence—he will be dead soon anyway.

I had thought the Vichy French were sullen collaborators, men and women who lamented their nation's defeat and consoled themselves that Germany had at least left them to "rule" southern France and the country's empire. In fact, most of them were fanatically pro-Nazi. Thousands of lives were lost when the British and Australians had to defeat them to stop them handing Syria over to the Germans.

In 1941, because of blinding headaches from earlier head wounds, Dahl was invalided out of the service and sent home to England. He wrote little more about himself. *My Year*★ (1993) is a short book based on a diary he kept during the last year of his life. Although he would have been aware of his impending death from leukemia, the book gives no hint of this. However, the changing seasons are vividly described as if they might be his last—the book is essentially a poem about the birds, trees, flowers, butterflies, and berries of the English countryside—and the reminiscences hint at a man summing up.

My Year has been aptly described as containing some of Dahl's best writing. I am a city person bored by the countryside except when it offers spectacular scenery. The fact it moved me is quite remarkable. Treat yourself to an hour of tranquility, rather like listening to the slow movement of a great symphony. For the non-English, a "conker" is a horse chestnut.

Anthony Burgess (1917–1993)
Between 1956 and 1995 Burgess published thirty-three novels. As well as being a leading English literary figure, his music put him among the second rank of English composers.

His first novels make up *The Malayan Trilogy*, which comprises *Time for a Tiger*★ (1956), *The Enemy in the Blanket*★ (1958), and *Beds in the East*★ (1959). They potently portray Malaya as British influence declines, and each character is more convincing than the last. I am not sure the third book matches the others but you will want to read it to follow the life of Victor Crabbe to the end. Crabbe's perspective and character, insights and blind spots, comedy and tragedy, give the tale an extra dimension. He knows how limited the minds and awful the lives are of many around him, but he cannot help falling in love with the place.

A Clockwork Orange (1962) was made into an excellent

film directed by Stanley Kubrick. The main character, Alex, is interesting and his slang appropriate, but much of the book is just one outrage after another. Alex's conditioning to make him harmless is a bit trite, as is the happy ending.

Burgess had a reputation as a comic novelist and therefore I began to read the four volumes of the Enderby series about an eccentric poet. The first book put an end to that. The initial ten pages of *Inside Mr Enderby* (1963) are so bad you suspect Burgess hated it as he wrote it. It begins with the sound of Enderby breaking wind. The author takes this as the height of humor, although he hilariously supplements it with belching, vomiting, and defecating ("his viscera loaded like a nightsoil-collector's bucket"). The vision of hell is of a realm of "sulphuretted hydrogen, unwashed armpits, halitosis, faeces, standing urine, putrefying meat", with the devil "farting prrrrrrp like ten thousand earthquakes". Even some of the purely descriptive passages are bad: "The sea whooped in … then grumbled back … grudgingly rattling many tambourines." I did enjoy some of Enderby's poetry.

The jacket blurb for *M/F* (1971) says it is full of wonderful humor and invention. Some funny passages do take over from bathroom humor, although not entirely. I liked the description of the local police—particularly the interrogation scene—and the exotics in the local circus appealed. Father Costello's wedding ceremony strikes the right note: "Do you, Catherine, take this man, Llewelyn, as your pillar, helpmeet, support and stay, as a source of joy and fury, of bread and brood, so long as lust shall last and love live?"

This novel seems to mark a fatal decision on Burgess's part. He became obsessed with showing he was smart, and as a result his writing features far too many passages that are simply pretentious. The first four chapters read like gibberish. Later he describes dawn in New York City as "Eolithic, yes—topless towers, rhodochrosite, rhodomel, touched by rhododactyls." For boredom read page 22 about hot beef sandwiches (they are litoric) and the historic dimension of French cookery. Or page 92, about a list ranging from "antipedobaptism to … zumbooruks", preceded of course by the smells of hell. Or page 102 about fat mothers who gave their children thick sandwiches and "thermoi".

Sadly, the new style becomes a disease in Burgess's most acclaimed work *Earthly Powers*★R (1980). This uses the reminiscences of a fictional gay character to tell the history of Europe during the twentieth century, with particular emphasis on the great wars and anti-Semitism, post-colonial Africa, the empty mindedness of modern youth, the plight of gays, and the recent decay of Catholicism, as he sees it. Kenneth Toomey's homosexuality is a thread that ties the novel together and I have no objection to frank description of its practice, but some of the repartee between himself and his paid lovers is too prolonged, and there is the eternal self-pitying conflict between being gay and being Catholic.

The pointless shows of erudition infect much of the book. Clearly, when you want to communicate with the reader, you say: "The moon was like a round of Breton butter with fromatical veins and a nightingale gushed ridiculous cadenzas." Or "If you saw the mansion from the back, you found something like Martino Lunghi the Younger's SS Vincenzo ed Anastasio." Or "the hall was a miniature Balthasar Neumann pilgrim church of Vierzehnheiligen". Some authors have an erudite style that teaches. For example, you come away from Aldous Huxley with new knowledge and an expanded vocabulary. Burgess was not interested in teaching anyone anything. He wanted to stun you with the fact you were reading the world's intellectual champion, someone whose mind and knowledge were simply matchless.

Some of the book is very amusing. When a modern American girl doomed to intellectual vacuity by her family and time is told who Christ was (Our Lord died on the cross for our sins), she remarks, "Poor guy. Did it hurt much?"

The Catholic priest, Carlo, is a wonderful character, full of surprises, and his monologues on Catholic doctrine resonated with a lapsed Catholic like me. I cannot recommend the book for the general educated public but I have given it a star with an "R" to indicate it is most appropriate for a restricted readership. Young people beginning to read seriously should set it aside for later: you have to already know a lot of history to profit from history as he presents it, and it may give you the impression that learning is simply the art of learning how to intimidate. The book shows Burgess has a first-rate comic novel in him but I was not willing to read another twenty-five books to find it.

By the time of the *The Pianoplayers* (1986) Burgess seemed to realize that going back to writing a decent novel would impress readers more than self-advertisement. It is primarily a book for those nostalgic about British music halls in their prime, the people who played in them, and their way of life. He uses his narrator to make some outrageous puns (she refers to "Low and Grin") and the scenes of her father playing the piano while drunk are pretty heavy-handed. There are long sections about a new method of learning to play the piano, and about every piece the father played during a marathon piano contest. These demand a reader who has some knowledge of music and an intense interest in all the pop music of the day.

The Kingdom of the Wicked (1985) reconstructs the lives of the Apostles between the crucifixion of Christ and their deaths. The degeneracy of Rome serves as a counterpoint to the sanctity of the Apostles—details are included about the vile ways in which each emperor amused himself. Burgess does a reasonable job of inventing how these men may have seen their mission, but the passages about how people thought, particularly Paul on his conversion, and the private musings of the emperors, are wordy. The Christian preaching (on the Trinity) and the descriptions of Nero's fear of hell seem a bit much. Those with an intense interest in the early church may find this book interesting.

Muriel Spark (1918–2006)
Graham Greene recognized Muriel Spark's talent before she was a successful novelist, and when she was recovering from dependence on amphetamines gave her money to

see her through. In *The Prime of Miss Jean Brodie*★ (1961) Brodie is a teacher in Scotland in the 1930s. Control of a coterie of her pupils is her raison d'être: "Give me a girl at an impressionable age and she is mine for life." She teaches the girls what she considers important—art, and admiration of Mussolini and Franco—and plans their lives, whether it involves going to bed with one of her lovers or dying in Spain for the fascists.

The characters are drawn with impeccable skill. A schoolgirl finds the god of Calvin exciting, particularly the doctrine that most of us are predestined to hell from birth. She notes that Calvin "made it God's pleasure to implant in certain people an erroneous sense of joy and salvation, so that their surprise at the end might be the nastier".

Spark's other novels are not as satisfying and after reading five of them I felt I had got as much as she had to give. In my view, two are better than the others but your taste may differ. She never writes a really bad novel.

The Bachelors (1960) is quirky and has complex characters, one of whom, Patrick Seton, verges on the improbable. Some of the dialogue is terrific and many passages are amusing. A séance begins with a hymn to the tune of "She'll be coming round the mountain". A departed husband who is going off to play golf speaks to the medium. He is described as very upset. A skeptic asks, "Why is he going for a game of golf if he is so upset?" A young man trying to be sympathetic to his aunt absentmindedly makes a rabbit out of a handkerchief.

The Mandelbaum Gate★ (1965) has too much about visiting the shrines of the Holy Land for those who are not devout, but the characters are plausible and it will educate you about the founding of the state of Israel. Some Israelis think this could have been done without incurring the implacable hostility of the displaced Palestinians. In fact, the influx of Jewish immigrants under British rule just after the Second World War turned the usual ethnic distrust into hysterical hatred. A doctor tells a Palestinian patient she is "without doubt" a victim of the germ warfare that Israel practices daily. A group of cynical young people ridicules the fanaticism of their elders, singing: "Long live Islam! Long live all fat men! Israel! My mother goes quack-quack all day."

The Public Image (1968) is a study of a not bright actress who has unexpected depth. Her husband despises her because her success is greater than his. He jumps off the top of a church and leaves letters that would destroy her career. She must, therefore, convince the world he was insane. She plants a rumor that women destroyed him by pursuing him relentlessly. The public seizes on this, and believes he was chased into the church by three women, one wearing a bikini.

The Driver's Seat (1970) is a short novella about a demented woman who (also) seeks death. The economy of style is impressive and the book is worth an evening.

Loitering with Intent★ (1981) is excellent. I don't usually like novels about an author—in this case Fleur Talbot—

writing a novel, but here the style, characters, and humor are a treat. In defense of a dubious priest, Sir Quentin, Talbot's employer, remarks, "One of his ancestors fought in the Battle of Bosworth Field." Sir Quentin's aged mother compromises his dignity. When he remarks that he will make sure a death certificate does not indicate suicide, she shouts, "Tell them to wipe their arse with the death certificate."

Doris Lessing (1919–2013)

I had sampled Lessing's work and not been engaged but friends urged me to read further. I did and enjoyed her first novel *The Grass is Singing*★ (1950). It analyses how the English settlers in Southern Rhodesia (now Zimbabwe) could treat blacks as simply beasts of burden: they dehumanized every relationship. They would have claimed a personal relationship with blacks was impossible, but since of course it was very possible it had to be forbidden by an unwritten law. A woman on an isolated and poor farm suffers a nervous breakdown and falls unwillingly into a platonic relationship with a black who becomes concerned for her welfare. The theme is rather like that of *Madame Bovary*, Flaubert's great novel, and ends tragically. The only flaw is the woman's unconvincing prescience of her fate.

Lessing's next novel *Martha Quest* (1952) is not outstanding, but it is a competent portrayal of how a young girl who values freedom above all is swept into marriage at eighteen with someone she knows she does not love. The description of the mindless social whirl of English youth in pre-Second World War Southern Rhodesia is well evoked. As an aside, the main character has mystical experiences as a young teenager, but since she cannot put them into a meaningful context she sees them as just exotic.

Retreat to Innocence★ (1956) is the best book by Lessing I read. A woman of twenty-one has her first affair with an older man, a Jewish refugee, most of whose family died in Auschwitz. Despite her hatred of his generation's politics—she sees them as fanatics who slaughtered one another—and their mores—she believes in one man for life—she is irresistibly attracted to this humane and cosmopolitan man. The young woman is utterly convincing: she knows the relationship is hopeless. When it ends, she anticipates a "happy" future with her fiancé but cannot suppress a sense of irreparable loss. Why did she have to discover that life could offer something beyond conventional happiness, something that will never come her way again?

The problem with *The Good Terrorist* (1985) is taking the central character seriously. She is a communist with an infantile mind and steals from her parents to make a nice home for her cell. If you think of her as a sort of drug addict with a habit that cancels out normal morality she is almost plausible, but her bleeding heart, "black" rages, and almost continuous weeping test your patience.

In *The Fifth Child* (1988) a couple who want a big family and a big house filled with joviality have their world destroyed by an offspring who is supposed to be a throwback to a troll. Aside from the reader having to suspend disbelief, the novel would have been more effective if the couple's dream had been dissolved by a less miraculous event. *Ben, in the World* (2000), about how the child fared as an adult, is no better.

The first half of *The Sweetest Dream* (2001) does a wonderful job of capturing the mixture of idealism and awfulness that characterized teenagers in the 1960s. The second half, which follows them through life, is sentimental and even maudlin. It also turns into a platform for the author's politics. It is not that her views are unsound: Stalin was a butcher; Mugabe and his Zimbabwe were evolving toward something horrible; the British Left was too blind to tell the full truth about either. The stand of the Campaign for Nuclear Disarmament against civil defense was not as foolish as Lessing makes out. There are far too many speeches and the villain, Rose, is so wicked as to be diabolical.

Lessing wrote *Alfred and Emily* (2008) when she was eighty-eight. The book is divided into two parts. The first is a novel about how happy each of her parents might have been if there had been no First World War. (They never marry in this scenario.) It nicely depicts how the inter-war British middle class built their lives around servants. When a woman suggests a small gathering, her husband responds, "But with no staff, surely a social evening is not possible?" They had only two servants.

The second part is a memoir about the actual lives of Lessing's parents after the war, living together on a farm in Southern Rhodesia. The war partially disabled her father.

His reminiscences about the "good chaps slaughtered"—he was the sole survivor of two companies—are heart-rending. The parents' impoverished and isolated life dooms Lessing's mother to total frustration. Lessing's own life as daughter of this family is marked by a terrible struggle to hold her mother at bay. Unfortunately, the style does not show the author at her best, and passages are awkward and contrived.

Doris Lessing also wrote six novels about an advanced interstellar society. These divided her admirers into those who liked and those who hated science fiction.

Barbara Vine (1930–2015)
Barbara Vine, who also published mystery stories under her real name, Ruth Rendell, has written novels about family trauma. The family portrayed in *The Chimney Sweeper's Boy*★ (1998) engages you immediately, and while it is not a great novel it is one anyone would enjoy. Not far behind is *A Dark-Adapted Eye*★ (1986), whose central character, Vera, and her interaction with her malicious son are depicted with great skill. When told it is vulgar to eat with the right hand, the son uses his left hand but manipulates his knife and fork rather like chopsticks. (He also tortures her by leaving ersatz suicide notes.)

The book will also make you aware, in a way no sociology text could, of what Britain was like in the 1940s. First, there was simply no teenage subculture: rather than prolonging adolescence, young people were impatient to become adults. Everyone from boys to aged men dressed alike. Brilliantly caught is how class poisoned the minds of almost everyone. People were unforgiving when their children married one inch beneath them and the gradations of class were infinite: nobility, lesser nobility, landed gentry, prosperous middle class, struggling middle class, middle class in trade, workers, and—utterly humiliating—someone in service. Vera is frantic to claim a noble connection and devastated when her son lets "slip" that a distant relative was a cook. She is intimidated when told that the word "auntie" is rather vulgar.

I suspect these two books are Barbara Vine's best. The central character in *Grasshopper* (2000) is less interesting. (Perhaps I am too old to appreciate a clueless teenager.) And the psychology of *The Blood Doctor* (2002) struck me as implausible. But none of Vine's books will bore you.

V.S. Naipaul (born 1932)
Naipaul is a Trinidad-born travel writer as well as a novelist, and has lived in Britain most of his life. His work in both genres has ranged across the globe. His exceptional book *The Middle Passage*★★ (1962) analyzes the West Indics, Guyana and Suriname circa 1960, in terms of the legacy of 400 years of European domination. Of the Rastafarians, Naipaul claims the sect's theology is based on the Bible, stray copies of *The New York Times*, and exciting historical hypotheses—the present queen of England is the reincarnation of Elizabeth I, and Prince Philip the reincarnation of her lover Philip of Spain. Rastafarians believe that Trinidad is hell (with some justification) and that Ethiopia's Haile Selassie was the

second coming of Christ. Christ was black but Christians have depicted him as white to suppress the truth and gain dominance.

Some of Naipaul's early novels were set in Trinidad. *The Suffrage of Elvira*★ (1958) is a light-hearted early work. Mr Harbans campaigns to be elected from a constituency called Elvira. It is 1950 and the electorate has never before been wooed but the voters' skill in extracting money from the candidate is unbelievable. There are hitches. When the campaign manager paints a slogan "Vote Harbans or Die", an opponent paints over it so it merely says "Die". Harbans' main rival is black and attractive because he wears a zoot suit and two-tone shoes.

In an effort to win the black vote, Harbans decides to contribute to the funeral of any black who dies before Election Day. When the leader of the black community is asked who is likely to die, he suspects the worse: Harbans is using curses to kill black voters. When a man finds a dead chicken on his doorstep, he realizes he has been cursed.

A House for Mr. Biswas (1961) describes an Indian community in Trinidad. Thanks to the death of his father, Mr Biswas depends on the charity of relatives as he grows up and the charity of in-laws later on. He has never had a stable home and longs for a house of his own. Many acclaim this as Naipaul's best novel. I did not find it so. I wished Mr Biswas well and was happy he got his house, but I did not empathize with him as I did with the characters in, for example, Naipaul's African novels.

The book does tell us something of what life was like in these communities in the mid twentieth century. Mothers compete to be known as the one who beats her children most vigorously; the status of both husband and wife is enhanced when the former beats the latter. When Seth tells Mr. Biswas a prospective bride is a good girl with a bit of reading and writing, he feels he may have put a foot wrong: "Nothing to worry about. In two or three years she might even forget." People still frighten their children by telling them that Alexander [the Great] will get them.

Naipaul has also published a book of essays: *The Return of Eva Perón,* with *The Killings in Trinidad** (1980). "The Killings in Trinidad" tells us more about the absurdities of European stereotypes about blacks and South Americans than about the people themselves. It paints a fascinating picture of a man, Michael X, whose whole life was unconscious play-acting. Although he and his cult met their demise in Trinidad, white intellectuals in England and America told him what they expected of a black leader: not someone doing anything to promote black progress but a man who met their stereotype: angry, violent, rootless, sexually attractive.

The book's other essay "The Return of Eva Perón" gives an excellent history of both Uruguay and Argentina up to 1972. Under the dictatorship of Eva's husband Juan Perón no criticism was allowed. The country's leading literary figure, Jorge Luis Borges, was such a great writer he could not be killed: instead he was offered the inspectorship of poultry and rabbits in the public markets. The book has a plug for New Zealand: "More gifted men and women have come from its population of three million than from the twenty-three millions of Argentines."

In another essay, "A New King for the Congo", first published in 1975, Naipaul's focus is Africa, and in particular Mobutu Sese Seko, dictator of Zaire (today the Democratic Republic of Congo). Like the kings of old, Mobutu claimed ownership of his country's mines, vacated land, and fruits of the earth. The task of developing the nation was immense. There was a veneer of civilization along the Congo River and the rest was essentially inaccessible jungle. As an escape from dwelling on this task and the fact nothing was being done, he used the slogan "African authenticity".

Later, in the novel *A Bend in the River*★ (1979), Naipaul brilliantly depicted what life was like under Mobutu, although neither he nor the nation are named. The book is beautifully written. A "big man" establishes his dictatorship. At least there is an intelligence at the center, rather than anarchy. However, it becomes apparent he is like most dictators, fostering a cult of personality, a rapacious army, and a corrupt administration. A white who has been removed from the center of power pathetically praises the man's virtues, hoping for reinstatement. Educated blacks have no doubt about their situation: "We're all going to Hell and every man knows that in his bones. … Everyone wants to make his money and run away. But where?"

The subsequent history of this nation is terrible. Two wars resulted in the death of more than five million of its sixty-eight million people. Since 2002, when a new constitution was written and a new president sworn in, there has been a fragile peace and things have improved. However, as of 2016, political instability, lack of infrastructure, and corruption were still impeding economic progress, even though the country has enormous natural resources.

Naipaul's earlier African novel *In a Free State** (1971) won the Booker Prize. The writing that gives the book its title is a 135-page novella surrounded by shorter pieces. The African "free state" is unnamed but appears to be a British colony in the Great Lakes region, which includes Uganda, Tanzania, and Kenya, all of which attained independence in the early 1960s. The action takes place at a time when one tribe, represented by a president, is decimating another once-ruling tribe, represented by a king.

Bobby is a white administrator in the south living in the Compound, a protected area. He drives there from the capital with Linda, the wife of another resident in the Compound. Over the 400-mile trip they see increasing evidence that independence is going to make the position of whites intolerable. Linda faces up to this; Bobby, who wants to stay, minimizes each incident and defends the blacks, pointing to their history of exploitation. There is a brilliant scene in which his disillusion breaks through. A service station attendant "cleans" his car windows with a scraper that has lost its rubber edge, leaving deep scratches. Bobby explodes in anger. Just before the trip ends, soldiers at a checkpoint beat him badly.

The book's shorter pieces (only one about Africa) are effective. An Indian talks to a compatriot opening a restaurant in Washington, D.C.: "No mortgages or anything like that. Cash or nothing." I understood him to mean he had tried to get a mortgage and failed. A West Indian refers to a woman he dislikes as "Miss Shameless Christian Short-Dress herself". There is a savage portrait of Italian tourists in Egypt and a sympathetic one of peasant soldiers.

More recently, Naipaul has published *The Masque of Africa: Glimpses of African Belief*★ (2010). He finds some commonalities throughout West Africa. Traditional African religions cannot withstand Christianity and Islam, both of which give attractive versions of an afterlife. Despite this, older beliefs in magic, witchcraft, and superstition are still strong and few feel safe from evil forces. Almost everywhere there have been population explosions, which eat up much economic development and threaten to impoverish the environment. For example, despite Idi Amin's reign of terror, wars, and AIDS, Uganda's population has gone from five million to thirty-two million since 1966. A student explosion has also put enormous pressure on the quality of university education: in fifty years student numbers have risen from 4,000 to 30,000.

The book gives a good introduction to several African countries. Uganda once had a high culture, but a history of cruelty and slaughter by successive rulers makes the reign of Amin from 1971 to 1979 understandable. He killed about 150,000 of his subjects. Nigeria is oil-rich and the élite appear modern until you find they believe in charms, pagan ritual, and that cats are demonic. Muslims are allowed four wives and Catholics do not practice birth control so numbers overwhelm public sanitation. Where the Koran governs education, graduates are literate in Arabic but untrained to do anything needed in a modern economy. The people of Ghana know that sneezing and the wind are portents. Ivory Coast was once a lush land, but even there overpopulation may soon mean starvation. Gabon is oil-rich but superstition, malaria, sleeping sickness, and the equatorial heat impede modernity. The Pygmy culture of the south is still intact and their "healers" much in demand.

The Enigma of Arrival (1987) is an introspective auto-biography. The narrator describes his feelings and thoughts between when he left Trinidad in 1949 at age seventeen to go to England to become a writer and when he returned in 1984 to attend his sister's funeral. He reflects on the differences between England and the Trinidad of his childhood, but the primary emphasis is on the deep satisfaction he took in his mid fifties when living in cottages near Stonehenge. He had a sense of timelessness, although aware that nothing is really timeless. From most writers we would get an exhibition of how boring their meditations are, but thanks to Naipaul's depth as a person and style the book is interesting. It is not really a novel. He treats certain neighbors as people worth portraying for themselves. However, this is secondary to how they suit his mood and expectations; they get the same attention as the trees and flowers that grow nearby. Read it only if you are interested in the man behind the books.

Naipaul has written three books about India. *India: A Wounded Civilization*★★ (1977) expressed deep pessimism about that country's future. *India: A Million Mutinies Now*★ (1990) was a bit more optimistic: the notion of freedom was beginning to undermine some of the rigidity of caste. Naipaul's 2002 book *An Area of Darkness* is said to be a masterpiece that captures India better than any other book ever written.

Naipaul's two books on Islam have enraged much of the Islamic world. *Among the Believers: An Islamic Journey*★ (1981) traces the rise of fundamentalism in Iran and Pakistan. One theme is undoubtedly valid: the tension in the Islamic world between wanting, if only selectively, the technological advantages of Western civilization, and rejecting those aspects of Western civilization, including secularization, that make the technology possible. In *Beyond Belief: Islamic Excursions Among the Converted Peoples*★ (1998) Naipaul revisited the same countries. He observed that the poor and oppressed had lost hope and saw their government officials as either indifferent or hostile. Religious hypocrisy prevailed: men grew beards for job applications and then cut them off.

Naipaul has published fourteen novels. With ten books starred as worth reading, it will not surprise you that I intend to read the rest. I rank Naipaul among the élite writers of our time.

A.S. Byatt (born 1936)

The Times listed this author as one of the fifty greatest novelists since 1945. I was recommended two novellas, *Morpho Eugenia* and *The Conjugial Angel*, published together as *Angels and Insects* in 1992. The formality of the style may be appropriate given the people and their historical setting but I found it cold and formulaic, and felt the characters suffered as a consequence. The first novella has a good fable about caterpillars and interesting information about captive ants. The insects seem more interesting than the people. There is a lot of tedious talk about the arts and the significance of ants for understanding human nature.

The second novella captures the peculiarities of English people obsessed with spiritualism and the atmosphere of their séances. It was hard to read through their endless speeches and streams of consciousness about what it all meant. There are lengthy excerpts from Tennyson's poetry, and he and his family emerge as pedestrian. This is probably true: Tennyson attained mystical experience through the method of endlessly reciting his name. I had to agree with the *Kirkus* review: "[it has] all the leaden scholarly pretension of that era"; "Too much learning can be a dangerous thing for a novelist who needs to separate the learned monograph from the illuminating tale"; "Dull and forced."

I then read the author's best-selling novel *Possession*★R (1990), which won the Booker Prize. It is often very funny although the humor assumes a restricted audience— namely people (I am one) who take delight in deflating the pretensions of current literary criticism. A feminist critic praises women for not describing the ocean as men do: women speak of "salty female wave-water ... which is not ... put together out of the crud of male semen scattered on the deep". Women writers and painters have created their own "evasive landscapes ... tactile landscapes which do not privilege the dominant stare." There is mention of postmodern criticism, namely "post-Derridean strategies of non-interpretation".

A literary scholar, Fergus, laments the difficulty of deconstructing something that has already deconstructed itself—a book about a painting that was itself a chaotic mass of brush-strokes. He gives a paper: "The Potent Castrato: The phallogocentric structuration of Balzac's hermaphrodite hero/ines." There is a passage in the book on the loves of a female academic: "After the professor, there had been Marge, Brigitta, Pocahontas and Martina."

However, there are long passages that could interest only someone who takes an intense interest in the Victorian poets, whose verse I consider awful. You may want to read only about 300 of the 500 pages, ignoring most of the poetry, references to mythology, and some of diary entries, and skimming the courtship letters. Even then you have to put up with a style like this: "And it is probable that there is an element of superstitious dread in any self-referring, self-reflexive, inturned postmodernist mirror-game or plot-coil that recognizes that it has got out of hand, that connections proliferate apparently at random, that is to say, with equal verisimilitude, apparently in response to some ferocious ordering principle, not controlled by conscious intention, which would of course, being a good postmodernist intention, *require* the aleatory or the multivalent or the 'free', but structuring, but controlling, but driving, to some—to what?—end."

Howard Jacobson (born 1942)
Jacobson is sometimes described as the English Philip Roth but he prefers the label the Jewish Jane Austen. I stumbled on *The Finkler Question*★ (2010) in a Salvation Army store in Auckland. The title is code for the Jewish question and the book is about what it is like to be Jewish in England today, surrounded by agitation against Israel, which easily translates into traditional anti-Semitism, both because anti-Semitism is there to be aroused and because the Jewish ear is tuned to hear it. Despite this dark theme, the first half of the book is hilariously funny.

Some samples. A young woman is recruited to cheer up a man of ninety who is depressed over his wife's death (and a bit deaf).

She: "What's your favorite color?"

He, thinking she said composer: "Mozart."

She: "What bands do you like?"

He decides against saying the Czech Philharmonic.

As evidence that good taste in music does not make you sympathetic to Jews: "When Mussolini visited Hitler in the Alps they played the Bach double violin concerto together." A gentile is a guest at a Passover Seder and keeps asking what each dish symbolizes. Answer: "The chicken symbolizes the pleasure Jewish men take in having a team of women to cook it for them."

Some of the humor assumes an awareness of Jewish culture. And the pathos of the second half is a bit diluted by the fact one of the main characters gets tiresome: he is a gentile who wishes to be Jewish. But even he is not without his merits. He offers women unconditional love, ideally consummated by their dying in his arms, bathed in his tears. And yet they leave him.

I think this book conveys two things better than any I have read: the way in which their history both burdens and benefits Jews no matter where they live; and how difficult it is for them to forge an identity independent of their awareness of "being a Jew".

I enjoyed Jacobson's earlier *The Mighty Walzer*★ (1999), although if you are bored by sport you may not be sympathetic. A Jewish boy in Manchester wants to become the world's best ping-pong player and thus reap the adulation of beautiful women. The World Veterans' Ping-Pong Championships and his nostalgic reunions with his childhood friends at the end of the book are moving. The humor is not as consistent as in *The Finkler Question* but you will enjoy it. The police question a suspect who says he was walking the streets brooding.

"And what, on the night in question, were you specifically worrying about?"

"Crimes against the Jewish people."

On being forced to attend his daughter's Orthodox Jewish wedding, where the sexes are separated: "One consolation though: later I was allowed to dance with my new son-in-law." Musing about his daughter's religious beliefs: "a universe … driven by One All-powerful God who happens not to be worth a pinch of shit either as a judge or as an exemplar."

The novels that separate these two books were disappointing. *Who's Sorry Now?* (2002) is burdened by pillow talk that goes on and on. *The Making of Henry* (2004) features tedious dialogues with Henry's deceased father. *Kalooki Nights* (2006) is an improvement in that you eventually get interested in the characters, but there is too much talk about things like nihilism. There is nothing the matter with that, it's just that great writers such as Fitzgerald and Dostoyevsky have done it so much better.

Jacobson's most recent novel is *J* (2014). A futuristic England has been designed to prevent ethnic violence. Name changes, adoption, and editing history render people ignorant of their ethnicity. Unfortunately, this does not eliminate murder or murderous impulses—for example, lovers often feel tempted to kill each other. People are filled with fury. The authorities decide that a partial renewal of ethnic tension is a desirable lightning rod, and deem Jews ideal for the role of a despised group (the Chinese are rejected). They select two people who are made aware of their Jewish ancestry. The plan is to wed them with traditional

Jewish rites, and make their offspring, together with those of similar couples, the nucleus of a new identifiable Jewish community. One is willing, the other commits suicide. I believe these futuristic people and this futuristic society are less interesting than real people living in the real world. It is hard to write a dystopia: Huxley's *Brave New World* and Orwell's *1984* are among the few that are successful.

Julian Barnes (born 1943)
You must read this author's eleventh novel *The Sense of an Ending*★ (2011). I thought it was one of the greatest novels I had ever read until it was spoiled by an utterly bad ending. Up to that point it seemed like a perfectly contrived work of art. Everything reflected light on everything else. For example, a history lesson at school characterized the attempt of the protagonist, Tony Webster, to tell his own story: history is not only the lies of the victors but the self-delusions of the defeated. The book comes close to Chekhov's maxim: "If you say in the first chapter that there is a rifle hanging on the wall, in the second or third chapter it absolutely must go off." As the events unfold, characters that seemed one-dimensional on the first telling take on depth at the second.

The ending springs a surprise that is unnecessary—it could easily have been foreshadowed with greater effect—and badly handled. The dialogue goes astray—for example, the epithet "You don't get it, do you?" keeps being put to someone who could not possibly have "got it".

When the chips were down the writer lacked judgment,

yet his touch was so sure up to that point that I decided to read some of his earlier novels. In *Flaubert's Parrot*★R (1984) Barnes uses a biography of Gustave Flaubert, the author of *Madame Bovary*, to range widely over literature and literary criticism. The book is somewhat uneven and perhaps of most interest to those curious about Flaubert. His summary of Flaubert's short story "*Un Coeur Simple*" ("*A Simple Heart*") will force you to read it.

There are wonderful quotations from Flaubert: "Language is like a cracked kettle on which we beat out tunes for bears to dance to, while all the time we long to move the stars to pity"; "[Life] is like soup with lots of hairs floating on the surface. You have to eat it nevertheless"; and when the Franco-Prussian war breaks out: "Whatever else happens we shall remain stupid." The indictment of literary critics is spot on and there is a great section on novels that deserve to be banned. Barnes offers a plot to render all novels of a certain sort unnecessary: A woman mates with a porpoise, symbolizing "the world [bound] together in peaceable companionship".

In *England, England* (1998) a megalomaniac replicates the greatest sights of England (Big Ben, Stonehenge, Manchester United, the royal family, Morris dancers) on the Isle of Wight as a tourist attraction. Martha is an adviser who briefly supplants him. Her personal history, particularly her childhood, is convincing and the megalomaniac is plausible, given what he is, but there are too many send-ups of postmodernism, such as people's play-acting roles becoming more real to them than their real-life roles, which are of course also play-acting, and too much about the meaning of life. England is portrayed as a bucolic refuge from the modern world.

You could treat this book strictly as a comic novel but the humor is too sparse. There are a few apt one-liners, such as: "What use would the Good Samaritan have been if he couldn't afford to pay for the innkeeper?" Barnes is never at a loss for an appropriate metaphor.

Arthur and George★ (2005) portrays two Englishmen from the first forty years of the nineteenth century who are so different from people today as to seem like Martians. Sir Arthur Conan Doyle, author of the Sherlock Holmes novels and short stories, never progressed beyond adolescence; he had the teenage code of a medieval knight, ready to ride forth to right all wrongs, and totally dependent on his "mam" for moral advice. For nine months he conducted a campaign to get a pardon for a man called George Edaji, who had been wrongly convicted of killing a horse. In Barnes' book George comes across as honorable and humorless beyond belief and Sir Arthur's commitment to spiritualism takes on a certain dignity. Spiritualists are the true religious skeptics. They see that all conventional religions are founded on sand, and therefore they are determined to rely on evidence. They are disgusted by the trickery of most mediums and accept the testimony of only a few as authentic. Some characters such as the mam and Jean Leckie, Doyle's second wife, are excellent.

Ian McEwan (born 1948)

On Chesil Beach★ (2007), for which McEwan was shortlisted for the Booker Prize, works on many levels. It is about Edward and Florence, a couple very much in love, who fall apart because they are sexually naïve, untouched by the sexual revolution of the 1960s. The brief account of the life Edward was to lead thereafter is a snapshot of how the lives of ordinary Britons altered from 1960 to the present. In a media interview, McEwan mentioned he had taken a few pebbles from Chesil Beach to keep on his desk for inspiration. The Weymouth and Portland Borough Council threatened to fine him £2,000 so he returned the pebbles.

McEwan's novel *Amsterdam* (1998), which actually won the Booker Prize, is his worst: excellent writing spoiled by a sensational and contrived ending. The same is true of *Solar* (2010). *The Child in Time* (1987), *Enduring Love* (1997), and *Atonement* (2001) sustain his stylistic excellence but some characters did not strike me as strong.

The best of McEwan's recent work is *Saturday*★ (2005), about a day in the life of a principled and intelligent man in London in 2003. His quality cannot shelter him from the forces the modern world has unleashed, and he is only too aware that it is too complex and ambiguous to tame, even conceptually. The overall excellence of the book makes up for the rather foolish dilemma of conscience he creates for himself: he "manipulated" a man who is becoming delusional to save himself from a savage beating.

Peter Ackroyd (born 1949)

I heard good things about Peter Ackroyd as a novelist and read ten of his books. Only three appealed. His early novels alternate between portraying the present and past and I thought that, as Ackroyd is an historical writer, he might do this well. *Hawksmoor* (1985) won the Whitbread Novel Award and the Guardian Fiction Prize. It is described on the dust jacket as a "meditation on the nature of time and causality". How did the disaster of encouraging novelists to "meditate" about these things, rather than write a narrative that illustrated them, get started? There are endless passages on causality ("I never know where anything comes from"), fate ("if he cared for anything, it was for oblivion"), and observation of self ("the shaddowes moving across … my Face"). The book ends with one of the protagonists "a child again, begging on the threshold of eternity". Once a character says, "I cannot change that Thing call'd Time …" If only the author had taken heed.

Ackroyd uses this novel to preach the message that "the generations jostle one another". The notion is that when dire things happened at a place in the eighteenth century, it is destined to be the scene of murders in the twentieth. After being stated over and over, the supposed link between the past and present becomes boring.

The notion also infects the thinking of the book's twentieth-century detective. He is obsessed with things such as that victims and murderers are predestined from birth, all is inexplicable, that he may have to invent a past, and if so "would not the future also be an invention?" He talks about this kind of thing to his team. It is not difficult to see why they lose confidence. On the plus side, the description of the horrors of old London is graphic.

Chatterton (1987) refers to Thomas Chatterton, born in 1752, dead by his own hand at age seventeen, perhaps suicide, perhaps because he was using arsenic to treat syphilis. Chatterton forged medieval poetry, and the plot turns on the authenticity of a newly discovered manuscript that suggests he survived his death, concealed his identity, and forged the work of the great poets of the day. As for the story, Charles, the hero, is a romantic twentieth-century poet who becomes obsessed with the possibility that the classics are Chatterton's forgeries. He and his acquaintances are undermined by the awful repartee they exchange about literary matters. I guess it is possible that literati in England talk like this but it is painful. Charles himself is a bit much. He eats books. His light-hearted exchanges with his son are very twee. A character called "Mother" sets your teeth on edge every time she appears.

First Light (1989) offers a story about the interaction of archeologists and locals during an excavation to reveal the distant past. The plot is interesting but the comedy is poor. A woman is guilty of persistent malapropisms: lesbian rather than thespian, coagulated rather than articulated, a wild fruit chase, a persona no thank you (for persona non grata), a mess of porridge. The characters muse about cosmology (half understood), nature, and of course time

("time is God"). The book ends with the resurrection of an aged seer with a profound message ("sound is the soul of all things"), followed by three pages of the seer's gibberish and then two pages of the author's gibberish.

The House of Doctor Dee (1993) evokes sixteenth-century London as it was before the great fire. John Dee was a thinker with a passion for alchemy, particularly the quest to create a homunculus, an eternally existing "human" being. Matthew is living in Dee's house today. The thoughts of both him and Dee are never-ending. Dee sees the world without love, or so the spirit of his wife tells him. He must climb the hill of forsaking, or so the spirit of his mother tells him. He must enter the garden of the true world (his wife again). Matthew tells a homunculus that he, the homunculus, does not exist. The homunculus seems convinced—he opens his mouth and screams. Matthew *becomes* Dee after a child instructs him that a door has been open for a thousand years and "lo, the thousand years have gone". The book ends with comments about history: "The imagination is the spiritual body, and exists eternally. It is done." There are a few nice surprises in the plot.

Milton in America (1996) starts badly with a dream about Menippus, Lycidas, Palinurus, Aeneas, Diana, Arthur, Arcturus, and the Pleiades. The pomposity and religious mania of the seventeenth-century poet John Milton are supposed to be amusing but rarely are. In colonial America the conflict between his Puritans and the Catholics is much like a Punch-and-Judy show. Milton loses and regains his sight and encounters Indian "magic". His impressions of the Indians—"feathers of angels" and "peacocks of Solomon"—make you wish you saw them through the eyes of almost anyone else. He has a knack for turns of phrase, among them: "I know no more of you than of the old man of Antwerp who ate his own feet."

The Plato Papers (1999) gets bad even before it starts, with a list of empty invented prefatory quotations. Plato is the main character and who would have thought you could make Plato seem silly. He reads *On the Origin of Species* by Charles Darwin, assumes it was written by Charles Dickens, and comments on it witlessly. The parody of creationists is not too unkind: they deserve it. Early in this book there is a list of definitions of words such as antibiotics (a death ray), brainstorm (believed anxiety changed the weather), daylight saving (light stored in containers), dead end (graveyard), and electricity (astral magic), that should tell you whether you will find it as amusing as the author does.

Despite all this I am glad I persisted with Ackroyd because his most recent novels are a leap forward. The style is better, the meditations mainly absent, the text free of ostentatious erudition, and the dialogue free of literary allusion. The plots are also better. In *The Clerkenwell Tales*★ (2003) he uses characters from *The Canterbury Tales* to bring alive the last year of the fourteenth century. The people are convincing, and convey what it was like to live in a time of violence, filth, superstition and religiosity. The book is tied together by a story about hatred of the Lollards, a harmless religious and political sect, and machinations of the "predestined men", who were by no means harmless.

The Lambs of London★ (2004) is often compared to *Chatterton* because of a similar theme. About 1795 a talented young man, William Ireland, seeks his father's approval by offering him what were supposedly Shakespearean relics and long-lost plays. All characters major and minor held my interest. The portrait of the "young" spinster whose life is enlivened by finding a soulmate and hero in William is outstanding, particularly as the woman's grip on sanity slips. The desperate lives of the London poor lurk in the background and are subtly conveyed: the anonymous suicide, the deceitful beggar, the bald-headed woman who would tumble in the streets for a halfpence, and little Anne, a street child, who befriends an indigent young man of letters. Her disappearance verifies that "the world itself seemed to breathe misery".

The Fall of Troy★ (2006) is loosely based on the character of Heinrich Schliemann, an adventurer who excavated the site of Troy in the late nineteenth century. Schliemann is larger than life, a fanatic who bends reality to his theories. This sets up an interesting interplay between himself and sanity, represented by his wife and other archeologists who visit him. Some of the extensive references to Homer may put you off but this is outweighed by the portrayal of the characters. Schliemann chose his young wife, Sophia, from photographs but she suspects she will learn to love him because he is a man of substance. She does grow to admire him, until gradually she becomes aware of his darker side.

Ackroyd's later novel *The Casebook of Victor Franken-stein* (2008) is not quite as interesting. Ackroyd retells the Frankenstein story with a twist. The ideology, life experiences, and psychology of Victor make you sympathetic to his mission of creating life and the "monster" is not bad. However, Ackroyd pays a price for the surprise ending. There is nothing in Victor's portrayal that prepares you to accept it. It is a matter of any person is capable of anything. Victor is a person. Therefore, Victor is capable of anything.

I don't know that it was worth reading ten books to find three good ones. I advise you to read reviews by someone you trust before you plunge into this author's work.

Martin Amis (born 1949)
The critics label *London Fields*★ (1989) Martin Amis's most significant novel, and it is worth reading. The author presents his usual dark view of the contemporary world, and the characters border on caricature because that is what Amis feels people have become. A man is writing a novel about three people he meets, one of whom can foresee the future and helps him shape events to give the novel the storyline he wants.

Amis can write, and while there are too many reflections on the human condition these are compensated for by his black humor. A hospital tries to cheer up its child patients: Welcome to the Peter Pan Ward. The British upper class cogitates: What is the proper way to eat a cockroach? Shall we hunt rabbits or weasels this weekend? The narrator defends the honor of Ireland: a proud but drunken nation.

Few of Amis's other novels are worth much. *Other People* (1981), about a young American woman who suffers from amnesia, is mildly interesting. The woman has to discover what living is like from scratch and eventually recovers her identity, which is much improved from her previous one. The novel relies a great deal on stream of consciousness and the stream of consciousness is dreary: "She wondered what happened when you lost it, your memory. Where did it go?" "The trouble with pain is that it hurts." "In the end the past will always be there." "Love is nothing without you there to feel it." "Don't eat fear soup." "All clichés are true." And so on.

It ends with a whimper, with life and death equated. Some critics thought this stuff was great but the book is far inferior to another that makes use of memory loss: *New Finnish Grammar* by Diego Marani.

In *Money* (1984) a would-be porno film director tells us what he is drinking and popping as he goes from one sex bar and brothel to another. Horribly, Amis himself is a prominent character in the book, chatting with the protagonist and giving him advice. The main character even blames Amis, partially, for his fate. He is like one of Norman Mailer's tough-guy characters gone to seed. Some of the descriptions of New York neighborhoods are deft and there are the usual funny passages. An actor has played Genghis Khan, Huckleberry Finn, Einstein, Zorro, Freud, and Jesus Christ. In a film a prehistoric man is transported to the present: a girl's flatmates find him a bit rough even compared to her usual pick-ups.

Amis has made a reputation for "experimenting" with fiction. *Time's Arrow* (1991) was an experiment in writing a novel where time runs backward: excrement leaps from the toilet into the anus and food exits the mouth to fall on the plate. Mothers lose their babies when they go back into the womb. A rape victim is un-raped and lifted to her feet by the rapist. Amis asks a "philosophical" question: would it make a difference if our lives ran backwards? Well, it certainly makes a bad novel worse. This book is dull, dull, dull. The experiment ranks with those of writers who see how long a story they can write without using the letter "e".

An experiment that did prove worthwhile was *Night Train* (1997), a psychological detective story written in the style of Dashiel Hammett. In passing, you may want to read Hammett's masterpiece *The Maltese Falcon*⋆ (1930), later made into a great film with Humphrey Bogart. That book, too, was an experiment: Hammett tells us only what the characters do or say, never what they are thinking. Amis's book does not match Hammett's but it is interesting and written with style.

Yellow Dog (2003) has been hailed as a comic masterpiece. It is filled with literary devices and puns. A Chinese woman gets the surname "He", so that when she makes love we get: "He touched him and he touched He." A duke dines with his mistress in a Chinese restaurant (wan tun a bit of privacy) but is pursued by reporters (we'll cashew). The caricatures have become too extravagant to be effective send-ups. They have names such as Izzat and Watban, and one uses a texting vocabulary. Still, there is some great dialogue and Amis retains his capacity to be funny. A yellow journalist writes a "think-piece": "Is The King Normal?" A mobile phone offers "hatecrammed music inciting you to act like someone crazy".

Koba the Dread: Laughter and the Twenty Million★ (2002) is not a novel but an account of the horrific crimes of Stalin in Russia, and the double standard of communists throughout the world who supported him while at the same time lamenting Hitler's slaughter of the Jews.

This was not true of the non-communist Left. Bertrand Russell wrote the scathing account *The Practice and Theory of Bolshevism*★ (1920) after meeting Lenin. The Socialist Party of America, to which I belonged, denounced Stalin from early on: too many communists we knew kept going to Russia to admire the regime and then being killed as "spies". And we believed the reports about slave labor camps.

The only defense of the Stalin supporters I can think of is that Hitler was appalling because he espoused an evil philosophy—anti-Semitism—while Stalin pretended virtue, with his stated goal a good society. However, it's hard to see how mass murder lied about is much better than mass murder boasted about. Naturally, once you closed your eyes to the real world you could dismiss negative accounts of Stalin as "capitalist propaganda".

All of this was a great tragedy for the Left. First, whenever there was a conflict between the interests of Russia and fighting evil in the United States, communists opted for Russia, which made the left look alien and insincere. The communists opposed the March on Washington for Jobs and Freedom of 1941, organized by the great black socialist A. Philip Randolph, whose aim was to end racial discrimination in American industry. The Communist Party thought agitation for racial equality in industry might disrupt American's preparation for war: their priority was a powerful America that would fight on the side of Russia. Their unions took a no-strike pledge. The Dunn brothers, who ran the Teamsters Union, were jailed for refusing to take it. They were followers of Trotsky (whom Stalin had murdered) and the communist newspaper *The Daily Worker* called their jailing a positive step toward "a better America". Less than a decade later, the communists were jailed under the same legislation.

Second, in Cold War-era America every protest group, whether endorsing racial equality or free speech, was split and weakened by the issue of whether to accept communist members. Those in favor saw good people committed to good things and hated the government's persecution of the Left. Those against could not stomach fighting alongside people who rationalized what was going on in the Soviet Union—namely ethnic cleansing, people being shot on the slightest suspicion of criticizing Stalin, and even anti-Semitism.

I have given *Koba the Dread* a star because even today people need to be educated as to just how terrible Stalin was.

In 1937 the Soviet Census Board's count showed his crimes had reduced the population by deaths among slave laborers and deliberate mass starvation. Stalin had all its members shot, and in 1939 the new board inflated the count and therefore gave a much higher estimate of the population.

Stalin did not neglect his home state of Georgia. Those who were shot were fortunate. The founder of the Georgian Republic had his eyes put out while his wife was forced to watch. The wife of the party leader was tortured to death in the presence of her fourteen-year-old son, who was then sent to a slave labor camp and later shot for pleading for his release. The ex-premier was tortured for three months and shot. His wife and four children were treated more kindly: they were just shot.

Children were encouraged to denounce their parents. The champion denouncer was a woman responsible for 800 deaths. She was finally recognized as insane. But there were risks if you denounced: you could be shot for not having denounced sooner, or for not having denounced more people. No one was safe. When Stalin decided that research on sunspots had become anti-Marxist, more than two dozen leading astronomers disappeared.

Amis uses his black humor to good effect. He notes that with great criminals such as Stalin you think you will find hints in their upbringing: "X was raised by crocodiles in a septic tank". Although Stalin's father was moderately violent and drank, he was fairly typical for his time. Both Stalin and Hitler were choirboys. The book has flaws. Amis's psychoanalysis of Stalin is extensive and repetitive. You may wish to read the first 180 pages and skim the rest.

Stalin poses a great mystery. He did not spare the families of his intimates. Night after night he watched films while surrounded by men whose wives had been shot or sons had died in camps. But no one ever picked up a chair and killed him.

Amis also wrote a book on America, *The Moronic Inferno* (1986). The title sounds exciting but it is just ordinary journalism without any sign he put his heart into it.

Hilary Mantel (born 1952)

Hilary Mantel is presently completing a three-volume series of novels about Thomas Cromwell. Friends had recommended *Wolf Hall* (2009) but I found *Bring Up the Bodies*★ (2012) better. It immerses you in sixteenth-century England, although if you know nothing about Henry VIII you may find it less interesting. The king's manner and psychology, essentially those of a passionate and precocious child, are the best part. Cromwell is entrusted with getting rid of Henry's second wife Anne Boleyn so he can marry Jane Seymour, whom he now prefers and hopes will give him an heir to the throne. Cromwell's interviews with the courtiers who must be convicted of adultery with the queen, and of course executed, are chilling. He is a highly intelligent and utterly ruthless (although not cruel) man, as he had to be to survive in the court politics of the day. Both books won the Booker Prize.

Sebastian Faulks (born 1953)

The Girl at the Lion d'Or (1989), *Charlotte Gray* (1999), *Human Traces* (2005), and *On Green Dolphin Street* (2007) are decent novels by this author, but none match the quality of the one that captivated me. *Birdsong*★★ (1993) tells of the terrible conditions in the trenches of the First World War. Toward end of the novel, a woman whose grandfather had fought visits the battlefield near Arras. There is an arch supported by four vast columns. Etched over hundreds and hundreds of yards of stone, furlongs of stone, there are names:

"Who are these, these…? [she asks]. Men who died in this battle?"

"No. The lost, the ones they did not find. The others are in the cemeteries."

"These are just the… unfound."

When she could speak again, she said, "From the whole war?"

The man shook his head. "Just these fields."

Elizabeth went and sat on the steps. … "Nobody told me. … My God, nobody told me."

I also found a first-rate piece of biography by this author. *The Fatal Englishman*★ (1996) is about three promising men who all died young. Christopher Wood's maturation as a painter is well described. So is the depiction of English apprehension, through the 1920s, of all things foreign. French art was pornography, the work of lunatics, a practical joke. Richard Hillary, the second of the men, became an icon during the Second World War because he insisted on flying after crippling injuries. He was a patient of A.H. McIndoe, the great New Zealand-born plastic surgeon: "He [McIndoe] was brought up in Dunedin, a dead-end town that had been enriched by a goldstrike in 1862." McIndoe's cousin Sir Harold Gillies told the Nazis he could supply a variety of nose bridges, so that anyone could "change his racial and facial characteristics by sleight of hand".

The life of the third man, Jeremy Wolfenden, takes us into post-war England. At Eton he experienced total segregation of scholarship boys, who were thrashed so they wouldn't think too highly of themselves, and exclusive little clubs whose members wore fancy waistcoats. He attended an Oxford that was "bitchy, complacent, and scared of itself". The ideal was to make an art out of repartee, drink, and sex. Wolfenden's gayness became a career and he drank himself to death. Faulk sums him up as someone who exemplified "the failure of the institutions that produced him".

Of Faulks' recent novels, *Engleby*★ (2007) is worthwhile for the sheer virtuosity of the writing. The young people at Oxford during the 1980s are vivid and the gradual darkening of the character of the narrator is chilling. I also think that *A Week in December*★ (2009) deserves a star. It falls just short on literary merit, but as social commentary on contemporary Britain and the madness that led to the crash of 2007 to 2008 it is fascinating. If teaching in an inner-city English secondary school is really like this, abandon all hope.

A Possible Life⋆ (2012) is divided into five parts, each a self-contained novella or long short story. "A Different Nan" is wonderful, with no moralizing or reflections on evil, history, time, or somesuch. Faulks conveys the horrors of Hitler's extermination camps using character and prose more powerful than any lurid description could be. A captured Englishman of unthinking decency is the vehicle. His "post-traumatic stress" is not analyzed endlessly but conveyed masterfully by his quixotic search for the woman (half loved) who betrayed him after she had been tortured. Faulks also captures the scene in Britain after the war: the penury, the traditions (boys seated in chapel according to their performance in Latin), and a former pupil whose touching act of kindness softens the lot of the "hero" in a mental hospital.

The second part, "The Second Sister", has a powerful impact. In mid nineteenth-century England a family is forced to send one of their four children, a seven year old, to the workhouse because they cannot afford to feed him. The oldest boy can work, the baby is not eligible, and the seven year old eats more than his six-year-old brother. The father, once a prosperous tradesman, soon joins the boy but is ashamed to acknowledge his existence. We know what slavery meant in terms of the separation of black families in America, but forget it was one of the horrors that poverty inflicted on the English working class. Later the household is partially reconstituted, although the mother has gone off to Australia with the baby. The boy marries a girl he met in the workhouse. Her eventual fate, and acceptance of it, affords one of the most moving passages in English literature.

The third part, "Everything Can Be Explained", is awful. It is melodramatic and its characters, motivated by silly accounts of science and its implications, are unconvincing. As a novella of ideas it reminds you of Nietzsche's assessment of Gogol: a wonderful stylist but child-brained. The fourth part, "A Door into Heaven", is better but I suspect your appreciation will be conditioned by how much you like stories in which simple piety is rewarded by the appearance of Christ. In the fifth part, "You Next Time", Faulks recovers his touch, evoking the pop music scene of the 1960s and beyond with characters that ring true. A decent man is divided between two women, with all the heartache that often entails. This collection does not match the consistency of Joyce's short stories in *Dubliners*, but who has ever done that? It shows that Faulks' talent is still fresh and by the end of his career may be judged truly outstanding.

Kazuo Ishiguro (born 1954)

I believe that Kazuo Ishiguro, born in Nagasaki but raised in England from the age of five, is perhaps the greatest novelist of our generation. His work is going to make him one of few novelists writing today who will be read throughout this century.

A Pale View of Hills★★ (1982) is about a woman, Etsuko, who went from Japan to England with a British man after the war, and her daughter with this man, who is her second husband. Etsuko's elaborate courtesy, self-control, and total rejection of self-pity are made all the more poignant by what she endured in post-war Hiroshima and at the hands of a traditional husband. It is a masterpiece of understatement. We are left to construct for ourselves how the woman's first marriage dissolved and why she exiled herself. Towards the end there is a flashback about an incident with a neighbor's child that leaves ambiguous whether Etsuko survived the war totally sane.

In *An Artist of the Floating World*★ (1986) a Japanese painter, Masuji Ono, committed "treason" by breaking with his mentor (some good dialogue here) and politicizing his painting. He was celebrated before the Second World War, when the military were ascendant, but in the post-war world the younger generation holds him accountable for promoting the war that wrecked their country. One of his daughters is finding it difficult to marry a man with a good family. Ono's family believes his tarnished reputation is responsible, and pushes him toward a humiliating apology when they meet with the family of a prospect. However, Ono is basically a decent man. His family loves him and fear suicide if they push him too hard.

England is the setting for *The Remains of the Day*★★ (1989). A butler goes on holiday. His whole self-esteem rests on the belief that he served a great man. He reviews the incidents that eventually tarnished his master's reputation— he was an appeaser—and tries to convince himself his master is a tragic figure whose virtues were turned into vices by history. This book will broaden your understanding of Britain in the 1930s. There were many good men who wanted peace above all and could not face the evil that was Hitler.

The Unconsoled (1995) was a mistake. Ishiguro tried to write a great novel in the style of Kafka, rather than writing his usual great novel. Naturally some critics call it his best book. Events occur randomly, dreamlike, half remembered from a past invented to give them a semblance of reality. Everything seems to make sense but nothing does. Life is a nightmare without shape or form, tasks never completed because of another task, conversations sidetracked by another conversation. Every event unravels. The book may be worth reading to see how a master can extract something from a literary convention that straitjackets most writers into utter monotony, but it just goes on too long.

There are some good scenes: a civic dinner punctuated by an outburst against a veterinarian for failing to return a garden fork borrowed six years before; a eulogy upon the death of a dog ("Your Bruno was … much loved by those of us who saw him doing his business around our town"); and a debate about whether there is to be a bronze statue for the dog and whether he is more worthy than a pet tortoise. The revered citizen who owned the dog rises to his feet: "You think that dog was so important to me? He's dead and that's it. I want a woman." The protagonist, a concert pianist, saves the day with a universally acclaimed speech: "Collapsing curtain rails! Poisoned rodents! Misprinted score sheets!"

When We Were Orphans★★ (2000) is a masterpiece, if marred by the improbability of how the main character thinks and behaves toward the end. Just after 1900 two boys, one English and one Japanese, play together in Shanghai. The English boy's father works for a company in the opium trade, and the boy's mother becomes estranged out of moral outrage. Opium smoking is destroying China, but England does not care because the country is making money out of it. England actually fought a war to force China to accept opium imported from India.

The appalling hypocrisy of the day is underlined: the company forbids hiring locals because they may be corrupted by opium. After Japan invades China in 1937 the English boy tries to find his parents, who have disappeared. His boyhood friend is now a soldier, totally brainwashed by Japanese nationalism but still human. He says he has a son back in Japan who does not yet know how awful the world is.

Never Let Me Go★ (2005) deserves a star for the virtuosity of the writing and the grimly compelling content. Read it if you want to be both fascinated and unhappy for a day or two. It will not fill out your picture of contemporary Britain very much because it based on a fiction that has, thank God, not yet become fact.

Ishiguro's latest, *The Buried Giant* (2015), is a failure. It is set in sixth-century Britain and written as if the world were populated with the objects of people's fantasies: dragons, ogres, and fairies. As a sort of enchanted land novel it is much inferior to, say, *The Hobbit*, where the dragon at least has an interesting personality. The book does pose this question: if we cannot recall the past, does that compromise enjoyment of the present? And even if it does, does not forgetfulness of historic injustices prevent acts and wars of revenge? But the question is treated simplistically. The speech of the time dominates Ishiguro's style and prevents his usual excellence.

Alan Hollinghurst (born 1954)
Hollinghurst's five novels include *The Line of Beauty*★R (2004), which won the Booker Prize. Nick is a young gay man who, thanks to a friendship with a member of a very wealthy family, lives from 1983 to 1987 in a home whose members travel in the aristocratic élite of the Thatcher era.

The party talk of these people reinforces the image of utterly worthless individuals who never doubt their superiority. Nick is obsessed with beauty in both men and art (music, painting, and décor) and his adopted family gives him access to both. This has a darker side in that basking in beauty is all he asks of life, and he thinks of little else, other than his erotic fantasies and the right thing to say to gain acceptance. The writing style is attractive, with the best at the end when Nick's patrons coldly dismiss him and all his illusions about friendship and acceptance are destroyed.

I have never understood why anyone would persecute gay men. However, I have zero interest in their sex lives, which makes much of the book tiresome. I have given it a qualified star as of interest mainly to readers who do not find gay erotica boring.

Patrick Gale (born 1962)

Patrick Gale's novels are also about gay men but most of the erotica is absent. For anyone who needs to be convinced that gay men are real people rather than stereotypes they are very successful. Beyond that, they do not belong in the first rank.

The dialogue in *The Aerodynamics of Pork* (1985) is not quite right. It often reads as if it were a script between a comic and a straight man: everyone is just so bright and quick on the uptake. The plot has a similar defect: every event is part of a tidy package. *Ease* (1986) is about a woman named Domina who calls herself "Minnie Mouse". It is not quite that horrible but it is very ordinary. *Kansas in August* (1987) shows improved style but the plot is very predictable. You know immediately who bore the mysterious baby. There are two weak characters. The thinking of Rufus (or Andrew) passes the bounds of plausibility. Sumitra Sharma is an eleven-year-old girl who has a crush on someone and invents a strange religion based on the belief that he has spontaneously given birth.

In *Little Bits of Baby* (1989) none of the characters are convincing, partly because of the uneven quality of their dialogue and the inappropriateness of their reactions to various events. They find people so lovely they "could just eat them up". You cannot fault Gale for failing to provide a happy ending: every character gets the best of all possible worlds. This author's work is improving. In *The Facts of Life* (1995), the best part is the description of a man's decline because of AIDS, if you can forgive the appearance of his deceased grandmother, who ushers him into death and then hangs around to appear to her still alive husband. Even here, drama sometimes edges into melodrama.

J.K. Rowling (born 1965)

Rowling is the author of very successful teen novels based on a schoolboy called Harry Potter. Her first adult novel *The Casual Vacancy** (2012) is not exceptional as a work of art but well worth reading as a social document on a slice of contemporary England. The portrayal of a welfare home, a household where violence and drug abuse is the norm, and the efforts of a girl, not bright but fiercely dedicated to a salvaging her younger brother, are too convincing to be comfortable. Some of the other characters such as Fats are less persuasive and it was not necessary to balance the overall tragedy with a spate of happy endings.

David Mitchell (born 1969)

Mitchell's *Cloud Atlas* (2004) is a collection of six distinct narratives, three bad and three good. Two are futuristic. One of these suffers because the main character—a "fabricant" with unusual intelligence—and the Korean Brave New World she inhabits are uninteresting, the other because the narrator uses an off-putting version of post-Hawaiian English. Another narrative features a precious character with lots of jokes about British railways.

On the plus side, there is a moving tale about the triumph of good over evil, with vivid descriptions of the fate of Moriori on New Zealand's Chatham Islands and the tyranny of the Christian missions in Polynesia. If you want a bit of stereotyped derring-do, a heroic journalist risks death to expose a dangerous nuclear power design. Finally, a young composer lives with a great composer and his family. These characters are interesting.

*Black Swan Green** (2006) is a real leap upward. A thirteen year old is the narrator and Mitchell does an excellent job of avoiding the dilemma this poses: pedestrian content because the psychology of a thirteen year old is not very enthralling, or better content at the price of a thirteen year old making observations that are jarringly mature. Part of the solution is brilliantly done dinner-table conversation between the parents, relatives, and older daughter, portraying a marriage in collapse and an emerging bond between the two siblings. The boys at the protagonist's 1985 Worcestershire school create a society more totalitarian and macho than anything I can recall from 1947 Washington, D.C. but it seems very real. The book has its faults. For example, there is too much moralizing, including a defense of the honor of gypsies. The author introduces a character from *Cloud Atlas* who says too much about beauty and truth and name-drops shamelessly.

Critics hailed these early novels as promises of greatness, so I also read Mitchell's last three novels. *The Thousand Autumns of Jacob de Zoet* (2010) is a historical novel, clearly written and meticulously researched, about the Japan of the late eighteenth century. I would not discourage anyone from reading it, but it does not rise above others of its kind and the plot is entirely conventional. In 1799 Jacob goes to Dejima, an island off the coast of Japan that is the trading hub of the Dutch East India Company. He finds he is the only honest man there, which damns his career. He falls in love with a talented Japanese woman, who is sent to a nunnery when her family becomes impoverished. The ending is exciting and satisfying and I will not give it away.

The Bone Clocks (2014) begins when Holly Sykes is fifteen: Mitchell has a real talent for portraying teenagers. Another storyline offers an image of student life at Cambridge in the 1990s which, if true, would justify mass extermination. A reporter describes how Iraq unraveled, with excellent detail about the tragic loss of his team, and his panic when, during a visit he made to the US, his daughter goes missing. A section on a novelist has some wonderful writing: his ex-wife wrote an "I will survive" piece for *The Sunday Telegraph*. However, a war between wicked vampires that feed off souls and virtuous horologists who enjoy transmigration of souls and do no harm introduces 150 unbelievably bad pages. Evil supermen confront Mary Marvel and shoot it out at the O.K. Corral, firing neurobolas. The good guys win with a resounding KA-BOOOOOOOOOMMM (really). The heroine kills a vampire with a rolling pin ("You will regret threatening my family"). There is a soppy ending: "So I just do my best to smile as if my heart isn't being wrung out like an old dishcloth".

The vampires are not just a passing aberration. *Slade House* (2015) is about a house inhabited by two vampires who feed on the souls of unwary guests. It reads like a ghost book for young readers. There is no suspense in that every victim meets the same fate until a horologist (see above) comes along and beats the vampires. Unfortunately, her victory is not enough to forbid another episode and thus another bad book. Still, Mitchell is only forty-seven and his best work shows he may wake up and write some real novels.

Lee Rourke (born 1972)

Reviewers do not necessarily make good novelists. Rourke's first novel *Canal* (2010) was lauded. *The Guardian* felt he had staked a "claim as heir apparent to greats such as James Joyce". (Where do they find these reviewers?) It is about "boredom" and consists mainly of conversations between a young man and woman sitting on a bench by a London canal. They find nothing interesting, not ideas, books, politics, art, sport, handicraft, travel—the poor things. All of their conversations are boring: "existence is essentially prolonged boredom" ... "the sheer beauty of boredom" ... "we are technology" ... "all is fiction" ... "everything is absolutely pointless" ... we live in the "endless here". The girl paints with her own blood because she wants to die. She risks her life to try and save a dying swan.

LOOKING BACK

A rereading of C.P. Snow's *The New Men*★ (1954) reminded me that it affords insight into those who created the nuclear weapons that Britain retains to this day. Blinded by nationalism, they convinced themselves that the best way to reduce the dangers posed by the bomb (which horrified them) would be to add another nation to the list of those who had the bomb. The only thing to recommend what they did is that it gives Britain an opportunity to unilaterally give up its nuclear weapons, although of course such a blow to its "national prestige" is unthinkable. It would be no more powerful than Spain.

I cannot leave England without a mention of D.H. Lawrence. Lawrence's first novel *Sons and Lovers*★★ (1913) is a fine nineteenth-century novel. It has long descriptive passages and the accounts of people's emotions are often florid, but Lawrence writes so well that the latter are convincing. This novel may not rival the best of F. Scott Fitzgerald or Isaac Bashevis Singer or Kazuo Ishiguro but it comes close. The depiction of the main character's father is wonderful: a miner who is attractive and kind, wanting to love and be loved, uncomprehending as to why his wife and therefore his children are alienated. The mother, and indeed all of the characters, are alive.

If your edition includes Lawrence's theological foreword, read it if you must but it is pretentious and foolish. He did not want it published. Unfortunately, he could not resist sermonizing in his later novels. *Lady Chatterley's Lover*★ (1928) has endless passages on being in touch with our instincts and the attractions of pre-industrial England: it was closer to nature. The sex scenes are sometimes banal, but understandable as a flaunting of the prudish taboos that got the book banned.

The first few chapters that depict the circumstances that made Lady Chatterley are wonderful. She was bathed in the ideal of freedom and yet was not taught to use freedom in any meaningful way. Her class was never going to provide her with a good way of living. Her lover, Mellors, is rightly offended by all the English class system has to offer. Her husband, brilliantly drawn, shows the futility of the life of the mind as it was practiced among the "chattering classes". The hopelessness of it all is colored by Lawrence's ideology. A purely instinctual life is impossible. However, thought offers nothing worthwhile compared to instinct—except his own novels, of course, which have the merit of making this message explicit.

IRELAND

Ireland has made an extraordinary contribution to literature published in English during the twentieth century—witness William Butler Yeats, James Joyce, George Bernard Shaw, Bram Stoker, Oscar Wilde, Samuel Beckett, John Millington Synge, Sean O'Casey, David Butler, Elizabeth Bowen, Kate O'Brien, Flann O'Brien, Seamus Heaney, and William Trevor. I wondered whether this were still true and found seven contemporary novelists of note. Many of them were obsessed with the early time of Troubles, 1916 to 1923, which saw the Irish War of Independence turning into the Irish Civil War. That period was utterly traumatic for very different reasons than the trauma the Jews suffered during the Holocaust. The Jews were being exterminated by a non-Jewish lunatic. The Irish embarked on an orgy of trying to kill one another.

Ireland's troubles did not end there. Between 1968 and 1998 the war with the Provisional Irish Republican Army (IRA) over merging Northern Ireland with the Republic of Ireland cost more than 3,500 lives.

Edna O'Brien (born 1930)
The Country Girls (1960) was banned in Ireland. At the request of O'Brien's parish priest, copies were burned in the church grounds after the saying of the rosary. L.P. Hartley, a prominent novelist, called the two girls in the story a pair

of nymphomaniacs. In fact, Kate has a conventional crush on an older man and Baba is mainly interested in the high life of Dublin. There is exactly one page in which Kate and Mr Gentleman look at each other in the nude and she briefly touches his "orchid". This is the closest to anything explicit.

The Country Girls is a very promising first novel. The girls go from elementary school to a convent high school (whose strictures, not that onerous, drive Baba mad) to first jobs in Dublin. There are some good descriptive passages. One girl said the nuns slept in coffins. Another feared that her dead mother was in purgatory. She had told a lie—when given too much change in a shop she had not returned the money. The style is not as mature as O'Brien's later work but more than good enough to merit the comments of those who said that here was a writer of promise.

In the 1990s O'Brien wrote a trilogy about the current state of Irish society. *House of Splendid Isolation*★ (1994) is set during the recent orgy of killing over Northern Ireland. A member of the Provisional IRA forces an elderly woman to give him refuge in her home. The IRA, the woman, the police who hunt the IRA, all of them love the very soil of Ireland, share a narrative of its history freed by heroes from English rule, and have a family background of relatives murdered, either in the struggle against English rule or by other Irishmen.

Everyone is at war with him- or herself: whether they castigate their enemies as "traitors" or "murderers", they hate killing fellow Irish. The IRA man prides himself on never targeting a "civilian". The woman tries to impress him with the fact her father was a freedom fighter. The sergeant who hunts him down has a little girl who asks him if he uses real bullets and cries when he says yes. Critics say O'Brien sometimes substitutes rhetoric for her usually elegant prose and there is some truth in this.

In 2013 Ireland passed a law allowing abortion if the mother's life was at risk, including from suicide, and women can no longer be prohibited from going abroad to access abortion services. By this time, the church was on the defensive because of a flood of cases about clerical abuse of minors. When *Down by the River*★ (1998) was published, the abortion issue still divided Ireland into passionate camps. O'Brien tells about a girl of fifteen who was impregnated by her father, fled to England, and was then forced to return. The anti-abortion camp gives her a fish. When it leaps out of its bowl she quickly puts it back: "Good girl … You saved its life … That is your true nature, you would not kill, you would not kill."

Why wouldn't she tell her solicitor about her father? "Shame … They feel dirtier if they tell it … They feel they're to blame in some way." The prose is riveting and intensifies your suspense about the girl's ultimate fate.

Why did O'Brien choose land disputes as an issue for the final volume of her trilogy? It too is something that pits Irish against one another because of the ferocity of these disputes. Which poses another question: why does land underlie the self identity and even the sense of national identity of so many Irish?

Wild Decembers★ (1999) provides the answer. English rule made personal ownership of the land all that was left of Ireland. The great famine of the 1840s killed millions and "pit neighbor against neighbor, and dog against dog in the crazed and phantom lust for a lip of land". Like Tom Jarndyce in *Bleak House*, Joseph disintegrates as he loses control of land he considers his own. He feels he has lost his heritage (the land was won at cards by his grandfather), his honor (his beloved sister falls in love with the enemy), and even his dog (killed accidentally on the disputed land). The story is told in O'Brien's usual excellent style. Joseph's dog wins a contest and "lifts one leg for it to be shaken". Hunting on the land as a child there were "eggs boiled in the same water as they used for tea, then a smoke, night coming on, the stars like pieces of diamond on the cloth of the heavens". The local church has "the stained-glass windows [with] virgins and martyrs with infants being born not from lower down, but coming out of their chests in clean and undefiled incarnation".

At eighty-four, O'Brien published *The Little Red Chairs* (2015). A Serb who masterminded the slaughter of Muslims in Bosnia seeks refuge in Ireland. He charms the locals but then is arrested and reviled. After he impregnates Fidelma, a middle-aged woman, Serbian brutes abort her forcibly and she flees to London. Fidelma's dreams belong in a melodrama. Each apparition is worse than the last. People around her say such things as "My victims are inside me", "I am a child of Africa", and "if it a boy I will kill him". They all have a sad past. Indeed even the dogs have a sad past.

John McGahern (1934–2006)

I read four of the six novels by this Irish writer. His style enhances everything he writes but his later work does not equal the quality of his second novel *The Barracks*★ (1963). Elizabeth, a woman in her forties, knows her life is under threat because of ill health. She had a lover who fell out of love with her only because he cared for nothing at all. She has married a policeman, a man desperately unhappy because he hates petty orders and routine, and she cares for his children from a previous marriage. The couple love one another, the children accept her with reasonable grace, and although she has a sense her life is without real significance it is enough for her, and the thought of oblivion is terrifying. The ending is a brilliant affirmation of her attitude. This novel does not pontificate about death but conveys how a person lives with it as an imminent threat.

In *The Pornographer* (1974) a man of thirty looks upon life as killing time between birth and death. His job typifies his pointless life. The style of the pornography he writes unfortunately carries over to the description of his own love life. He impregnates an attractive but boring woman eight years older. She is totally enamored with him and the ideal of their life together. He does not love her and the prospect of a future with her fills him with horror: he has always feared being swallowed by others. The conversations in which she tries to win him over are repetitive. There are some dismal passages about life: "We have to go inland … and there make our own truth … even if that proves nothing too"; "We were outside change because we were change"; "But I don't need kindness." "You will," a ghostly voice said. "You will."

Amongst Women (1990) describes a self-obsessed man who totally dominates his family. To maintain the peace, everyone must spend all their time diagnosing his moods and catering to him or they suffer angry outbursts. The wife and two daughters—who worship him as the guarantor of their sense of identity and worth—achieve this, but one son in particular is alienated. The family's dynamics and the characters of the children are beautifully conveyed. However, the father is the centerpiece, and I found him altogether too predictable to hold my attention. Every family scene is dominated by his hypersensitivity, suppressed rage (a tool of domination), and self-righteousness.

That They May Face the Rising Sun (2001; also entitled *By the Lake*) was McGahern's last novel. In the late 1980s Joe and Kate Rutledge go to Joe's boyhood home to find a better life than in London. They run a small farm in a rural area by a lake. They and their neighbors, some local characters, are very real but the book is interesting only if you want to linger in the routine of their daily lives, punctuated by minor events such as the sale of a business and the death of a local boy whose life unraveled after he went to England.

Descriptions of the lake, its birds and animals, flowers and trees, the change of the seasons, and the chores of the farmers take up much of the text. The Catholic church is revered but sometimes resented: Americans believe America is the greatest country on Earth but "the greatest country in Ireland was always the world to come".

John Banville (born 1945)
Banville's style is wonderful despite a touch of preciousness here and there. I first read *The Sea*★ (2005). Every character from major to minor is authentic, even when summed up in a few words. The colonel is outstanding but so are the narrator's mother and sister and another family that entranced him as a boy. Banville's descriptive powers extend beyond people to, for example, a discussion of Bonnard's painting *Nude in the bath, with dog.* The narrator drinks heavily. Inebriation permeates several of the Banville novels I have read, particularly those set in Ireland.

The Untouchable★★ (1997) is a fictionalized account of the Cambridge Five, men who spied on Britain for Russia during the Second World War and after. Victor Maskell is an art historian based on real-life Anthony Blunt. He finds his wholly virtuous family, whom he loves, an embarrassment and feels guilty that he is embarrassed. The scene when he takes his retarded brother to a "home" is terribly affecting. His wife and her parents and his parents and his brother are vivid portraits. Maskell marries at thirty-one but later comes out as homosexual.

The atmosphere the five spies breathed was a blend of idealism and self-definition. Maskell needed to be a man of action. His life as a spy, particularly his involvement with Russian minders, is beautifully conveyed. He felt he belonged to an exclusive club, an élite of the best and brightest. One critic of his politics remarks: "The trouble with you … is that you think of the world as a sort of huge museum with too many visitors allowed in."

This book is not just about the psychology of a spy: Banville elevates tragedy to the highest level. Maskell's life of deception leaves him deceived about every facet of his own life and awakens an emotion in the reader for which pity is too weak a word. Art creates an empathy that is rare, even in great literature.

Does Banville rank with Ishiguro? He is seventy-one and Ishiguro sixty-two, so both have time to add to their achievements. Banville's prose is slower to captivate but the magic is there in the end. *The Blue Guitar* (2015) is his most recent novel and, like Ishiguro's *The Buried Giant* is a step backwards. The style is inhibited because the narrator is a self-obsessed man. For most of the novel his "indulge me please" attitude and inner life dominate. But Banville cannot write badly for very long, and eventually others—his wife, his sister, his father—not only impress but add a dimension to the man's life that had somehow escaped him: he had been incapable of registering love. The last page is very touching.

Banville also wrote a trilogy about great men of science. *Doctor Copernicus*★R (1976) is about an historical figure whose life was a tragedy. Copernicus was born in 1473. He hated the world and sought personal salvation by trying to depict an ideally ordered universe. He saw that the Greek astronomy of Ptolemy did not cover all observations, had a blinding revelation that a sun-centered universe was true, lost faith in his solution, and yet could not shake the conviction that all was centered on the sun.

At thirty-three he was old in the way medieval people were old, including losing his teeth. He had already lost faith in God, and at times simply wanted to be left alone with his misery. Despite fear of persecution—it was near heresy to deny the immobility of the Earth—he published a brief sketch of his astronomy, the *Commentariolus*, and was half pleased that it was largely ignored. He busied himself with administrative duties of considerable importance. Just before his death at seventy, he published his full theory, *On the Revolutions of the Celestial Spheres*. Its defects, some inherent and some later repaired, meant it attracted only a few converts before Galileo.

Banville wrote this novel almost forty years ago. I do not recommend it as literature; for example, the book begins and ends—a deathbed scene—with florid prose. But I was glad I read it. The sheer awfulness of life in Europe circa 1500 left an indelible impression: torture for fun, public hangings, runaway servants nailed to a post by the ear and given a knife to cut themselves free, people lying in open drains, boys offering themselves for a bed, peasants reduced by drought to praying to the Roman god Mercury, good husbands who beat their wives rarely and are sometimes sober, an ambassador who realizes his lifelong ambition to be assigned to Paris and is strangled in a brothel.

Kepler★ (1981) is about a German astronomer who was born in 1571, twenty-eight years after Copernicus's death. He believed the heavens obeyed eternal laws that integrated mathematical equations, the perfect solids of geometry (a cube composed of six equal squares, a pyramid composed of four identical triangles, and so forth), and the musical harmonies. His image of the universe did not survive him, but while elaborating it he discovered the three great laws of planetary motion, including that planetary orbits around the sun are elliptical rather than circular. This solved a key problem that had seemed to invalidate Copernicus's theory.

Kepler's life was in turmoil because of religious persecution (he was Protestant and his mother was thought to be a witch), a wife who saw him as a failure, and the times (the plague, six children dead). The book begins in 1599 when he is twenty-eight, with flashbacks of the previous five years. He hopes for security by joining the staff of Tyco Brahe, a Danish nobleman who has devoted his life and riches to astronomy and is somewhat mad. Kepler gets data from Brahe that are essential to his task, which he will complete in 1619, eleven years before his death.

After Brahe dies, Kepler is employed by Emperor Rudolf II, who is also somewhat mad: he keeps a zoo with apes, a hermaphrodite child, and a statue that sings when exposed to the sun.

Banville had calmed down by the time he wrote this book, and captures the interplay between genius and a manic mind. Kepler once wrote: "I do not speak like I write, I do not write like I think, I do not think like I ought to think, and so everything goes on in deepest darkness."

The Newton Letter** (1982), the third in the trilogy, is a very short novel of only eighty-one pages. A historian lives in a cottage. He is supposed to write a book about Newton, but becomes obsessed with his subject's nervous breakdown in 1693. He believes Newton realized that his science did not really address the question of what was the point of it all, hence his retreat into alchemy and Biblical interpretation. Explaining the universe did not teach him how to live.

The historian starts to share Newton's sense of utter futility. He cannot finish his book and begins an affair that means love to the woman but nothing to him, particularly since he really loves her ethereal aunt who, it eventuates, is spaced out on drugs. Everyone he meets seems hollow. A boy makes every effort to break a birthday toy. A visitor is destined to sire "a brood of pale neurotic daughters … doing needlepoint and writing hysterical novels". He cites an article that epitomizes futile endeavor: "Interface tribal situations in southeast Ireland". A random fact: "Young men of the Ipo tribe in the Amazon basin pledge themselves with the nail parings of their ancestors." Banville's style has now fully matured. He describes nihilism far better than books that emote about it.

I have not read Banville's other trilogies but I have no hesitation in recommending them. The second consists of *The Book of Evidence* (1989), *Ghosts* (1993), and *Athena* (1995). The third includes *Eclipse* (2000), *Shroud* (2002), and *Ancient Light* (2012).

Under the name Benjamin Black, Banville has written eight crime novels, most featuring Quirke, a Dublin pathologist. When I read the first, *Christine Falls*★ (2006), I was initially disappointed by what seemed to be stylistic signals to his "real readers" that he was doing something he did not take seriously. But then his usual style took control. A detective answers a question about new developments in a case: "you must go to the pictures an awful lot. We have a full set of fingerprints … and a couple of locks of hair … and a cigarette butt … and a lucky monkey's paw dropped by a person of Oriental origin".

As a mystery there is a bit too much melodrama, but as a period piece it works. It conveys the atmosphere of Ireland in the 1950s: church-dominated, Catholic versus Protestant a yawning chasm, and most characters (except a few abstainers) drunk as often as they can manage it. And the pre-war poverty of Ireland: "I used to go to school with my boots tied around my neck to spare the shoe leather."

It also describes the Boston Irish, "still with their race memories of the Famine and the death ships", gives a one-page summary of their bitter history, and shows how Catholicism permeated their lives. The loveliest girl in South Boston is a Mother Superior. The cardinal takes an interest in who gets a state haulage contract. Wealthy Irish wish to be known as loyal sons of the Church and get Papal knighthoods. It reminds me of my own Irish-Catholic upbringing in Washington, D.C., being told: "Every time you take the Lord's name in vain every angel in heaven has to genuflect." For those curious about a world very different from their own, a sort of alien species that once lived in their midst, this book opens a window. Today, it is a world in decline in both America and Ireland: the grandmother attends mass daily, the mother on Sunday, and the grown children hardly at all.

The second in the crime series is *The Silver Swan*★R (2007). The central characters are the same but two years older, and there is no additional local color. Banville/Black has his heart in this book from the start, and as a mystery novel it is somewhat better plotted than the first. It gets a star for those who want crime novels that are superior to the general run, something on the level of P.D. James.

I read one other in the crime series. *Vengeance*★ (2012) is better still. The detective friend of Quirke and all the new characters are substantial. There are touches of humor. A public notice says "Planting in this area restricted to dwarves." (Presumably it means dwarf trees.) Ireland is diagnosed: it is likened to a man beating a cart horse with a stick. Mysteries aside, this book is well worth reading.

Sebastian Barry (born 1955)
Barry is another Irish writer (also a playwright) blessed

with an excellent style, but one quite different to Banville's. He writes on the level of whatever character is featured but does it wonderfully well.

A Long Long Way★★ (2005) joins *All Quiet on the Western Front*, *Paths of Glory*, and *Birdsong* as a chronicle of the First World War, this time from the point of view of Willie Dunne, an Irish volunteer who joined the British army and fought in Belgium. These Irish thought that Ireland would be given home rule after the war. But during the war, in Easter 1916, the Irish Republican Army rebelled in Dublin seeking total independence. British troops crushed them and their leaders were shot.

Willie was involved as a soldier, unwittingly, thinking Germans might have been invaded Dublin. He reports back to duty with Irish blood on his British uniform. To the terrible tragedy of mass slaughter in Europe—Irish villages were left without even one young man surviving—was added a conflict of loyalties. The Irish fighting in Europe, which side were they on? Were they to write off the deaths of thousands of their comrades as a mistake, or take pride in their heroism? Were they to strip off the now hated uniform and back the rebellion, or condemn the Irish rebels as misguided fools? Willie's favorite passage from the Bible was "And I saw heaven opened and behold a white horse and he that sat upon him was called Faithful and True". But where did these virtues lie? To this second tragedy was added a third: Willie's fate was to be stripped of all he cherished.

I wish I could adequately convey the language. The chaplain "whispered last rites to headless men, and also to men with only a head left". A British officer says, "What's wrong with you fucking Irish, can't you take a bit of [poison] gas?" He later weeps and hangs himself. Irish soldiers sing "God save the King" to defy their German enemies. A rebel boy says the act of contrition as he dies. Willie visits the mother of a dead officer and feels inadequate: "How could there be comfort in a fool sitting in the kitchen with his tongue tied?" She says, "It means the earth to me to see what he meant to you."

On Canaan's Side★ (2011) is about Lilly Dunne, who appeared, nicknamed Dolly, as a child in Willie's story: the little sister who loved him so dearly. Aside from childhood memories her story begins at age sixteen, after Willie's death in France in 1918. Her fiancé, Tadg, has a price on his head because he was on the wrong side during the Irish War of Independence, a member of the hated Black and Tans, an Irish paramilitary unit recruited by Britain. This constabulary was organized so hastily that the uniforms were thrown together from both the police (who wore black) and soldiers (who wore tan). When Tadg learns his name is on an assassination list the couple flee to America, where the IRA tracks him down.

Lilly flees Chicago, baffled by an America in which Catholics cannot go to the local priest and complain about victimization. Eventually she works as a cook for a beloved Irish-American mistress in a town near New York. Along the way, she has a son who fights in Vietnam and a grandson named Bill who fights in Iraq. It is Bill's suicide that makes her old age unendurable.

I found the language about the son and Vietnam less effective than Barry's usual but there are impressive passages: "there is a little touch of Englishness to him. … he is very austere, and depressed-looking, and he never smiles"; "He said people were plain stupid, and broke laws like Christians broke bread"; "Joe convinced the bootleggers not to kill him and at Christmas they sent him a card thanking him, for had they killed him they would have got the electric chair"; "Christopher Robin was going off to boarding school, and Pooh wanted to know if he would still exist when Christopher Robin was gone". The final pages are very beautiful.

An earlier novel, *Annie Dunne* (2002), is about another of Willie's sisters, hunched thanks to polio and therefore unmarriageable. The book is well written but its slow pace is more akin to nineteenth-century than contemporary literature. If you have a special interest in the hardships of the Irish rural poor circa 1959 you will enjoy it: labor unrelenting, using grass to save on toilet paper, the main treat sugar in your tea so you can live like a lord. Those of Irish background will enjoy Annie's claim that she is descended from kings. Every Irish person can claim this, thanks to the fact that every hamlet had a "king". Hers was ruler of Kelsha, a tiny area in Wicklow County.

The Secret Scripture★ (2008) introduces a character outside the Dunne family. Roseanne, a 99-year-old woman in a mental hospital, reminisces about her time on the "outside" between 1918 and 1957. Her history mirrors that of Ireland after independence. The treaty of December 1921 ended the war with Britain but divided Ireland. Was Ireland to accept independence without the north, Ulster, which was left under British rule as part of the United Kingdom? Thus began the terrible civil war in which the Irish focused exclusively on killing one another.

Roseanne's father is the best portrait of a wonderful person I know of in literature. (Usually such a character is clothed in sentiment and unrecognizable as fully human.) He is eventually broken by misfortunes arising out of the war, and what poverty does to his wife. He can abide it but she cannot. She burdens him with her utter depression and her desperation (she starves the family to try to buy an expensive clock). Young Roseanne finds herself alone: father dead and mother insane. Between then and her incarceration in the mental hospital her life is a fable of what it was like when the church and its mores ruled Ireland. Only cinema and dances and song illuminate the gloom.

The book is like a slow waltz well played: Roseanne's mother lived her life in Sligo "like a lost shilling on a floor of mud, glistening in some despair"; her father had "that rare ability to let things ease in himself in the company of a child, and be stupid and gay in the parched light"; the priest "carried a highly ecclesiastical umbrella … that said its prayers at night in the hatstand"; "The river, drowned in its own water, and drowned a second time in the rains of February, was not in a position to throw its light"; "How much of such kindness the war had covered over with corpses and curses I do not know"; "You could slave all week in a rotten job in the town, but as long as you had the Plaza … It was bigger than religion, I can tell you, the dancing"; "If I were a horse they would have shot me out of mercy." Usually Barry's style makes all the characters that populate his books seem totally real.

Roseanne has a child fathered by the protagonist in *The Whereabouts of Eneas McNulty*★ (1998), the brother of her husband and the subject of Barry's earliest novel. When Eneas is twenty-one the IRA puts him on its death list. His closest friend, Jonno Lynch, cannot persuade him to enlist in the IRA and join in the killing and the two young men become politically estranged despite their personal ties. After Eneas pays a clandestine visit to his home, he is told he will be killed no matter where he goes. He eventually heads to Africa and binds closely with a Nigerian named Harcourt.

In 1970, at the age of seventy, he and Harcourt are running a hotel in London. The IRA's struggle to merge Northern Ireland with Ireland has begun and has revived old memories. Jonno seeks him out. Rather than dying at Jonno's hand, Eneas dies in a fire trying to save Jonno's life. They may be eternal enemies but they are also eternal friends.

Barry's style is already mature: "His grandfather died, it was said, during the hunger … killed by a mob for feeding Indian grain meant for paupers to his fattening pig"; "the ticket of terror [is] flying in the wind, but they don't speak about it"; "it's worse than being shot by patriots, being shot by his father's obvious love"; "things in his head find their places, hammer to its niche, sextant to its shelf and box, and he is fiercely content to dig the canal".

Everyone sees betrayal in everyone else and everything is remembered ("And didn't your grandfather make his money in the hungry days …?").

I hope the subject matter of Barry's writing does not destroy your pleasure. The killing is interspersed with many scenes of sentiment and compassion. The hatred the Irish bore for one another was an index of their hatred for English rule. In a 1935 film *The Informer*, based on a book of the same name by Liam O'Flaherty, a character says: "The soil of Ireland is sacred, it is like a holy church." The obsession with country we call nationalism is the great disease of our time.

If the Irish had waited one hundred years, they may have had a chance to vote for freedom in a referendum, like the Scots in 2014. The chances of their waiting for that were too small to be measurable. My Irish grandfather used to say, in a bewildered way, "But why did the Scots not rise as well?" That is another story. Scotland was predominantly Protestant (some of whom were anti-Catholic), not as poor, and divided between the lowlands, called in Gaelic "the place of the foreigner", and the highlands, persistently referred to as "uncivilized". By the twentieth century, most of the population lived in the central lowland region from Glasgow to Edinburgh to Stirling to Dundee, and their ties to England and its empire were stronger than their ties to the north.

Colm Tóibín (born 1955)

Many Irish writers refer to Tóibín as the best of their generation. I read five of his books and all of them are beautifully written. *Nora Webster*★ (2014) is his most recent novel. It is about a woman of forty-six struggling to come to terms with the death of her husband. Her two young sons are living at home with her, while her two daughters are away studying.

Nora's story is uncomplicated by dramatic events, or money troubles, or a new man, so the portrayal of sheer grief is unadulterated, and done with great sensitivity. Over three years Nora finds her way back to life, partially because by chance she discovers the joys of music and training her voice. She and her two daughters grow as they gradually liberate their minds from convention, and both boys are convincing. The book gradually captures you to give a quiet satisfaction.

Brooklyn★ (2009) features Eilis Lacey, a young woman who in the 1950s emigrates to America from her small town in Ireland simply because there is no work. Father Sullivan, an Irish priest in New York, is a tower of strength, arranging a job and accommodation, paying Eilis's fees for night school, and providing a sense of community in the city for Irish, particularly aged men. He is a welcome reminder that many priests were guardian angels rather than pedophiles, and that the church was an asset to Irish Americans, which is why they remained so loyal for so long.

Eilis finds a new life and marries in New York City. The

book explores her homesickness and her growing realization that her mother will have to live out her old age without her children. The book has been made into an excellent film directed by John Crowley and written by Nick Hornby.

I think these two books are Tóibín's best. They are about perfectly ordinary people and eschew adding "interest" to their lives by injecting dramatic events. However, neither rises to the level of a truly great book such as Ishiguro's *The Remains of the Day*. It too is about an ordinary person, an English butler who goes on holiday, but Ishiguro raises his story to the level of Greek tragedy. History has turned his master's virtues into vices. Thus, the butler's self-esteem collapses: pride in having served a great man becomes despair at having worshiped a false god.

Tóibín's earlier novel *The Story of the Night*★ (1996) is about Richard Garay, a young Argentinian who lives with his British mother. The major theme is being gay at a time when gay rights are non-existent. However, lurking in the background are the terrible disappearances under the military regime in Argentina between 1976 and 1983, estimated at from 20,000 to more than 30,000—all dead, most tortured first—and the 34,000 in Chile between 1973 and 1990, 4,000 dead, the rest tortured. The latter occurred under the Pinochet regime that came to power after a US-backed coup overthrew the Allende government. Richard's mother cares nothing about this. She is the eternal émigré, longing for Thatcher and the queen: "They both looked so well in blue."

Richard is concerned with getting out of a dead-end job and finding a gay lover. Two American friends get him on the payroll of the CIA and the International Monetary Fund, the IMF. The latter audits the Buenos Aires transit system. The cost of ticket sellers and checkers is greater than the income from tickets; it would be cheaper to let everyone ride free.

After Richard finds his first love there are a lot of gay sex scenes. It may be said that these will excite gays and bore heterosexuals. I think there are just too many. Even were they male–female scenes I would still say let's get on with the story. Nonetheless Tóibín achieves something significant: he converts the agony of the gay community threatened by AIDS into the despair of the individual for whom "pills are our children. … We have no favorites. We brought them all into the world and we love them equally." This is a moving book.

Two of Tóibín's novels focus on great personages and I found them less interesting. *The Master* (2004) explores the interior life of Henry James. As such, it is a masterpiece. However, it will appeal only to those whose reverence for James sustains an endless interest in his interior life. It was one dominated by artistic taste, sensitivity to every mood of his associates, and obsession with who knew about his whereabouts and might disturb him. You get what lodgings he liked, what furniture he liked, and countless observations about his friends: "As his friend crossed his legs again, Henry noticed how beautiful his shoes were and how slender his feet." You have to care about his sexual identity. (He emerges as not much interested.) His older brother William James comments on Henry's novels: "your style has suffered from the strain of constantly dramatizing social insipidity. … something cold and thin-blooded and oddly priggish has come to the fore in your content. … I have to read innumerable sentences … twice over to see what they could possibly mean."

In *The Testament of Mary* (2012), a novella, an aging Mary lives alone, fed and housed by Christ's disciples. She is quarantined because she says the Resurrection was merely something she dreamed. This is the most pointless attempt to secularize the Christ story I have read. It compares unfavorably with José Saramago's *The Gospel According to Jesus Christ*, which at least gives some insight into Mary's status as an orthodox Jew of the time.

Colum McCann (born 1965)

McCann is Irish but sets his novels elsewhere. *This Side of Brightness* (1998) is about a mixed-race family in New York whose history covers most of the twentieth century. The men are construction workers who do the most dangerous possible jobs: tunneling, high-rise building. The family faces unrelenting bias and persecution. With one possible exception, the characters did not excite me enough to feel involved.

Dancer (2003) is based on the life of Rudolf Nureyev. His father is a true believer: he fought in the "great patriotic war" and his biggest fear is that he will be expelled from the Party. Book One begins with a horrific description, the best I have ever read, of the sufferings of Russian soldiers on the sub-zero Eastern Front from 1941 to 1944. The post-war conditions—economic privation and political repression— of the ordinary Russian are made more horrible by the fact that most believe the party line. We learn what it was like to live in Soviet Russia with an intimacy that few histories can touch.

Book Two does not live up to Book One. The dancer's performances, thoughts about the dance, and swinish behavior are repetitive. Book Three is better, at least when minor characters take the stage. Book Four is very brief but excellent and evocative. The dancer goes back to Russia to see his dying mother. His sister slaps him when it appears he may not even taste the banquet they prepared, food their poverty makes almost prohibitive.

This description makes the book seem a mix of good and bad, but what spoils it for me is something that runs throughout. The dancer's character is blurred by a stereotype, the romantic hero of the nineteenth century, a genius beyond the bounds of convention and decency but forgiven everything because what else can you expect of a genius. He is often simply a swine. He calls a friend a miserable Jew-boy and accepts another friend's favors with an airy, "Why not, she is more cultured than a slave?" He is always throwing coffee on people and slaps a girl who wants an autograph. His idea of a good time and sense of humor are infantile. Perhaps that is the point: that a great artist can be a worthless human being.

There is empty talk about art: "The known way leads us to the unknown, and the unknown way back to the known." The author has a habit of lapsing into a machine-gun style of one-, two- or three-word sentences. There is also a thirty-two-page sentence, manufactured by omitting obvious punctuation, with one decent line.

Zoli (2006) is the story of a Romani singer and poet born in 1930. It too is based on an actual life, that of the Polish Romani poet Bronislawa Wajs. Rather like the Orthodox Jews of Eastern Europe a century before, the Roma, or Gypsies, are cemented by tradition and persecution and fragmented by the attractions of the modern world. During the 1930s the fascists hunt them for sport, and during the war they join the Jews in the concentration camps. Zoli's group survives and the communists in Slovakia hail her as the ideal proletarian the new order will create.

However, the communists decide Gypsies must abandon their nomadic life and settle in houses. Zoli's community expels her for treachery and various infractions: women, for example, should be illiterate. She never resents this and lives stateless, alienated from both Gypsy and non-Gypsy, until she marries a worthy man and lives with him in virtual isolation. After a visit to her daughter in Paris, she understands the youth who want assimilation but knows it can never be for her. It is a decent novel, but only distinguished by its clean prose.

Let the Great World Spin (2009) is about New York in the 1970s. The machine-gun style reappears but fortunately McCann reverts to normal prose a bit more quickly. The best parts are about the desperate lives of those in housing projects, mothers who lost sons in Vietnam, and two painters semi-corrupted by the good life as lived by young New Yorkers who take drugs. There are perceptive remarks about racial stereotypes. However, the author may not have shed these. A black woman who is an honors university graduate writes a half-literate note: presumably she would not qualify as black if it read grammatically. The worst parts are details about the preparations of a tightrope walker who walked from one Twin Tower to the other (this was prior to their destruction) and the communications of computer hackers.

Book One of *TransAtlantic* (2013) is a series of short stories about people who happened to cross the Atlantic: two pilots in 1919 become the first to fly between the continents. Frederick Douglass, a black escaped from slavery, whose talents made a mockery of the claim that blacks were inferior, goes to Ireland in 1845 to raise money for the anti-slavery cause. A US senator in 1998 gets an agreement that stops the latest round of Irish killing one another other over the fate of Northern Ireland.

Douglass sees the irony of the "free" Irish who are servants (he amazes them by shaking their hands when he leaves) and starving (a man eating bark). He reads Daniel O'Connell—was it true that Irish harpists had their fingernails plucked so they could not play?—and meets him.

They are at one about freedom for Ireland and for blacks. The fifty pages about the senator add little. He comes across as an ideal mediator but not much more than that. There is one wonderful touch: the grief-stricken Irish mothers who put an extra teacup out every night in hope of a miracle.

Books Two and Three are about four generations of women who happen to interact with these men or dramatize the importance of their achievements. The last loses a son killed by one of Belfast's warring factions. Like all of this author's books, there is interesting material but it is uneven.

John Boyne (born 1971)
Until recently, John Boyne did not write about Ireland but when he finally did he chose a theme of great contemporary interest. In *A History of Loneliness*★ (2014) he uses the eyes of a devout priest to chronicle how pedophiles among the clergy tarnished the Irish Catholic church. The devastation was far more dramatic than in any other nation because of the church's unique role. It was in control. The clergy was virtually worshipped by the people. An archbishop could veto any story in the press. Parliament was intimidated. In America in 1945, when I was eleven, Sister Margaret Francis happened to mention in class that Ireland was much to be preferred to Italy because it was a truly Catholic country.

The dialogue in Boyne's book is as fine as anything in literature. Two scenes wonderfully convey the contrast between before the scandal and after. In 1980, as a young man, a priest gets on a train and people compete to serve him. A highly pregnant woman and a doddering old man both offer him their seats. Instead, a little boy is shifted to his mother's lap. The mother offers him little Anthony's potato crisps. "No!" roars the boy in horror, looking at the priest with fury. He is duly slapped. Unbidden, the old man buys the priest a cheese roll and offers a Kit-Kat for dessert.

By 2010, the priest cannot go into Dublin in clerical garb without risking derision and jostling by teenagers. He cannot be alone with the altar boys without a layman present. In many parishes altar boys are abolished. If the layman leaves the hall to go to the toilet, the priest has to leave as well.

How did the abuse of boys happen and who knew? The priest reviews his past life and has to admit he half knew. His best friend among the priesthood had been a molester from his first parish onwards, but at first he could not bring himself to believe it. And then he could not face the truth and expose it. The church was so revered that the hierarchy would not hear of the slightest hint of wrongdoing. Bishops deceived themselves into thinking some of it was lies, and that shifting priests from parish to parish protected the boys from men who were mainly too "demonstrative" for their own good.

The "few" complaints from parents were solved by a phone call from a bishop or a cardinal or (once) even the Pope. (This is assumed, not proven.) Nearing retirement, the priest feels the church destroyed the soul of Ireland and he was complicit, but fortunately for his sanity he has restored good relations with his abused nephew (the scene is movingly described) and another nephew and their families.

Boyne's earlier novels are not of equal quality. *Crippen* (2004) is based on the famous case of Dr Crippen who, after his wife's suspicious death, fled England with his lover by ship, and thanks to telegraph communications was apprehended before he reached Canada. Erik Larson documented the same events in *Thunderstruck* without departing from history. Boyne novelizes the story and takes liberties by creating many minor characters and altering the outcome. I have rarely read a more disastrous ending; perhaps *Amsterdam* is comparable. The revision of history adds nothing except to make us wonder what the point is.

Some of the minor characters invented are caricatures and some, such as Victoria, are well done. There are funny passages. Crippen's mother says, "Give thanks … to the good Lord for creating dirt all around us that we may have the honor of cleaning up in His name." The widow and Mr Munyon "could enjoy their senility together, mistaking each other for a lamp post or a stick of celery."

The Boy in the Striped Pyjamas (2006) is a novel for young readers and has sold in the millions. The style is aimed at teenagers or even pre-teenagers and I found it condescending. A boy aged nine calls the Führer (Hitler) "the Fury" and calls Auschwitz "Out-With". The Fury has appointed his father commandant of Out-With and they live in a house near its perimeter. He has no friends but makes one out of Shmuel, the boy in the striped pyjamas on the other side of the wire fence. The innocence of the boys—they are rather obtuse—contrasts with the horror of the camp. The style flows but is nothing special. *Next of Kin*★R (2006), published in the same year, is a mystery novel in which the corpses accumulate, rather than there being one murder at the start waiting to be solved. There are some well-written characters and well-crafted plot lines, including a suspenseful court case. The book is recommended for those who like a thriller.

Boyne has a sense of humor and in *The House of Special Purpose* (2009) it occasionally breaks through. The head of the British Library circa 1923 comments: "Too many books being produced, that's the problem. Most of them written by half-wits, atheists or sodomites, but God help us, we're obliged to carry them all."

However, the account of the Russian revolution and the couple who live through it to find refuge in England is very ordinary. It is not improved by the husband's presence among the great figures of history. Although of humble origin, he is the teenage love of Anastasia. How sad, they can never marry—or can they? He relates the death of Rasputin, who has a hideous smile; witnesses the abdication of the tsar; and briefs Winston Churchill. Even his London neighbor has to have been a onetime neighbor of Charlie Chaplin. Most readers will anticipate the ending but the later the better: it spoils the book, with a final scene in St Petersburg that is pure corn. It is as if a fine composer wasted his time on a bad libretto.

The Absolutist (2011) is a First World War novel, told from the perspective of Tristan, a gay shunned by his family. Tristan falls deeply in love with Will, a comrade in the army. Despite a few encounters, Will spurns their love and ultimately him as well.

Will becomes a conscientious objector at the front and is executed. The trench warfare is graphic, and the scene in which Tristan learns about the deaths of all those he knew in boyhood, including his best childhood friend, is moving. So are the sufferings of others: He fears for Sergeant Clayton's sanity. "Williams has told me that Clayton is one of triplets and that both his brothers were killed in the opening weeks of the war by hand grenades that exploded too soon as the pins were pulled out."

The book is not improved by the roles assigned to the two main characters: Will is too much of a saint and Tristan too much of a villain. The book ends with Will's sister Marian delivering a diatribe labeling Will a brave man and Tristan a coward, and Tristan accepts this verdict as a death sentence.

Boyne has a tendency to manufacture a surprise ending (note *Crippen* and *The House of Special Purpose*) as if his books needed something out of the ordinary to win the reader over. However, he is only forty-five and it may be prudent to judge his promise by his most recent novel. *A History of Loneliness* has an ending that is a bit flat but not disastrous. Boyne may be learning to let his fine style and narrative stand on their own merits.

LOOKING BACK

James Joyce (1882–1941) wrote the best book of short stories I have ever read. *Dubliners*★★ (1914) is set just before the Easter rebellion of 1916, which eventually led to Irish independence. Joyce's characters transcend time and place in a way that is the mark of great literature. The story about Farrington is almost too real to bear. He has a soul-destroying job as a copyist of legal documents—this was before the typewriter—and only the pub offers him any relief. He goes home to brutalize his small son, who desperately pleads, "Don't beat me, pa! … I'll say a Hail Mary for you. … if you don't beat me … I'll say a Hail Mary."

EUROPE

Sándor Márai (1900–1989)

Perhaps Hungary's best novelist, Sándor Márai fled that country in 1948 to settle in America. Between 2000 and 2011, five of his novels and a memoir were translated into English. I first read his last novel *Embers*★ (1942, translated 2000) and the purity of style captivated me. The story—the testament of a general reflecting about a love triangle, one that has dominated his life although the woman has been dead for many years—unfolds gradually. Some passages are too long—the analyses of the nature of friendship are too often repeated—but my heavens, Márai can write, and the significance of what was done and said holds surprise after surprise. The evocation of the Austro-Hungarian Empire is vivid: its psychological unity (the emperor, loyalty, rules, order); the military and its code (nothing to do in peacetime except hunt as a substitute for killing); the utter futility of the life of the rural nobility after the empire was gone; the romantic suicide of a twelve year old for reasons no one can imagine as operative today.

The Rebels★ (1930; translated 2007) is stylistically elegant, as are all Márai's books, and by no means ordinary. It is about a group of young men in 1918 who are unraveling psychologically when confronted by a world that has nothing better to do than send them to war to be killed. On the debit side, the descriptions of their intense bonding with one another and their fantasies were prolonged. Still, the young men are understandably on the verge of hysteria. There are some excellent older characters, including a father possessed by religious mania and a pawnbroker whose impotence captures the impotence of the time, and some vivid scenes.

Esther's Inheritance (1939, translated 2008) is a step down. The best part is its account of a kind of person known to us all: someone who has no transcendent purpose and tries to give their life significance by lifestyle and self-analysis: "There were times when life in the house and garden was like real life that has a purpose, a project, some inner meaning. It was just that it had no meaning." The self-wounding behavior of the main character towards something she realizes is a fraud is not plausible, unless you believe women are creatures who obey laws that are "stronger than the laws of reason".

Casanova in Bolzano (1940, translated 2004) uses Casanova's psychology—love tames him—and that of a woman who loves him to analyze the nature of love. This goes on far too long. The duke's pages of commentary on the sentence "I must see you" is a sad example ("you" is a fearsome word and so forth). Márai is drunk on his own style and writes for himself alone.

The first version of *Portraits of a Marriage*★★ appeared in Hungarian in 1941 but a posthumous manuscript, published in 2003, updates it through the post-war communist regime. The story concerns a man and his two wives. Just as *Embers* paints a picture of the aristocracy, this outstanding book analyses the remainder of the class hierarchy. Peter hates the life of the upper bourgeoisie: the "delicate, decadent, exciting, stuffy, superior, hopeless, cold conspiracy" that kills joy. The lives of him and his wife are regulated to the point of insanity: they dress for breakfast as if for a wedding. He withdraws into a love of solitude that makes it alien to offer anyone unconditional love.

His first wife is a romantic of the lower middle class and yearns for nothing less than unconditional love. He tells her, "I married you because I didn't know you loved me as much as you do." Her confessor addresses her as "dear soul" and advises that unconditional love is a sin: it aims at the possession of a soul that belongs only to God.

The second wife is from the impoverished peasantry and her family lived in a hole in the ground to survive the winter. She looks at him through a servant's eyes and saves in secret for the day when she might be dismissed. He never realized just how much his father treated her like a servant (pinches and so forth) and how much like a servant she felt. When hired, she was inspected for venereal disease. She became infected by their lifestyle but eventually, as his wife, she wants to wipe off his face the superior smile of the rich.

When Peter realizes his wife has become his enemy, he politely says, "I think it might be best for us to separate." When the communists come to power, he flees to America. In New York he meets a bartender who is also from Hungary and was his wife's last lover. The bartender detects in him a sense of superiority that he hates, but is disarmed when they joke together about the bartender being a "stinking prole". The bartender philosophizes: what bond can be stronger than that between men who have slept with the same woman: that is real democracy. Minor characters—for example, an enigmatic friend—have style. At any time, perhaps when given a kiss, he "might say something like: did I know that with each step a giraffe takes it advances by fifteen feet?"

Also in English is *Memoir of Hungary: 1944–1948* (1972, translated 1996). Márai describes the invasion of Germany by Russian troops, the advent of a communism that enslaved literature, and why he left: "I'd rather be eaten by vermin, than eat vermin." Ironically, the Russian soldiers admired writers: "if you are a writer, then you can tell us what we are thinking". The soldiers were in fact not monsters but men whose poverty bred pathetic looting: one treasured a broken thermometer.

Márai believed the educated middle class and its intelligentsia create the literary culture that defines a society and binds humanity together. He foresaw its demise in the West, and therefore the demise of humanism. The book suffers by comparison with Miłosz's masterful *The Captive Mind*, which covers the same period in Poland. However, Márai conveys something interesting about Hungary: its unique language bred psychological isolation from both East and West.

Romain Gary (1914–1980)
Romain Gary died thirty-six years ago but I discovered him

only recently. He won France's *Prix Goncourt* twice, even though no one can get it more than once: he wrote under three names other than his own, and received the prize the second time under one of these pseudonyms.

In *The Roots of Heaven*★★ (1956, translated 1958) a Frenchman, Morel, conducts an armed crusade in French Equatorial Africa to ban the killing of elephants. Preserving the elephants is emblematic of all that is good but is dying, primarily liberty and compassion. Many oppose Morel because they see him as opting for elephants over people, God, or ideals like African independence. (As he says, there are already plenty of independent nations that slaughter animals.)

When reading a book I often mark passages that exemplify excellence of style. Here I was overwhelmed by the sheer number and will offer only one. A man defends his decision to accompany Morel: "For three years, I was a bus conductor in Paris. [That] taught me a good, solid knowledge of humanity which prompted me to change sides and go over to the elephants." Gary seems to write without pause and some passages are repeated virtually verbatim.

The Life Before Us (1975, translated 1977) was published under the pseudonym Émile Ajar. The narrator is an Arab boy named Momo. A boy narrator often imposes the handicap of seeing the world through a child's eyes. In this case the result is far worse: Gary uses the boy to express a list of aphorisms or brief observations that are totally out of character. And like all such, most are empty: "I already needed somebody to hate like other people"; "Jews are very

obstinate, especially when they have been exterminated";
"Pediatricians look after babies, later it's psychiatrists."

Momo is told he has his whole life ahead of him: "Was
the bastard trying to scare me, or what?" Also: "Cholera
never asked to be cholera, it was just born that way"; "She'd
forgotten about it all, it was an attack of amnesty"; "When a
child refuses to have anything to do with life, the condition
is known as artistic."

This goes on page after page—such wisdom out of the
mouth of babes. There is a touch of redemption at the end
when Moro's "mother" dies. The concept behind the novel
is not the problem, it's the presentation. How could he write
something this bad? How could anyone give it a prize? (It
won the Prix Concourt.) Another nine of this author's
novels have been translated into English. It is probably
worth sampling them to see whether they feature Gary at
his best or at his worst.

José Saramago (1922–2010)

Saramago won the Nobel Prize and is acclaimed Portugal's
best novelist. *Baltasar and Blimunda* (1982, translated 1987)
is a story of love in an eighteenth-century Portugal still
haunted by the Inquisition. It combines historical narrative
with fantastic events. (They fly about on an airplane.) The
magic realism cannot disguise the thinness of the plot.
However, the early chapters recreate the time wonderfully:
the awfulness of urban life; the omnipresence of religion
combined with rampant hypocrisy; the army becoming

dysfunctional; the corrupt church bureaucracy. There are hair-raising descriptions of both an auto-da-fe—burning of a heretic—and a bullfight. If you think they are barbarous today, read this.

After that, there is one good section on the religious mania of the Portuguese king. It is the sole reason to keep reading unless you have been captivated by the story. Within a few years this author, who really could write, had been totally corrupted by fashion: streams of consciousness, boring musings, and the compulsory long sentences. He cheats in that he prolongs sentences by using commas where most people would use periods.

The History of the Siege of Lisbon (1989, translated 1996) begins with a ridiculous six-page sentence and it is all downhill from there. It describes a battle that took place in 1147 and foreshadowed the demise of the Moors. We do not get an account of the siege of Lisbon but rather what might have happened if a fleet of Crusaders had not done what they did—namely come to the aid of the Christian forces. Saramago seems bored with historical recreation compared to a love story set in the present, and the two often dilute each another as paragraphs bounce back and forth.

Some of *The Gospel According to Jesus Christ* (1991, translated 1993) is worth reading. It shows what it was like for the holy family to live together as Orthodox Jews, as distinct from faultless plaster saints. Joseph regarded Mary as his inferior, just as the ultra-Orthodox today treat women as inferior, however they may try to explain this fact away:

"at the hour of death, each man must give an account [to God] of any idle conversation he may have held with his wife"; "the malice of women knows no limits, especially when they feign innocence"; "Better that the Law should go up in flames than be entrusted to women."

Saramago goes on to discuss God's psychology and theology. God was disappointed because few worshiped him, and chose Jesus as the means to attract wider adulation. God needs the devil because otherwise he could not be wholly good. Where does the responsibility of God for evil end and the responsibility of man begin? Some call this wry humor, but humor ought to be deft rather than soporific.

Blindness (1995, translated 1998) is a tour de force and I am not sorry I read it. Here Saramago adapts his style to the narrative and it flows powerfully. Inexplicably, people are stuck by a blindness that is clearly infectious. Therefore, the first ones afflicted are strictly quarantined (food is left for them) until everyone has gone blind, which means there is no one to guard them and they can walk free. The events under quarantine are dramatic, and described with imagination. However, the post-quarantine material deteriorates. I hesitated to give it a star, despite the author's powers of description, because readers may find the style trying and the content uneven.

Italo Calvino (1925–1985)
Calvino has been hailed as the greatest Italian writer of the twentieth century. *The Path to the Spiders' Nests*★ (1947,

translated 1956), which is about Italian resistance to the Nazis during the Second World War. Almost 100,000 Italians lost their lives in battle, concentration camps, or as civilians killed as collaborators. Calvino aims at neither branding the resistance fighters as criminals (as fascists did) nor worshiping them as proletarian heroes (as communists tended to do). His narrator is a young boy to whom crime seems natural and who has no heroes. The resistance unit is composed of a few criminals, some there only by chance, others men of conviction but to whom communism means little more than a world where people will treat one another decently. Some are filled with hate: one just loves guns and shoots cats when he cannot shoot people. The ending is quite moving.

I decided to sample some of Calvino's later works. The concept that inspires *Invisible Cities* (1972, translated 1974) is interesting. Kublai Khan, who lived from 1215 to 1294, realizes his empire is so vast he doesn't know anything about most of it, except that his armies conquered it. Therefore, he converses with the great traveler Marco Polo, who tells him about the cities he has visited. The fifty-five cities are imaginary: collectively they are supposed to describe Venice. The descriptions are boring: "victory over the termites left the city at the mercy of the woodworms." The conversations are empty. Kublai: "We have proved that if we were here, we would not be." Polo: "And here, in fact, we are."

If on a Winter's Night a Traveler (1979, translated 1983) is a novel that evolves into a whole series of novellas. The writer parodies everything from literary chat to James Bond to crime novels to hostage novels to intellectualizing sex to *The Teachings of Don Juan*, tales of a sage high on peyote. There are a lot of funny one-liners. A publisher tries to say something nice when rejecting a book: "We much admired the atmosphere of fantasy." The book is about Trotskyite splinter groups in New Zealand.

When a female accomplice suggests that if a body will not fit into one bag two may be required: "I had to admit that girl's intelligence was superior to what you would expect from one of her background." Others:

"I knew [my daughter] was working in nightclubs but the idea that she exhibits herself in public with a crocodile seems to me the last thing a father could wish".

To depict sex "would require a three, perhaps four-dimensional model."

Sadly, the strand of character and plot that glues all this together is thin. Endless passages tell us about what it means to be a reader or a writer.

There is much speculation in literary circles about what living novelist is a worthy successor to Calvino. The three Italians usually nominated are Umberto Eco, Antonio Tabucci, and Elena Ferrante. As you can see, I am not sure that Calvino was a giant whose shoes were so difficult to fill.

Amos Elon (1926–2009)
Elon wrote a book that reveals much about the mindset that prepared the Aryan Germans to massacre Jews. *The*

Pity of It All: A History of the Jews in Germany, 1743–1933★
(2002) gives a full picture of the contribution Jews such
as Moses Mendelssohn, Karl Marx, Sigmund Freud, and
Albert Einstein made to German culture. This did not deter
the Nazis from exterminating Jews as "cultural parasites".
They had trouble with Heinrich Heine's poem "Lorelei",
which had been set to music by Friedrich Silcher and was so
popular they dared not suppress it. They printed it in song
collections as "traditional" and to this day some Germans
think the author is unknown.

Elon shows how even the best of the Germans, including
Jewish Germans, were swept away by the mad nationalism
that created the horrors of the First World War. Thomas Mann
had long felt the need of a war to subordinate materialism
to German "Kultur". Rilke called the outbreak of the war
the resurrection of "the God of hosts". Max Weber gushed
"this war is great and wunderbar". Even the saintly Martin
Buber, who later opposed the identification of Zionism with
Jewish nationalism, lost his mind: "I know personally that
Belgian women amused themselves by putting out the eyes
of wounded German soldiers and forcing buttons ripped
from their uniforms into the empty sockets."

Umberto Eco (1932–2016)
Eco published seven novels. His first, *The Name of the Rose*★R
(1980, translated 1983) was an international bestseller. It
is 1327. A Franciscan monk and his attendant, modeled
after Sherlock Holmes and Dr Watson, try to solve seven

murders that have occurred in a monastery. The plot is often ingenious but unfolds against a background of medieval debate about theology, heresy, and faith that consumes at least 500 of the book's 600 pages. I enjoyed much of this because I teach theology and am familiar with many of the principal actors of the time. The general reader will need a passion for being immersed in the climate of medieval ideas. Even then, the galaxy of names mentioned and detail on religious symbolism are an indulgence, an exhibition of erudition for its own sake.

However, the book does show how the world seems to those who find in it God, God, and only God—rather like the Islamic fundamentalists who tolerate no faith but their own. What Christians did to their own heretics makes anything Isis does pale by comparison. These are people who see in the fact that dogs eat their vomit the tendency of sinners to sin again, who wonder whether enjoying memories is not a temptation to ignore the here and now of saving one's soul, who debate passionately about whether Christ ever laughed (thus justifying jesting). After all, mockery can kill fear, including the fear of God. Thus, any book that dignifies mirth must be suppressed. This last proves of more than academic interest in that it underlies the plot.

Eco's second novel *Foucault's Pendulum* (1988; translated 1989) is about three men who invent what they see as a fictitious plot: a secret cabal, descended from the Knights Templar, possesses a "force" that will give them total power. It turns out that a cabal of sorts really does exist, but it is ignorant of the location of the force and therefore targets the three men as people who can reveal its whereabouts.

The story is interrupted by long sections in which Eco talks about the history of the Knights Templar and the myths that they survived the suppression of the order. Since those myths intertwine with every other cabalistic or occult theory of history, Eco covers those as well.

The three men also run a vanity press and the lunatic books submitted give Eco a chance to comment on virtually anything. Some of this is very funny. Book titles: *Panther without Eyelashes* and *Did the Egyptians Know about Electricity?* Advice: "you will approach the frog several times and will utter words of worship." A diabolic priest has the crucifix tattooed on the sole of his foot so he may tread on Christ.

A preface on Foucault's pendulum, a device that demonstrates the rotation of the Earth, and cryptography contains a few passages clearly designed to be incomprehensible, even to the most informed reader. If you read Eco, be prepared for the price you must pay: hundreds of pages in which he displays his learning. There is no doubt he was a great writer. It is a pity that he could not stick to writing a novel. *Foucault's Pendulum* has been called the thinking man's *The Da Vinci Code.* However, most people would prefer to read the latter.

J.M.G. Le Clézio (born 1940)
The Swedish Academy awarded this French writer the Nobel Prize in 2008, making special reference to *Désert*

(1980; translated 2009). The French have a long tradition of idealizing noble savages. In *Désert* the desert peoples of Morocco, eventually subdued by the French, have amazing eyes and spend much time looking into each other's. Lalla is a young girl who gives birth assisted by a fig tree. She has conversations with the desert and sees it as splendid, partially because of phenomena created by a boy magician. The desert tribes are the last "free men", free in the sense that they are isolated in a harsh environment. My admiration for them is tempered by the fact they own slaves. Le Clézio does capture the utter misery of Africans who migrate to France.

He can write well, particularly in the scene where the tribes come together to praise Allah. However, his descriptions of the desert and the sea and the wind and even the misery lose their impact because they are repeated so often. There is a much better novel about nomadic tribes: *The Wandering Falcon*, see pages 260–261. I decided to find out what Le Clézio could do with characters that were more real than ideal. I set aside his early novels, which explore insanity, language, and "writing", and read two of his post *Désert* ones, of which only three are in translation.

The Prospector (1985, translated 1993) also offers noble savages. Alexis becomes one as a child, raised in an isolated area of late nineteenth-century Mauritius. If you want almost 300 pages of lyrical description of the sea (his great love), forest, and mountains, and do not mind that the characters are childlike and the message that life in accord with nature is better than gold, you may enjoy it. Perhaps it is intended for the very young? At age eighteen, Alexis departs on a ship without a word to his beloved mother, leaving her in abject poverty. He thinks only: *The sea! The sea!* He finds love with a noble savage girl (beautiful of course) who has a mute brother (not just beautiful but extraordinarily beautiful and a special gift of God).

Wandering Star[*R] (1994, translated 2004) gives us something better. It is about two teenage girls. While in occupied France and then Italy during the Second World War, Esther, a Jew, is threatened with death everywhere, until she arrives in Jerusalem just before the proclamation of the state of Israel. Nejma is a young Arab uprooted by the victorious Israeli army. She spends years in a camp, starving, surrounded by children longing above all for a drink of pure water, and visited by bubonic plague.

I recommend this book for those who want to understand why the Jews of Israel are obsessed with absolute security, and cannot see that this always becomes a threat to the security of others, and why the Palestinians treasure the "right of return" to their homes, which if granted would tear Israel apart. There is an arresting passage about Rachel, a young woman who does not flee the Nazis. Her mother begs her to stay with her father who is ill. She knows they are all doomed but "tries to think of the words she'll say to her mother and father, to reassure them, so they won't know right away." She finds she loves them so much she could die, and didn't even know it.

Antonio Tabucchi (1943–2012)
Seven of this Italian author's novels have been translated into English. *Pereira Maintains*★ (1994, translated 2010) has been singled out as his best. Pereira tells his story to an anonymous narrator, who passes it on without comment, except to remind us continually that the story is what Pereira *maintains* to be true. This device is best ignored and once this is done the style is simple and elegant.

Since the death of his wife, Pereira is only half alive, living on the memories of his youth and their time together. His intimate conversations are mainly those he has when addressing her photograph. He lives in Lisbon in 1938 when Portugal is ruled by the dictator Salazar, an ally of Franco in Spain and Hitler in Germany, and whose regime murders dissidents with impunity. Since the present and therefore the future mean nothing to Pereira, he manages to ignore current politics, finding solace in his Catholicism and in his work as a minor editor of a newspaper in which he publishes translations of foreign authors as a tribute to great literature.

Over a year the outside world intrudes, particularly after he hires a reporter who turns out to be a recruiter for the Republican army fighting against Franco. He ends by giving him refuge, "watching" the secret police kill him, smuggling an account of their brutality into his newspaper, and fleeing Portugal for France. He evolves from an undefined sense that he has something to apologize for but cannot identify what, to a realization that his whole life is an evasion that ignores present evil and its consequences. Along the way he finds, often to his surprise, that those in whom he confides, his "psychologist" and his confessor, are dissidents. His lack of insight into how his mind is changing, his sleepwalking to a new state of political awareness, is very effective.

I suspected this novel was probably Tabucchi's best. For one thing, it does not include devices I normally find irritating: the dead rise and speak in some of his novels, for example. However, I read other books to see what I thought. In *Indian Nocturne* (1984, translated 1988), a man travels in search of a friend in India circa 1980. There is no narrative but the style is excellent and the snapshots interesting. At the time only Untouchables—Dalits—were willing to look after a patient's bodily needs. The book offers a few hours of pleasure (it is about 100 pages) but is hardly compulsory reading.

The English translations of three short books by Tabucchi have been published in one volume. In *Vanishing Point* (1986, translated 1991), a mortician unsuccessfully seeks to identify a corpse through investigations that first make sense, then have no plausible connection with one another. The book's dust jacket excuses this waste of time as "metaphysical". *The Woman of Porto Pim* (1983, translated 1991) has one decent short story and the rest is a miscellany about the Azores, their geography, visitors, and selected inhabitants, plus information about whaling. *The Flying Creatures of Fra Angelico* (1987, translated 1991) has two decent short stories and uses the author's clean prose to present a useless correspondence and a series of mood pieces. None of this was worth publishing except in little literary journals.

Herman Koch (born 1953)

This Dutch writer has produced eight novels, two of which have been translated into English. I chose *The Dinner** (2009, translated 2012), which had attracted the better reviews. Its merits certainly outweigh its demerits but I am not sure that the author aims at much more than popularity.

Two couples, brothers and their wives, meet at a restaurant to discuss what to do about acts of violence committed by their two fifteen-year-old sons. One brother is the narrator and initially appears normal. The gradual realization that he, and his child, and his wife, are psychopaths is accomplished with great skill. There is a tedious discussion about race, but it may be designed to show how an unprincipled person can be convinced they really have principles. There is a nice counterpoint in that an adopted black boy behaves as if tainted by his heredity. The digs at middle-class Dutch society are heavy-handed and somehow the French middle-class seems exempt. The very end is a little too pat: father and son bonded in love by their sadistic traits.

Stieg Larsson (1954–2004)

Writers who achieve huge popularity can write worth-while books: look at W. Somerset Maugham. With this possibility in mind, I read a series of Scandinavian crime writers beginning with Stieg Larsson. A journalist and Trotskyite, Larsson exposed right-wing extremism in Sweden despite death threats. He died at fifty of a heart attack after climbing seven flights of stairs. At the time of his death he was the second bestselling novelist in the world: his novels have now sold almost seventy million copies.

The first was *The Girl with the Dragon Tattoo* (2005, translated 2008). This book makes a reasonable first impression, thanks to the development of one of the two main characters, journalist Mikael Blomkvist, in greater depth than is the case in the usual pop novel, and because it has a plot with some surprises. The long passages about corrupt business practice in Sweden and computers and computer hacking will appeal to a limited readership. The chief villain, Nils Bjurman, is so wicked he is trivialized. The life of the heroine, Lisbeth Salander, is so horrific that Larsson trespasses on bathos. Life has made Salander so hard she can scarcely tolerate anyone who treats her as a real human being.

Larsson's next two books, *The Girl Who Played with Fire* (2006, translated 2009) and *The Girl Who Kicked the Hornet's Nest* (2007, translated 2010), go downhill. There is a lot of silly stuff about the heroine being so bright she solved Fermat's last theorem. (She forgot the solution and, knowing she had solved it, lost interest.) She is so expert in martial arts she can cripple any roomful of professional killers. As she's a superwoman, a superman must be invented to give her an appropriate adversary; the giant who can feel no pain turns out to be her half-brother. This is action comics writ large. We learn something more about Mikael Blomkvist: no woman in the world can resist him.

Andreï Makine (born 1957)

Born in Russia, Makine went to France at the age of thirty. He has published fifteen novels, and twelve have been translated into English. His most acclaimed book is *Le Testament Français* (1995). In 1997 it was translated with the title *Dreams of My Russian Summers*, although there is another translation that retains the French title. It became the first novel in history to win both of two great prizes, Prix Goncourt and Prix Médicis. The story concerns how incredibly sensitive the narrator and his grandmother (perhaps fictitious) were about everything and ends with his deciding to write a book about it. The style is a bit too sentiment-laden for my taste and there is much talk such as "The essential was unsayable. … The unsayable was essential." Flag-waving may account for the prizes: Makine praises the French for exactly what they like to believe about themselves.

The book vividly depicts the horrors Russians endured from the First World War through the Stalin era, but these are better presented in his later book, *Requiem for a Lost Empire*. There is one memorable anecdote. A young boy about to be shot begs the soldiers to be allowed a few minutes so he can go home and give his mother his watch. They are amused by such a naïve subterfuge and let him go. Almost immediately, he returns and falls into line with those waiting to be shot.

Although I did not think Makine's "best" book was worth a star, I read two others. *The Crime of Olga Arbyelina* (1998, translated 2000) has a promising first two chapters, which delineate the Russian princess's character, particularly her attitude towards aging. However, it quickly turns into a stream of consciousness full of "Who am I?", "Who was he?" (he being her son, other people being "the other"), people being amazed that their experiences are unknown to others, and how strange everything is. Makine is at times a virtuoso of style, but this piece is unworthy of his talent.

Requiem for a Lost Empire (2000, translated 2001) shows the horrors of Russia's twentieth-century history. There is an anecdote about the war on the Eastern Front during the Second World War. A German general holds up a dying Russian who spat at him as an example to his troops: "This is a true soldier." The psychology of those risking their lives as spies for the Soviet regime after having lost all faith in the regime's integrity is interesting. The streams of consciousness are less claustrophobic here because more than one character dominates. I recommend this book as the one to read if you wish to assess Makine's novels for yourself. As for me, I felt that by now I had enough insight into the minds of those damaged by Russian history and personal misfortune, and enough of a style that mixes excellence with nonsense.

Ildefonso Falcones (born 1958)
The second novel of this Spanish writer, *The Hand of Fatima* (2009, translated 2012), was a bestseller, as was his first, *Cathedral of the Sea*. Its 961 pages reminded me of the movie

serials I saw as a child: the hero was seemingly doomed at the end of each episode, only to rise again unscathed at the beginning of the next.

It is hard to take this man's personal dramas too seriously in that it is hard to take him too seriously. His mission to reconcile the Spanish and the Moors (the book is mainly about the persecution of the latter) is ridiculous. Instead of a faithful horse he has a faithful mule—although he gets a horse eventually. The book's popularity may be enhanced by lots of explicit sex but the descriptive prose—"young milky breasts", "starting at her shamelessly with lust in his eyes", "voluptuous curves"—went out of fashion a long time ago.

However, the book does give a vivid picture of sixteenth-century Spanish society, with all its fervor and flaws. Is it worth reading for that? The portrayal is arresting but the detail is endless. You may find it easiest just to read the first few pages of Chapter 28, which are succinct and powerful: Spain was a mix of generosity, the noble mindset that despised work in favor of an insane code of honor (there is a wonderful vignette exemplifying this), slavery, and a licentiousness that tainted even the clergy. After all, nuns from good families were in convents not because of any vocation but to save their fathers the extra money a dowry would entail.

I did not read *Cathedral of the Sea* (2006, translated 2008) or *The Barefoot Queen* (2013, translated 2014) as I suspected the critics were reliable: "A very readable adventure novel" and "quickly consumable entertainment for a broad public".

Diego Marani (born 1959)

Marani is an Italian novelist of considerable reputation. Described as his best book, *New Finnish Grammar* (2000) was translated into English in 2011. It is not a classic but has an interesting plot. Long tales from Finnish mythology and frequent philosophizing—"we have need of the body in order to gain a sense of the soul"; "we can never perceive the infinite"—add little. Two more novels now in English, *The Last of the Vostyachs* (2009, translated 2012) and *God's Dog* (2012, translated 2014), are both described by *The Guardian* as excellent thrillers. A third, *The Interpreter* (2015, translated 2016), the final in the author's trilogy on the relationship between language and identity, was released as this book went to print.

Jo Nesbo (born 1960)

This Norwegian author was recommended to me as better than Stieg Larsson. I tried *The Redbreast* (2000, translated 2006), which was voted the best Norwegian crime novel ever. It is the third in a series of ten about Inspector Harry Hole. Hole is a real tough guy in the Dashiell Hammett tradition and is very impatient. Slow time (waiting for something to happen) is like "sitting in the electric chair before the current [is] turned on". The humor is pretty low: when Hole undoes his top shirt button, the woman at the next desk whispers "More, more" and claps encouragement; when he mentions that Nazis call a thug who batters people "batman", she exclaims, "Got it, *baseball* bat". Why be concerned about a death when every year sixty percent of all hedge sparrows die?

Some minor characters are better. Nesbo paints a disturbing portrait of the idealism that inspired Norwegian Nazis to fight for Hitler, even after hope was gone; one of them is even made to seem worthy of love. I was unaware of the depth of Nazi sympathy in Norway not only during the war but also up to the present. As with Larsson, the typical man in authority tends to be utterly brutal toward women. Is this true, or at least true enough that readers accept this behavior as normal? I did not read other books in the series: I did not want to meet Harry Hole and his mates again.

Arnaldur Indriðason (born 1961)
This Icelandic author is a world bestseller because of his Detective Erlendur series of fourteen novels, many of which have been translated into English. I read *Jar City* (2000, translated 2004). The characters are plausible, some excite your sympathy, and none embarrass you with their antics or repartee. It is a very competent no-frills mystery novel that will appeal to those who do not want more. It always seems to be raining in Reykjavik and that is true: precipitation there varies between seven and eight days out of ten according to the season.

Elena Ferrante (pseudonym; born perhaps 1962)
Ferrante is the third Italian novelist nominated as the successor to Calvino. Her first novel, *Troubling Love* (1992,

translated 2006), is good but not outstanding. If Neapolitan men are really the kind of sexual predators she portrays, it is a wonder all women there do not carry mace. Ferrante's second novel *The Days of Abandonment*★ (2002, translated 2005) is about a woman of thirty-eight with two children. Her husband leaves her for a twenty-year-old blonde with whom he has been having an affair for five years. For some reason, this enrages her. You are gripped by a nightmare that lasts for almost 188 pages.

By now, nine of Ferrante's novels have been translated into English. Four, all published since 2010, have put her in the first rank. They are known as the Neapolitan novels and all of them document the lives of two girls born in a Naples slum in 1944.

In *My Brilliant Friend*★ (2012, translated 2013) the girls are aged six to sixteen. In *The Story of a New Name*★ (2012, translated 2012) they are sixteen to twenty-four, in *Those Who Leave and Those Who Stay*★ (2013, translation 2014) twenty-four to thirty, and in *The Story of the Lost Child*★ (2015, translation 2015) thirty to sixty-six.

Their neighborhood is full of violence. Mothers and grandmothers are "as angry as starving dogs". Lila's father throws her out of the window and breaks her arm. Lila is the more brilliant of the two girls, but only Elena continues her education beyond the fifth grade. Lila's brilliance shows forth in whatever she does. She becomes highly paid thanks to her expertise with computers, and eventually opens her own business. Elena becomes a successful novelist.

Lila marries at sixteen, Elena at twenty-four. Both abandon their marriages because they fall in love with Nino, a childhood friend. Lila wins and leaves her husband to live with Nino. This lasts twenty-three days before he gets sick of her. Later, Elena wins him and abandons her husband to live with her two girls. Her liaison with Nino lasts some years, presumably because they do not live together. He remains with his wife and maintains Elena in an apartment as his mistress. She has a child by him. When she finds out about his many infidelities, she finally shuns him.

At the age of sixty-six Lila disappears from Naples. She had long expressed a desire to do exactly that and has taken all her possessions. Everyone assumes she is still alive somewhere creating turmoil. Elena receives a package that could have come only from her.

Partly because she has risen from poverty, partly because of Lila's brilliance, Elena has an inferiority complex. She is obsessed with her image in other people's minds, not just what people think of her novels, not just whether she appeals to men, but whatever anyone she encounters thinks of her at that moment. As she is the usual narrator, her psychology dominates and I was pleased there was no attempt to reconcile her contradictions. She is open to radical feminist ideology but totally at the mercy of her adolescent crush on Nino—which is to say she is his slave, even tailoring her reading to cater to his interests—even though she knows he moves from woman to woman, leaving children behind to their fate. He is a bore, delivering long political diatribes without regard to the interests of his listeners. She judges these as brilliant because she loves him. On the other hand, since she does not love her husband she labels him as boring because he rejects the romantic imagery of the new Left. In fact, he shows great courage in defending traditional academic values against colleagues who would turn the university into a propaganda rag, and faces down a student who confronts him with a loaded gun.

Elena never feels at ease with her colleagues, convinced that because they have been raised in professional homes they have an acquaintance with politics and the arts she can never absorb. This bought home to me how fortunate I was to attend the University of Chicago in the 1950s. Thanks in part to the high proportion of Jewish students, whose exposure to political and artistic culture was intense no matter what their class origins, and in part to the curriculum, which exposed us to the great books of Western civilization, we emerged without any sense of inferiority toward America's intellectual élite. It never occurred to us that we could not compete on an equal footing.

I have given a star to all four novels in the Naples tetralogy, but want to add that collectively they are like reading one long novel whose psychological content and style vary little. I would recommend you read the first and see if you want more of the same. As for the style, it is electric and intense rather than elegant, but perhaps suits the subject matter, and it carries you along. Elena is pleased to find a woman in her old neighborhood reading her book—"How many pages do I have to read to get to the dirty bits?" the woman asks. Another woman, estranged from her grandfather and hoping for reconciliation, greets him on the street with her son in tow. He addresses the child: "If you see your mother, tell her she is a whore." On the psychology of women: "If a man tells a woman he loves her, she wants him to write it down and sign it so she can show other women."

Carlos Ruiz Zafón (born 1964)

Zafón is a Spanish author who first wrote for teenagers and has an international following. *The Prince of Mist*★R (1993, translated 2010) gets a star but only for that audience. The prince is the devil. Despite this, the youths who do battle with him do so on fairly equal terms. These young people are realistic and the tension, as they gradually come to realize who is behind certain events, is sustained enough to keep you turning the pages. Demons must be popular with younger readers. In *The Midnight Palace* (1994, translated 2011) a corrupted ghost is eventually banished by appeals to his better nature. In *The Watcher in the Shadows* (1995, translated 2013) a doppelgänger (created when a person's shadow escapes and becomes evil) is destroyed after, at least for me, too many close calls with its teeth and claws. If you enjoyed the first book, read *The Watcher in the Shadows* rather than *The Midnight Palace*.

In 1999, Zafón began to write for adults with *Marina* and I wanted to see what he could do on that level. And what do we get? A self-created Frankenstein, more fangs and claws, a handsome young couple, a revered older man, a mystic symbol, and evil destructive but ultimately vulnerable. Like Agatha Christie, this author hit on a successful formula early on and repeated it. Blurbs about gothic horror, supernatural horror, and so forth put me off his other novels. In passing, all of them have elicited high praise.

Finally, he wrote a book he decided to take seriously. *The Shadow of the Wind* (2004, translated 2005) was a bestseller. It gives a picture of what Barcelona was like after the Second World War. Zafón is sometimes quite funny—for example, in his send-ups of the attempts to glorify Franco. But he is an accomplished pop writer, nothing more.

Karl Ove Knausgård (born 1968)
Joshua Rothman of *The New Yorker* calls Knausgård one of two titans who dominate current literature. (The other he deems to be Ferrante.) The first two books of Knausgård's six-volume autobiography are said to be the best and I read the first, *A Death in the Family* (2009, translated 2012). The style flows. The tale of the author's life as a child, adolescent, and adult in Norway and Sweden is told with effect, particularly passages about his thoughts after the death of his father and his subsequent visit to his grandparents' home. This was not enough to enliven 480 pages of meticulous detail about very little: "locked the door, undressed, clambered into the bathtub, adjusted the shower head away from me, and started the water." One critic remarked that he was interested even when bored. I was not. The "essays" about

the world, death, knowledge, chaos, and understanding are pedestrian or silly; the best ones are on painting and clouds.

Autobiography automatically supplies a hero, characters, and a plot, which poses a question: can Knausgård supply these out of his own imagination? This is particularly apt in that the autobiography itself is hardly going to guarantee him a permanent reputation. He published two early novels, the second of which is *A Time to Every Purpose under Heaven* (2004, translated 2008). This uses the appearance of angels to a sixteenth-century man as a pretext for essays on the mutability of angels, Christian theology, the crucifixion, the history of ideas, and seagulls—plus embellishments on Biblical stories: Cain was a nice guy, Noah clubbed to death people who tried to get on the ark, and so forth. These stand or fall in terms of their intrinsic quality, which is slight. A former associate of Knausgård reviewed this novel under the title "Between the Bible and blah-blah".

The book ends with reminiscences about Knausgård's father and a bit of introspection, masturbation, and self-mutilation. At that time Knausgård declared he was sick of writing novels. Recently he published *Autumn*, a set of essays to an unborn daughter, on subjects ranging from the virtues of forgiving to the joys of women's labia.

Julia Franck (born 1970)
Julia Franck won the German Book Prize and her novels have sold in the millions. Two have been translated into English. I enjoyed *The Blindness of the Heart*★ (2007,

translated 2009). The fact it suffers in comparison with some really outstanding portrayals of Germany between the two world wars is no reason not to read it. I refer to Erich Maria Remarque's two great novels, *The Black Obelisk* and *Three Comrades*, Christopher Isherwood's *Goodbye to Berlin* and *Mr Norris Changes Trains*, Sebastian Haffner's memoir *Defying Hitler*, and also to Erik Larson's *In the Garden of Beasts* (see pages 36–37).

Frank's book begins in 1945 at the end of the Second World War. Helene abandons her eight-year-old son at a train station on a trip from East to West Germany—she pins on him a note with the address of an uncle they have never met. She makes no effort to contact him for ten years and does not want him back even then. The rest of the book examines her past in an effort to explain how she could have done this.

Whether or not the book succeeds on the psychological level, it succeeds on an ideological level. There is a terrible truth in the saying, "The death of one man is a tragedy. The death of millions is a statistic" (falsely attributed to Stalin). Huge numbers deaden our hearts to the horror of it all. Helene's life reminds us of the terrible suffering that a sheer wayward accident can inflict on one person. It thereby provides a metric that brings home the collective horror of the Holocaust. The Nazis were a historical accident that brought personal tragedy to every one of millions of Jews and the host of people who loved them, not just to the people killed but to the millions destroyed by the absurd deaths of friends, neighbors, and loved ones. Our feelings are reawakened and multiplied.

Back to Back (2011, translated 2013) is no better than any run-of-the-mill tearjerker about youth suicide unanticipated by an unfeeling mother. It takes place in East Germany so there is an "I must be free" theme. Despite the mother's awfulness, people inexplicably seem to like her. The son loves her. A brother will not help the son escape because it would kill the mother. What is meant to make the boy appealing—pretending to be a dog, his adolescent poetry—is counterproductive.

LOOKING BACK

Joseph Roth (1894–1939)

Roth was a German-Austrian novelist who committed suicide through alcohol abuse in 1939. His novel *The Radetzky March*★ (1932) is about a doomed family whose demise parallels the demise of the great Austro-Hungarian Empire that controlled most of south-central Europe before the 1914 war. It is slow moving but eventually I got involved with the characters, perhaps because some of them are elderly men. With hindsight, we all know that the Austro-Hungarian Empire, which embraced many nationalities, was doomed by the rise of nationalism and the desire of the subject peoples for their own nation states. Roth wonderfully captures the forces that kept this strange state together for so long: duty to the emperor, to your assigned role (the utterly barren life of a soldier on the frontier), to your family honor.

The portrait of the emperor is excellent. He carefully conceals insights that might make him appear other than the stereotype of an emperor. He knows that his role is vital at present even if futile in the long run. The final chapter, in which the mental worlds of all the characters collapse as they die, is very affecting.

Federico García Lorca (1898–1936)
Lorca was the greatest Spanish poet and playwright of modern times. An anti-communist death squad executed him early in the Spanish Civil War. Just as Camilo José Cela describes the rural poor of mid twentieth-century Spain, Lorca depicts the lives of the "respectable" rural middle class. I rank his three greatest dramas in this order: *The House of Bernarda Alba*★ (1946), *Blood Wedding* (1936), and *Yerma* (1937). A great poet shines through the translations, all published first in 1987. The plays owe half their beauty to the singing and music, which give the words depth. Read the texts and decide whether you want to seek out a performance.

The House of Bernarda Alba is about a family trapped in the countryside by the fact they are rich in those surroundings but would be lost among the genteel poor in Madrid. The mother, obsessed with their status, turns all her daughters into spinsters, except the eldest, who has inherited money. The tension between propriety and humanity dominates all three plays, but in this one the scenes have an especially powerful cumulative effect. What a tragedy that Lorca died at thirty-eight.

An Oddity

Javier Sierra (born 1971)

How Sierra got on my original list of promising novelists, I cannot imagine. However, since I am not only recommending books but also issuing warnings, I will proceed. His novel *The Lady in Blue* (1998, translated 2008) follows the path of religious science fiction blazed by *The Da Vinci Code*, which was at least a page-turner. But incredibly it has been translated into twenty-three languages. Angels, including one who likes red shoes, intervene in history in the form of humans who have special powers. You may be sitting next to one of them. They are dedicated to resolving a great issue: did the Virgin Mary appear more than once, or were most of her appearances really of nuns who had learned how to be in two places at once?

NEW ZEALAND AND AUSTRALIA

Whenever I ask scholars I respect to recommend books from these countries, five author's names keep appearing: Maurice Gee and Janet Frame from New Zealand; Patrick White, Tim Winton, and David Malouf from Australia. Here I also identify other authors of note, and one whose work in my view deserves more prominence.

NEW ZEALAND

Janet Frame (1924–2004)

Janet Frame has received almost universal praise for her three-volume autobiography: *To the Is-Land* (1982), *An Angel at My Table* (1984), and *The Envoy from Mirror City* (1985). It was therefore a surprise for me to discover that her novels are more honored by New Zealanders than read. Some of my literary friends had read nothing by her, and most only *Owls Do Cry* (1961), her first novel. When I arrived in New Zealand in 1963 this book impressed me. Recently I reread it and found it a disappointment. It is unusual in that it alternates between outstanding passages only an accomplished novelist could write and something close to schoolgirl emotive prose. It feels as if it were written in a rush of fluency, without reflection on what was effective.

There are four children. Francis dies young: this section is well written. The others are Toby, Chicks, and Daphne. The italicized summaries and introductions are showy: "And we walk like Theseus or an ashman in the labyrinth, with our memories unwound on threads of silk or fire; and after slaying by what power the minotaurs of our yesterday …"; "I talk of the woodlouse and his traffic across the wall, the turtle-turn of him and his legs writing in the air his telegram to pity"; and much more.

The section on Toby goes downhill to "And one or all [of the witches] answered, We are afraid of you, Toby. You will take a fit"; and "We have dug the pit and he who diggeth the pit shall fall into it." The fact that Chicks keeps a diary salvages the prose but she is painted as too crass for anything but a morality play. Daphne in the asylum starts badly but improves as irony begins to dominate and the medical staff is well done indeed. The epilogue is very potent.

Living in the Maniototo (1979) won the New Zealand Book Award for Fiction. By now Frame's prose is mainly unadorned. A lot of the book is well written and some passages are beautifully written. Others are not ("There are some who live forever in the manifold"). There are poems that offer random images ("I am Hypotenuse"; "The fed cat / sleeps on the mat") but the one about Italy is not bad. She plays some games with who is dead and who is alive, and someone disappears in a flash of light, an event that has no significance except to put on record that someone disappeared in a flash of light. There are some good descriptions of the immiserated people of Baltimore. It is a superior novel but not brilliant. I wish she had not coined the name Alice Thumb.

The Carpathians (1988) was Frame's last novel. She introduces the "Memory Flower" and the "Gravity Star". Without language human beings could not speak and would be scarcely human. Deprived of it, people scream, shriek and wail, although cats can still howl. It is sad to see this talented writer waste pages on this, thanks to the seduction of the literary fashions of our time. Despite this flaw, there are perceptive descriptions of the residents of a town of 13,000 near Palmerston North and of the American narrator's life and marriage. I would rate it about equal to *Living in the Maniototo*.

Maurice Gee (born 1931)
The Plumb Trilogy will interest everyone who wants to know exactly what it was like to be a certain kind of New Zealander during the first three-quarters of the twentieth century. Taken as stand-alone novels, *Plumb*★ (1978) is the best of the three.

George Plumb, a clergyman, is a sympathetic enough character to make us empathize with his dilemma: the godly man who can never be at peace with others unless they are religious and benevolent or happen to live a virtuous life by instinct. He feels a special pain at the to him unfulfilled lives of his children when they fall short of this ideal. Others have, of course, described the God-centered person as inherently alien to his time, but the paternal despair is, as far as I know, uniquely portrayed here. Plumb rejects Christianity because he also takes reason seriously, and suffers for this and for his radical politics. He has had the introverted mystical experience—a blinding experience of unity with God—that makes conventional religion irrelevant at best and superstitious at worst. He challenges ordinary Christians to purge their religion of its historical baggage.

Readers will find that Gee has anticipated the controversy that surrounds theologian Lloyd Geering in New Zealand today. Therefore, they may find the debate too familiar to have the sort of impact the book would have had at the time. But the mysticism adds an extra dimension that Geering (as far as I know) lacks: why not simply stop trying to make people religious if the god of Christianity has left the scene? Plumb's answer: nonetheless I know there is a god that is real.

The other two novels in the trilogy suffer because none of Plumb's children or grandchildren has his substance, and because they, far more than Plumb, are prone to irritating one-liners that are supposed to be insightful. There is a lot of effective writing in both, but in *Meg* (1981) the narrator's reminiscences as a child are not very interesting. Things improve at adulthood but there are too many passages along the lines of "know thyself", "too complicated for me to understand", "It might have given me life", "It was unreal. It was our new reality." *Sole Survivor* (1983) is about the evolution of a swine into a politician who meets a quite arbitrary demise. The description of the narrator's marriage is acute but neither the narrator nor the anti-hero come across with the force of the occasional references to Plumb himself.

Going West★ (1992) is a novel I can recommend. Gee's novels turn on a few central characters, and I find that whether I am sympathetic to those he treats sympathetically makes a big difference. This book reveals the inner life of an Aucklander and his best friend, an excellent poet, between 1930 and 1990. Do not be put off by the first forty pages, which describe the characters in generalities and worse, and psychoanalyze the narrator on why he is writing the book, who it is really about, and so forth. (Gee has a tendency to do this.) After that, Gee begins to tell his story in an attractive and revelatory style that gives depth to interesting characters, including many minor ones, and isolates what made them what they became.

In an earlier novel, *Prowlers* (1987), the thought processes of some of the characters are less than convincing, but the main character's love of science and his interaction with his grandniece, a contrast between personalities and generations, are perceptively described.

Josef, the narrator of *Live Bodies*★ (1998), is forced to flee Austria by his parents just in time to escape Hitler's takeover. His parents do not flee and are duly exterminated. The flashbacks to the social and political situation in Austria and Germany are so vivid they make the book almost worth reading in themselves. The gradual understanding of Josef's family as to how their world is collapsing and the description of how left-wing youth fought with the Hitler Youth for dominance is so real as to give a sense of participation.

Josef arrives in New Zealand just before the country's entry into the war. The authorities show a total lack of sophistication about the world beyond their borders and intern him, a Jew, on Somes Island as a dangerous alien. When he marries, his wife's family reacts with horror, illustrating how much insularity and anti-Semitism existed in New Zealand, without the tinder that made it lethal in Germany. In some quarters it still exists. Since I have a Jewish wife who does not "look" Jewish, she and I have occasionally had to listen to comments such as "He was a Jew and of course just interested in money." After a few such incidents, she decided to wear her grandmother's Star of David necklace at gatherings where she was unknown. *Live Bodies* tails off at the end, but I think it may be a bit better than *Plumb*.

Joan Druett (born 1939)

In this book I focus mainly on novelists and review only a few authors of histories, but I want to call attention to Joan Druett, who has twelve to her credit. I read *Island of the Lost*★ (2007) and liked the way she told the story without distracting asides. In this shipwreck survival story the prose is unadorned and the characters ring true. Although the demise of the men always threatens, there are no deep thoughts about death. The book deserves a star: it is almost perfect of its kind.

Charlotte Randall (circa 1955)

This New Zealand novelist deserves special recognition. Her first book *Dead Sea Fruit*★ (1994) reminds me of Elena Ferrante's *The Days of Abandonment* as a study of the ravaging effects of unrequited love. (Interestingly, like Ferrante, Randall writes under a pseudonym.) Randall sums up Alma's life: "The rich, attractive girl with the world at her feet became a doctor, became a mother, became a widow, became a cast-off lover, became a drug addict, became a maffled old woman with a headful of imploding stars."

Alma's frenzy as an abandoned lover is the main theme, although her demise is very moving. Her neighbor Frank is equally troubled. He is destroyed by an infatuation. Even though he sees it as no more than that, once it is over he is has no hope of anything beyond mere living. The description of the effects of the adults' relationships on their children is chilling. Alma's daughter praises the man who has traded in her mother for a new mistress: "Oh, he's got his head screwed on right—get one a bit younger so all her last hopes don't crush him; and a bit stupider so she can accept things as they are."

Randall's second novel *The Curative*★ (2000) is very interesting. A man is committed to Bedlam, a London asylum, from 1802 to 1815. The medical theories of the time about treatment of the mentally ill are paraded before us, each solemnly proclaimed as scientific. Being half drowned then heated is rejected because it is "discovered" that heat is fatal to internal air passages and that perspiration gives rise to miasmas and unpleasant vapors. What is required is being confined to icy cells. Then the fact that air is neutral (composed of gases plus phlogiston, an element that was thought to make things flammable) implies that miasmas are no problem. Next, biology shows that a diseased body has a tendency toward putrefaction, which is best impeded by cool rather than icy conditions. These follow in quick succession. Throughout, spinning the patient to insensibility (while surrounded by burning sulphur) plus bloodletting, purges, and enemas are standard fare.

Much of the book consists of observations about the man's life, the human condition, and current events, but in this case what the man says is genuinely interesting. On how handsomeness corrupted his son, for example: He "caught sight of himself in a mirror one day and was instantly transformed into an oozlum bird, satisfied to spend the rest of his days secreting oil from his preen-gland and lubricating his fine feathers."

The story behind why the man was committed to the asylum emerges, with each step beautifully paced. One of the proofs of his insanity was that he gave a woman large sums of money without demanding she sleep with him.

Randall's third novel, *Within the Kiss* (2002), is based on a bad idea, namely, a satiric reworking of the "Faust who sold his soul to the devil" theme. This results in a soirée between Faust (a woman), the Devil, Lord Byron, Goethe, Faust's husband, and his mistress that offers little. Faust and the Devil quibble endlessly about writing a novel within the novel.

Her fifth novel *The Crocus Hour*★ (2008) is set in Crete, which is vividly described. A girl of seventeen disappears on the island. Henry, her father, arrives to search for her, meets her best friend Jane, and acquires a young man as a companion. They are all engrossing characters. Jane's upbringing has isolated her emotionally. The young man says to her, "Do you think we can manage without Henry … Maybe we won't be enough for each other?" She replies, "Enough for what exactly?" When she has a child we know, without being told, that her anonymous husband was only a fleeting means to an end.

As an aside, the young girls went to Crete without the slightest knowledge of its history, or of European history in general. At their Dunedin high school they had studied the unification of Germany and Italy. "I had no idea what they were talking about," Jane says. "How can you unify a place that's already whole?"

I feel the quality of Randall's writing is close to that of Maurice Gee and have embarked upon reading the rest of her novels.

Eleanor Catton (born 1985)
Eleanor Catton's second novel, *The Luminaries* (2013) won the Booker Prize so she is one to watch. Catton writes very well but needs to bring her talent under control. *The Luminaries* is over 800 pages long. The author had that much good material, but good material sometimes has to be sacrificed to produce an artistic whole. The next to last

draft of Fitzgerald's *The Great Gatsby* has been preserved, and it is universally agreed that by pruning the material he enhanced the final novel.

The Luminaries concerns the machinations of various people trying to profit from the 1860s gold rush near Hokitika in the South Island of New Zealand. The plot is initially so complex you are continually pausing to try to remember the state of play. The number of major characters, around sixteen including the twelve "luminaries", tests your ability to call to mind their personalities as they reappear.

Some of the portrayals are very effective—particularly those of the young man Emery Staines and the two Chinese men, Sook Yongsheng and Quee Long—but all the characters are continually psychoanalyzed. Only about two-thirds of these passages work and many are unnecessary. Half the length, half the characters, and a simpler plot would have been better. Still, the writing holds your attention to the end.

The Luminaries is a big leap up from Catton's first novel *The Rehearsal* (2008). This was based on her thesis for her Master of Arts in Creative Writing and, rather than a finished piece of work, shows someone learning to write a novel.

AUSTRALIA

Patrick White (1912–1990)

Patrick White is to date the sole Australian-born Nobel prizewinner for literature and most critics list *Voss* (1957) as his best work. Voss, a German, leads an unsuccessful expedition—none will survive—that attempts to trek across Australia in the mid nineteenth century. Before he departs, he and a young woman fall in love and much of the novel describes her fears for him and his fixation on her during his trials. For comparison, it is not nearly as good as Romain Gary's *The Roots of Heaven.*

Some minor characters stand out and there are excellent descriptive passages. However, these are outweighed by an often pompous style peppered with the worst kind of rumination about the human condition: In Australia "it is possible more easily to discard the inessential and to attempt the infinite"; Voss is "the ugly rock upon which truth must batter itself to survive"; "The man in the cave should have felt wet, and aching, and cold but the woman's smooth instinctive soul caressed his stubborn, struggling spirit."

Voss's poems are horrible, and there is a lot about religion: "Ah, the humility, the humility! This is what I find so particularly loathsome. My God, besides, is above humility"; "When man is truly humbled, when he has learnt that he is not God, then he is nearest to becoming so. In the end he may ascend."

In *Riders in the Chariot* (1961), God sends to Earth a few in every generation who are "riders in the chariot" and offer balm to humanity. Four of them recognize one another and think and talk about truth, God, the omnipresence of evil, and so on, with vacuity and pomposity. One is a recluse, one a thoroughly good woman, one a half-Aboriginal painter, and one a Jew who escaped a concentration camp. The gentile couple who hide this man in Germany are done wonderfully well: proof again that White really can write. If only he had let his characters convey his message, like Graham Greene in *The Power and the Glory*, rather than endlessly discussing it. I do not think anyone could enjoy this book without having to pause frequently and remind themselves that White is a "great writer" and therefore they must be at fault if they are not edified. The Jew dies after being semi-crucified, an apostate Jew hangs himself (like Judas Iscariot—get it?), and the artist is inspired to paint both the crucifixion and the chariot.

The Vivisector (1970) uses vivisection as the epitome of evil. God is the great vivisector, the agent of enlightened evil against which man's evil is childlike, if only because God ends everything in death. The first 200 pages (the book is 642 pages) offer portrayals of intriguing characters. You hope the remainder will merely be overwriting. But when the fictional Australian artist, Hurtle Duffield, reaches maturity, he talks a great deal about truth. (Have any of you ever spent an evening conversing with anyone about "truth"?) He laughs "uncontrollably"; he works "in exhilaration, exhaustion, hunger, black hate, then an orgy of messy uncooked food". When he cuts his hands on the tins "the blood worked in with the paint". "Reckless purples began to stain the premeditated." Sex scenes feature "burning ear lobes" and "half-melted skins" and "the ultimate in depravity". One lover has a "tortured, dripping, shivering soul". Luckily a thirteen-year-old love, a young woman who makes her appearance late, is excellent.

White's artists are Artists: romantic heroes who are beyond convention, the sort James Thurber sent up when he described a writer as being best known for being able to trash someone else's apartment faster than anyone else. They are not simply people with an unusual talent. (Compare this with Sebastian Faulks' portrait of Christopher Wood, who comes across as a real human being.) Perhaps this is a matter of taste. After these three, I did not have the heart to embark on White's ten other novels.

David Malouf (born 1934)
The Great World (1990) won the Commonwealth Writers' Prize and France's Prix Femina Étranger. It follows two characters through the First and Second World Wars (both were imprisoned by the Japanese after the fall of Singapore in 1942) and thereafter up to the stock market crash of 1988. Digger lives out his life in a town north of Sydney. Vic, an orphan, was adopted by a respectable Sydney family at the age of twelve. He becomes a man of substance and financial irregularity. Malouf's writing is always smooth, and in the background Australia evolves from a strange mix of propriety and frontier rawness into a modern society ruled by smart young men. However, the two main characters lack something—namely, the psychological depth to make attractive the detail of their everyday lives.

Remembering Babylon★ (1993) is just as well written and here the characters did arouse my curiosity. The book lays bare the hardships faced by white Australians as they pushed their settlements north of Brisbane: the heat, torrential rain, mosquitos whose bites made their eyelids swell, and cockroaches as big as wrens, which ran over their faces in the dark. Gemmy, a man who has spent sixteen years with Aborigines after being shipwrecked, comes to the village and is sheltered by the McIvors. Malouf uses him as an instrument to dissect the apparent unity of the settlers and analyze them as individuals in terms of temperament, character, and self-awareness. Gemmy had been an orphan in early nineteenth-century Britain and his background characterizes the society he had left. When little more than a toddler, he had swept all day in a timber mill. The best food he had got was a meal of oil grime mixed with sawdust. When "adopted" by a rat catcher, he had graduated to household slave, as well as being horribly bitten when assisting at rat fights.

The English novelist and critic David Profumo hailed Malouf's next novel, *The Conversations at Curlow Creek* (1996), as his best. Three children share a well-off Irish childhood that makes them more important to one another than anyone else is. At maturity Adair loves Virgilia who loves Fergus, despite which Adair and Fergus remain close friends. The plight of Ireland's poor in the early nineteenth century, even before the Great Famine, was terrible. Those with a mud shack were comparatively fortunate. Even they lived in fear of families of beggars who roamed the countryside ready to loot and kill. Thousands were transported to Australia, and many of them became policemen or rural outlaws.

Fergus, a champion of the poor, goes to Australia, as Jack Dolan, to try and transform the downtrodden settlers into rebels. Virgilia hears vague rumors that Fergus has left. Adair, now a soldier of fortune, goes to Australia as a trooper to see if it's true. Much of the book consists of Adair's conversations with the sole surviving member of Fergus's band of rebels on the night before his execution. During this the truth emerges.

The depiction of the plight of the Irish is gripping and the style can be compelling: "his pen traced the magic words 'My dear Virgilia' and his soul added, silently, 'My dearest.'" When Virgilia reads to her paralyzed father: "It's like the tiniest tiniest air-hole that he's breathing through. If it wasn't there he'd have no will to live." But there is too much pedestrian correspondence, and conversation that is supposed to enlighten us about the workings of fate.

Thomas Keneally (born 1935)
Keneally is an Australian writer noteworthy primarily because of his account of a German who defied Hitler during the Second World War. *Schindler's Ark*★ (1982) (called *Schindler's List* in the United States edition) won the Booker Prize, which slightly enhances my regard for that award. It is the story of two men so strange that if we did not know they actually existed we would be likely to dismiss them as

implausible fictions. Oskar Schindler, before and after the war, was a businessman in Kraków, Poland with few scruples. Yet during it he risked his life repeatedly to save around 1,100 Jews. The local Nazi commandant used to shoot Jews for fun with a rifle while sitting on his front porch, but since he was simply a sadist rather than an ideologue, and since he liked Schindler, he colluded in his friend's unaccountable mania for saving Jews.

Peter Carey (born 1943)
Touted as Australia's next Nobel Prize winner, Peter Carey has won the Booker Prize twice. I have read only two of his books but they are enough to convince me I must read some of his other eleven novels.

Oscar and Lucinda★ (1988) is about two young people who eventually fall in love in mid-nineteenth-century Australia thanks to a shared mania for gambling. Oscar's upbringing shows just how the English at that time managed to use religion to drive themselves insane. It was not just that religion colored every facet of life, it was the division of Christians into sects, each of which was totally convinced that everyone outside their sect, however small, was damned. Oscar, for superstitious reasons rather like reading the entrails of an owl, abandons his father's church, the Plymouth Brethren, for the Anglicans, and feels he must leave his father's home to be raised by an Anglican priest. He and his father know the other is going to hell, and each prays for the other torn by agony and love. Some of the best passages are about a sporting gentleman who finds, to his amazement, that he has become friends with this religious "Odd Bod".

Lucinda is an heiress who bitterly resents the condescension of men and is a total romantic. Neither she nor Oscar are in any way suited to dealing with the outer world. In this book Carey shows he has everything a writer needs: convincing characters, excellent dialogue, a clear plot, and expressive prose. He is certainly superior to Patrick White, Australia's only Nobel winner for literature thus far. (The 2003 Nobel winner J.M. Coetzee is also credited as Australian, but this South African-born novelist became an Australian citizen only in 2006.)

True History of the Kelly Gang★ (2000) is longer still at 500 pages but held my interest throughout. Ned Kelly has a place in Australian folklore as a daring outlaw: he was hanged in 1880 at the age of twenty-six. His last words were "Such is life", and these capture the fate of a man who had to end up on the gallows if he behaved honorably.

Honor consisted in obeying the code of an Irishman whose family was under siege in a hostile country. At this time the plight of the Irish in rural Australia was even worse than that of the urban Irish in America. Both populations were considered violent, ungovernable, potential criminals, and thieves. However, the urban Irish controlled their own neighborhood, into which many police did not dare to trespass. The isolated Irish family on a farm was fair game for any police force that wanted to arrest them on suspicion, harass them to try and extract a confession, or jail them for months on the flimsiest of pretexts. You never betrayed another Irishman to the law, even when you knew he had committed the crime of which you were accused.

By the age of five, thanks to the nuns, Kelly could name all the traitors and heroes of Irish history: "John Cockayne Edward Abby even poor Anthony Perry who finally betrayed the rebels after the English set his head alight with pitch and gunpowder … Tom Murray and Owen Finn they would not betray the rebels though they was flogged and tortured the whole town echoing with their screams."

Family honor came above all. You fought to defend your mother's name at school even though you knew she had done what she was accused of. When Kelly was on the run his little brother offered to keep guard all night but dozed off, "and I laid his ferocious little 8 yr. old body upon his crib". He begins to rob banks because he needs to arm a gang so he can rescue his mother from prison and then escape with her. His lover curses the police who come to arrest him: "O I curse your seed … May your children come to the straw with feet like toads and eyes like snakes … Your wife will lie with soldiers. You will wander the roads with sores and weeping warts."

His image of English and Irish is fixed: "there were not an English eye could see her no more than an English eye can picture the fire that will descend upon that race in time to come". A friend tells him he saw the devil. He asks:

"Did he have an Irish voice?

"What do you mean?

"When the Devil spoke were he Irish?"

True History of the Kelly Gang is a tour de force that is written in language of Kelly himself, a nearly illiterate man, without sacrificing anything in the way of insight.

Tim Winton (born 1960)

Tim Winton's novel *Cloudstreet*★ (1991) is unique. Three readers' polls have called it the best Aussie book, and the Australian Society of Authors voted it their favorite Australian novel. My decision to award it a star wavered back and forth.

It is a wonderful depiction of two working-class families living in the same huge house in Perth from 1944 to 1964. The Lambs own the house and live off the rent the Pickles pay, and the Pickles run a shop from its premises. There are a lot of good touches of humor: when a boy's birthday cake is sold to a customer from under his nose he is given a florin as compensation. He asks, "You want change from this?" A husband, trying to mollify his irate wife who wants to slaughter a pet pig, says, "There's another thing. … The pig talks." When Toby brags that someone has taken one of his poems, Sam Pickles is sympathetic: "Don't spose you're insured?"

Some passages are affecting. Dolly never got to travel—"by sixteen she found herself out on her back under the night sky with a long procession of big hatted men". At school lunch, out of pride, Wogga McBride and his brother go "through the motions of unwrapping, passing, commenting on, eating food that doesn't exist".

Young Rose Pickles and Quick Lamb gradually take on depth. This is spoiled by a ridiculous passage in which Rose's middle-class lover humiliates her, and an embarrassing passage in which Rose and Quick discover love. The book has many annoying pages you have to wade through. Some are painfully maudlin, some muse poetically. A brother who suffers from mental retardation and converses with the pig is the subject of a lot of bad writing.

Dirt Music (2001) won the Miles Franklin Award and was shortlisted for the Booker. In the first half, characters grow on you. The second half is less attractive. There is too much detail about Luther's search for solitude and Georgie's search for him. Their thoughts dwell on one another at length. The main characters become marvels of psychological complexity, with much brooding about atonement for their sins. The dialogue is generally sharp, except for a tendency for everyone to make intelligently ironic replies, which level their differences. This book has none of the defects of *Cloudstreet* but lacks its virtues.

Hannah Kent (born 1985)

Kent is a writer with an impressive first novel that has won nine literary awards. *Burial Rites*★ (2013) is set in Iceland in 1829. Agnes, condemned to death, spends the winter before her execution captive in a household whose women are reluctant to have her. (There is no prison in the isolated area.) All the people ring true, with the possible exception of Agnes's former lover, one of the two men she has been convicted of killing. The evolution of Agnes's hosts from revulsion to sympathy is beautifully done. Just before Agnes is taken away to be killed, Laura, the daughter who at first loathed her the most, calls out to her. When Agnes remarks that this is the first time Laura has ever addressed her by name, Laura is stricken. The book also lays bare just how grim and close to starvation the lives of most Europeans—not just Icelanders—were two centuries ago. Watch for Kent's next novel.

AFRICA

J.M. Coetzee (born 1940)

I believe Coetzee is a competent rather than outstanding novelist. Recently I reread his two Booker Prize-winning novels and found them interesting, although more for their theme than their literary merit.

Life and Times of Michael K (1983) describes the travels of the protagonist in the South Africa of the 1970s, when it seemed to be drifting towards civil war. Thus, it underlines the horrors that were somehow avoided. Michael is simple-minded and has a harelip. He is well portrayed but, sadly, is used to muse about that graveyard of serious novels—time. Time turns life into a series of precious moments.

Disgrace★ (1999) is worth reading to get the flavor of South Africa since the end of apartheid: no civil war but much interpersonal violence, often with an underlying theme of race hate. To vacate your urban flat for any length of time is to assume it will be pillaged. Whites who farm in an area dominated by blacks are at risk. The best character is the black farmer, Petrus. He recognizes that a great evil has been done to his white "patron" (who was brutally raped) but looks upon an adolescent kinsman who was present as innocent. He wants control of the woman's land but is prepared to put her under his protection. The main character David Lurie, a professor of English, is less satisfactory. His preoccupation with an opera he wishes to write is too prominent and distracting.

Rian Malan (born 1954)

In *The Masque of Africa*, V.S. Naipaul recommends an autobiography as the best account of modern South Africa. *My Traitor's Heart*★ (1990) tells the story of Rian Malan's father's family, who arrived at the Cape from France in the seventeenth century. In moving prose, you get South African history from the beginning of European settlement to the end of apartheid and Nelson Mandela's release from prison.

Apartheid refers to the system by means of which whites dominated the overwhelming black majority. Residential areas were segregated, sometimes by means of forced removals. Blacks were deprived of national citizenship, legally becoming citizens of one of ten "homelands" called Bantustans, where they lived in poverty and neglect. The government segregated education, medical care, beaches, and other public places and services, and forbade interracial sex.

The book shows what a miracle it was that the transition to black rule came without wholesale slaughter. Nelson Mandela was released from prison on February 11, 1990. Over the next few months violence did escalate. In September 1992 the Zulus massacred forty-six black followers of

Mandela's African National Congress (ANC). In April 1993, riots followed the assassination of Chris Hani, an ANC leader. But nothing was as horrific as predicted.

Writing in mid 1990, Malan is still pessimistic: "We did not learn to love before they learned to hate." His heart is divided between goodwill toward blacks and fear of a race war in which whites will be killed indiscriminately. He recognizes that he himself is a member of a tribe, the Boers or Dutch Afrikaners of South Africa.

It took both sides to end apartheid without disaster. The Boer leaders realized they were going to be overwhelmed eventually and the prime minister then president P.W. Botha began to relax apartheid. He established a good relationship with Mandela before suffering a stroke in 1989. The following year the new president, F.W. de Klerk, announced he would end apartheid and release all political prisoners. In 1994, the ANC won a free election and Mandela became president.

However much de Klerk respected and trusted Mandela, why did he make an act of faith that Mandela could control black rage? Malan knew black Africa as a reporter and saw violence everywhere. The brutality that blacks suffered from whites defies description. Blacks were also violent towards one another. Thieves would go on a train and drive a sharpened bicycle spoke through their victim's thigh. This nailed him or her to the seat and the thieves could rob at leisure. Black factions burned one another alive. Zulus warred against one another simply because the young men enjoyed war. Imagine what they would do to whites. (They killed Neil Alcock, a saintly white who was trying to negotiate a peace between two warring tribes.)

It is easy to say that de Klerk knew the handwriting was on the wall and had to take the risk, but even buying a few years, or time to flee, seems worth it if the alternative is extermination. It is enough to make you believe that the hand of God was on Mandela's side. The only serene man Malan met was an Irish priest. He was less concerned about what would happen at the end of apartheid than about the ills Britain had heaped on Ireland.

The story is not over because the economic benefits poor blacks have enjoyed are few. The new South African government has thrown its borders open, and impoverished immigrants overwhelm the cities. Race still dominates everything. But only a few extremists want a race war.

SOMALIA

Ayaan Hirsi Ali (born 1970)

The autobiography of this Somalia-born writer and former member of the Dutch parliament, *Infidel: My Life*★ (2006, translated 2007), will give you an unparalleled insight into what Islam means for those who interpret the Koran literally. Islam dominates all of Northern Africa, most of West Africa and Somalia, and has a smaller but substantial following in other parts of East Africa, including Eritrea, Ethiopia, where thirty-four percent of the population are Muslim, Kenya, Tanzania, and Mozambique. Hirsi Ali was subjected to female circumcision at the age of five: her clitoris and inner labia were cut off and then her outer labia sewed together to guarantee her purity until marriage. This practice is pre-Islamic. It is done in a few places outside Islam, and not done universally within Islam, but it is widespread, justified by its advocates in the name of Islam, and goes unopposed by most imams in nations such as Somalia.

As a young woman Hirsi Ali was initially devout, but then began to question her faith in Islam and was shocked to find that what she found objectionable was actually in the Koran: the husband's right to sexually access his wife whenever he pleases—"even on the saddle of a camel"; wife-beating for disobedience (wives must ask permission even to leave the house); disguising any hint of female attraction that may entice a male; holy wars; and child marriage—Mohammed married a six-year-old girl and consummated the marriage when she was nine.

Hirsi Ali's father was not a literalist and interpreted the Koran as a document of charity and peace. She herself is also well aware there are fundamentalists who make other scriptures, such as the Christian Bible, into instruments of oppression. But her point is that partially due to the efforts of Saudi Arabia, literalism—practiced by what she calls Medina Muslims—is coming to dominate the minds of far too many in the Islamic world.

After Hirsi Ali sought refuge in Holland and eventually became a member of parliament there, she crusaded to stop the Dutch government's policy of subsidizing Islamic schools. Many of these not only preached violence, anti-Americanism, and anti-Semitism (hatred of Jews, not just of Israel) but also perpetuated family tyranny, female circumcision, and honor killings. The Dutch, unwilling to compromise their cultural tolerance, liked to pretend that honor killings were rare. She forced the authorities to list deaths by cause. In a sample of two regions over an eight-month period, Muslim families had executed eleven girls.

EGYPT

Egypt, an Islamic nation, is the largest Arab state, with a population of over eighty million, and perhaps the most modernized. This does not mean a great deal in areas such as law and gender. The fertility bestowed by the Nile has sustained a large population here from ancient times. The extent to which black or sub-Saharan Africa influenced its ancient culture is a political football, unlikely to be settled. There is a consensus that the country's present mix has a strong continuity with ancient times, the Middle Eastern component having been strengthened since the Arab conquest of Egypt in AD 642. DNA studies suggest modern Egyptians have genes divided almost equally between those current in Europe, the Middle East, and Africa, with the latter split between sub-Saharan blacks and the Berbers of North Africa.

In any event, the divisions of contemporary Egypt are not racial but religious and cultural. The government likes to underestimate the number of Coptic Christians, who are not racially distinct but go back to the time before the Arab conquest when Christianity was the majority religion. Some eighty to ninety percent of the people are Sunni Muslims, the rest mainly Coptic. The majority are split between an urban élite, whose culture has tempered religious fervor and made them advocates of democracy, a larger group of Muslims more fundamentalist in belief, including the Muslim Brotherhood and those more fundamentalist still, and the army, which sees its rule as essential to national unity and modernization.

Hosni Mubarak, a military careerist turned politician, was president from 1981 to 2011. He struck a balance between the three groups that favored the army. The urban élite objected to military rule. They led demonstrations and the Islamists joined them. In 2012 the Islamists won a free democratic election and installed Mohamed Morsi, a member of the Muslim Brotherhood, as president. Unwilling to abandon its pivotal role in government and the economy, the army under General el-Sisi deposed Morsi in 2013. The Muslim Brotherhood was outlawed—it is now labeled a terrorist organization.

Sisi was elected president in 2014 and Morsi was sentenced to twenty years in prison. Ironically, a new balance has evolved that gives the military an even greater role than under Mubarak, and has weakened not only the Islamists but also the urban élite, the only group really committed to democracy.

Naguib Mahfouz (1911–2006)

Mahfouz has an enormous reputation as Egypt's best fiction writer and a Nobel Prize winner. I found *The Mirage* (1948, translated 2009), the first of his books I read, a disappointment. It is well written and the main character, Kamil Ru'ba Laz, is vivid enough, but he is so one-dimensional he failed to hold my attention. A psychological novel has to be about someone whose character contains a few surprises and this man is simply an archetype of the smothered son. The novel does show how the weird courtship dominant among the Egyptian middle class, smoldering looks but no real knowledge of the person until after marriage, can lead to tragedy.

The minor characters in the book, particularly Kamil's grandfather, father, and in-laws, were more fully developed so I hoped for better things from Mahfouz's other works. *Children of the Alley*, sometimes called *Children of Gebelaawi* (1959, translated 1981) portrays Mohammed as an historical figure. In addition, there is a character who represents the rise of science, whose "magic" makes God unnecessary and whose psychology means the death of God. The book's style has an appropriate dignity, but if you are not caught up in the ethos of an Arab world in which it is courageous to advocate religious tolerance and treat Islam as merely one of the world's great religions, the book is not very exciting. Adam, Satan, Moses, Christ, and Mohammed come and go.

The book was banned in Egypt. Five years after the Nobel Prize gave it new notoriety, two men stabbed Mahfouz in the neck and damaged nerves, which made it hard for him to write over the last twelve years of his life.

The writer's excellent style is manifest in his most ambitious publication, the Cairo trilogy: *Palace Walk*★ (1956, translated 1989); *Palace of Desire*★ (1957, translated 1991); and *Sugar Street*★ (1957, translated 1992). I have awarded them each a star with some hesitation. You need to be engrossed in the everyday life of urban Egyptians and prepared to ignore some long internal monologues by characters who lament their plight to enjoy this trilogy. It runs over 1,200 pages and follows a middle-class Cairo family from the British occupation during the First World War until the overthrow of King Farouk in 1952 ended British–Egyptian collaboration. The following year Egypt became a republic. You become involved in the fate of some of the characters, and the social history is engaging.

The story begins with a husband who totally dominates a wife preoccupied with spirits and ghosts. She is never allowed to leave her home, and addresses her husband as "Sir". His life is one of drink, sex, and the company of old friends who meet every evening in town. Each night his wife waits up for him, undresses him, and shampoos him, tasks she does with pleasure and delight. Over the years, women make gains. In the last volume, one female character is a Marxist and independent journalist, but the status of women still falls far short of that of women in the West.

Quite recently, Islamic fundamentalism has eroded some of what was gained. A man can divorce his wife at whim without recourse to the courts. A woman has no automatic right to divorce, even if her husband marries a second wife, as is common. Proceedings often take years in backlogged and biased courts: only sixty-two out of 5,252 divorce cases filed in a Cairo court one year were resolved the next.

The true position of women is captured in a description by an Egyptian woman, Amira Ahmad, in a report called *Divorced from Justice*, published by Human Rights Watch in November 2004: "I told him, 'Divorce me and leave. At least that way when I go to beg from people on the street, they'll know I have no one.' He said, 'No, I'll kill you. Leave the house if you want a divorce. Give up the house, the children, the furniture, and the clothing that you're wearing. I will not give you anything. You will go to your family's house and they'll bring you back to lick my shoes.'"

The rise of nationalism is charted. Although it was strong among men, even in 1900, many women did not care. A son tells his mother that a delegation has been sent to the queen requesting that British troops leave Egypt. She replies: "That is in very bad taste … after the time we have spent living among them as neighbors to tell them bluntly, and in their country at that, to get out. … Son, they don't kill us and they don't interfere with the mosques." Why would anyone care about the English when the important thing is to marry off your children advantageously?

Mahfouz acknowledges his debt to a book *Return of the Spirit* (1933, translated 2012) by Tawfiq al-Hakim. The first novel in the European style published in Arabic, it is mainly about unrequited love, but closes with the first spark of nationalism among the Egyptian masses, which resulted in the revolution of 1919 and Egyptian semi-independence. However, Britain refused to withdraw its troops, which were there to protect the Suez Canal, defend foreign interests in Egypt, and "protect" Egypt against aggression. It was 1953 before full independence was achieved. The book itself is better than most pioneering books but falls short of the caliber that would much interest a contemporary reader.

LIBYA

Libya's land area is larger than Egypt's, but, having nothing like the Nile, about half of it is uninhabited desert and its population only five million, plus a million or more black immigrants from the south. From prehistoric times, Berber were the indigenous people along the north coast of Africa, including Libya. They are not black Africans but akin to an early population that originated in upper Egypt (southern or inland), with some affinities to the Semites, and spread throughout the whole Mediterranean area. Arabs overwhelmed these people in Libya. Today their distinctive genes account for only thirty percent of the population and, particularly after Muammar Gaddafi took power in 1969, they were forced to give up their traditional languages for Arabic, although some sense of difference remains on the tribal level.

Today ninety-seven percent of Libya's permanent citizens are Arab or Arabic-speaking Berbers. They are also Sunni

Muslims. During the uprising against Gaddafi during the Arab Spring of 2011, there was an upsurge of racism and many blacks were killed or fled. There is a foreign Christian minority of about two percent, split between Coptic Christians from Egypt and Roman Catholics originally from Europe. The Toubou, or Tebou, are nomads scattered around the desert regions. Although they are racially distinct and have their own language, they are also Sunni. There are numerous tribes and sub-tribes, particularly in the east, deeply divided by enmity and embittered history, and some east versus west antagonism. Gaddafi's tribe, the al-Gaddafa, was dominant in the city of Sirte. Members held out even after his death and were slaughtered when defeated. Those remaining are bound by honor to try to avenge him.

After a coup put Gaddafi in power in 1969, his record, rather like that of Saddam Hussein in Iraq, was of a tyrant allied to what he saw as progress. There is no doubt about the tyranny. He killed thousands of dissidents and conspired against his neighbors, including a plot in 2003 to assassinate Crown Prince Abdullah, the de facto ruler of Saudi Arabia. There is no doubt about the progress. He advanced the position of women. He spent much of the nation's oil revenue on free health care, free education for both boys and girls, adult literacy, housing, pensions, and accident compensation.

Many who plotted against him were sincere idealists, but it was only when tribal loyalties were aroused that they overthrew him. Whether a veneer of Westernized liberals can establish an effective democratic and progressive government remains to be seen. The alternative is the fragmentation of the nation along tribal lines, or suppression of the tribes again by a new tyranny, perhaps one based on conservative Islam.

Hisham Matar (born 1970)
Born in New York to a diplomat father, between the ages three and fifteen this Libyan writer had a life divided between Tripoli, Nairobi and Cairo. His family fled Libya in 1979 because Gaddafi considered his father suspect: he wanted a democratic regime. In March 1990, in Cairo, his father "disappeared": the Egyptian police kidnapped him and handed him over to the Libyan authorities. It used to be thought he might be still alive but when prisoners were released from Libyan jails in 2011 there was no sign of him.

Since the age of fifteen Matar has lived in London. His father's disappearance was the defining moment of his life and his two novels both feature parental loss. I recommend *In the Country of Men*⋆ (2006) because of the light it sheds on both traditional Libyan society and the insecurity of any dissident living under Gaddafi's dictatorship. A boy's mother is forced to marry at fourteen to preserve her reputation: she has been seen in public seated across a table from a male. Fortunately, the marriage bed proves she is a virgin or her father would have had to kill her. She hates the lot of women and serves as a counterbalance to those who tell us Islamic women never feel more fulfilled than when they embrace the submission that is their lot. She freezes with alarm on an occasion in which she might seem remiss for not having prepared lunch.

She eventually comes to love her husband but has become alcohol- and drug-dependent. She respects her husband's integrity but cannot understand his persistence in risking everything by clandestine political activity. Her father is arrested and tortured and betrays his comrades. There is a hair-raising description of a public hanging. The writing at times descends into a sentimentality that lessens its impact.

Anatomy of a Disappearance★★ (2011) is much better. There are no jarring notes and the style is purified. Contrary to some critics, I count this in its favor. The book has the slow pace that only a writer confident of his power to charm and captivate the reader can afford. It borders on the quality of the great Ishiguro's work. Could it be that fluency in two languages, Japanese and English in one case, Arabic and English in the other, acts as a sieve that tends to refine language?

A man aged twenty reviews the effects on his life of his father's disappearance. Before this happened, the family lived in political exile in Egypt. His despondent mother died when he was ten. His father was attractive to women and took a second wife. She is a captivating woman, and cannot resist the gratification she enjoys when her stepson falls in love with her, particularly as he matures. The interaction between the boy, his father, his stepmother, and the father's mistress are the substance of the plot. After the family goes to Geneva the father vanishes, presumably taken by Libyan agents. The boy does not feel endangered: he is most disturbed by the fact that his father was living in the past, obsessing about a problematic day when he could return home.

Given the quality of this book, I have only one reservation about Matar's future: Can he transcend his personal history to paint on a larger canvas?

MOROCCO

The Muslims conquered Morocco early in the eighth century. Between 1172 and 1222 the state they founded dominated the Moorish portion of Spain. It lost influence in Spain after 1248, when the Castilian king Ferdinand III succeeded in reconquering the major cities of the south. Morocco remained independent until 1912, when the Treaty of Fès divided it into French and (ironically) Spanish protectorates. In 1956 it regained its independence.

King Hassan II ruled from 1961 to 1999, not without challenge, although these were not popular revolts but rather attempted coups by army officers. The present king, Mohammed VI, has been more liberal and has granted women reforms in family law although, as we shall see, women's rights have far to go. The country is a North Atlantic Treaty Organization (NATO) ally and has arrested thousands of Islamic extremists. Arabs outnumber Berbers by about two to one but there is considerable assimilation. Almost all are Sunni so there is no real religious divide. Slow growth and unemployment were acute before 1990, not much better before 2000, but there has been significant progress since.

Tahar Ben Jelloun (born 1944)
According to Islamic inheritance law, still in force, if there is no male heir two-thirds of a deceased person's estate is divided among the deceased's brothers. Without male offspring, fathers are not real men or mothers real mothers. The Koran was a step forward: it forbade the tradition of burying unwanted female infants alive.

In *The Sand Child* (1985, translated 1987) a Moroccan woman lives as a man so her father's estate can be kept intact. She embraces the role because it offers an escape from the awfulness of being a woman. Eventually, though, the pretense drives her into miserable isolation and she is tortured by regret. The style of this book has been highly praised and the passages about the family and the woman's "marriage" are powerful. However, there is flowery prose about the outrageousness of it all, and the last third is devoted to the prospect of the woman's death and to meditations about death: a chronicler admits defeat because "death was turning [him] into a clown"—that sort of thing.

Fifteen years later, in *This Blinding Absence of Light** (2001, translated 2002) Ben Jelloun's style is under control and far more eloquent. However, you must have the stomach for reading about twenty-three men held in a special prison. In 1971 senior officers attempted unsuccessfully to assassinate King Hassan II and commanded their junior officers to obey. Most of the latter were unaware of what was afoot, and had they resisted they would have been shot. The senior officers were executed and the junior officers held for twenty years, eighteen in a desert prison where they were deprived of light and given just enough calories to keep them alive. Their cells were only five feet high so they could never stand. Anyone who got gangrene was eaten alive by cockroaches. Aziz is one of only four who survived, albeit with no teeth and a hump back: he lost fourteen centimetres in height. He kept himself alive by first persuading himself he had had no past, then by having something close to a mystical experience, which made him trust in God.

*Leaving Tangier** (2005, translated 2009) tells why people risk their lives, usually by drowning, to enter Europe illegally. The time is the late 1990s. Every ambitious youth, unless he has money or a taste for corruption or violence, wants to leave Morocco. Young men with degrees sit for years in cafés living off whatever pittance their mothers or sisters provide. Mobsters and the police administer brutal beatings. To escape this life, women are willing to accept false marriages, prostitution, or servitude. Azel, a young male graduate, is willing to be sodomized by a wealthy Spaniard. Malika, his childhood neighbor, sees her dream of emigration slipping away as she shells frozen shrimp and faces reality—fingers eaten by eczema and becoming arthritic, pneumonia a year away, death not long after. These last two books have convinced me Ben Jelloun's many other novels are worth reading. At least fifteen have been translated into English.

Overview

If you have read the recommended books about Africa, both here and in *The Torchlight List*, you now know something about ten nations. Seven of these are below the Sahara. If you feel ready for an overview of this part of the African continent, read *A History of Sub-Saharan Africa*★ (second edition 2013) by Robert O. Collins and James M. Burns. You will find particularly interesting their account of the slave trade. What you have learned about North Africa, or at least Morocco, Libya, and Egypt, will connect you with the great Islamic world that runs from North Africa to the Middle East and extends across the southern half of Asia.

ASIA AND THE MIDDLE EAST

JAPAN

Shūsaku Endō (1923–1996)

A Catholic, Endo is hailed as Japan's Graham Greene. *Silence* (1966, translated 1969) is about the persecution of Catholics in Japan in the seventeenth century. Kichijiro, a cowardly Christian who begs a Portuguese priest for forgiveness for betraying him, is convincing but the mind of the priest is less so and is analyzed at too great a length. An analogous novel would be Greene's *The Power and the Glory* about the persecution of Catholics in Mexico in the early twentieth century. Endo's book is not the equal of Greene's. An index of its merit would be A.J. Cronin's *The Keys of the Kingdom* about a Scottish missionary in China.

Endō's early novel *The Sea and Poison*★ (1958, translated 1992) is also marred by an excess of introspective anguish, but several characters engage you and the book acknowledges something Japan is reluctant to acknowledge to this day: the barbaric things done prior to and during the Second World War. That great atrocity the six-week Nanking Massacre, in which 20,000 women were raped and 300,000 civilians slaughtered, is a matter of casual reminiscence. Speaking of a neighbor, a man says, "He raised hell in Nanking", as if this were a bit of fun that soldiers had when they went overseas.

The novel focuses on why a medical team agreed to participate in experiments on captive American servicemen. It shows how all of their consciences had been anesthetized, partly by the hopelessness of their lives as the war dragged on, but partly by their own psychology as Japanese: the complete sense of superiority to foreigners, the worship of authority (nurses think of doctors as a different species), and the class hierarchy. In school, boys who are middle class are addressed by their formal names—even by the farmer's sons whom they despise. All of this is conveyed without overstatement. The central character survives the war. He cannot live with what he did, but believes the man he was would make the same choice even if given a second chance.

Yukio Mishima (1925–1970)
Mishima wrote 273 books, including fifteen novels. I have not read all of these but will discuss six, including his last four that completed a set he considered his masterpiece.

Mishima's autobiographical novel *Confessions of a Mask*★ (1949, translated 1958) reveals that the author, real name Kimitake Hiraoka, suffered a dissonance between sexual desire and love. Desire was focused on sadomasochistic fantasies about young men but these were devoid of affection. Love had a young woman as its object but she aroused no lust. The plight of the woman, who is ignorant of the hero's lack of desire and therefore baffled by his behavior, is extremely moving. Despite his tragic themes, Mishima injects a wry humor. During the Second World War a father is reconciled to the fact American bombs may kill his daughter, but appalled that her corpse might be found attired in slacks.

The Sailor Who Fell from Grace with the Sea★ (1963, translated 1965) is a chilling story about thirteen-year-old nihilists who represent the antithesis of the Samurai tradition. Respecting nothing, in total rebellion against their own society, they conclude that only outrage can lend them significance. They must show they can do anything, no matter how awful, and murder is the obvious test. They graduate from cats to people before the age of fourteen, because at that age they can be held responsible under Japanese law. Their victim is eligible because he loses heroic status and goes soft, beginning to show some humanity. The prose is elegant: "Yoriko's flaws and her vulgarity were apparent as always, but they seemed as cool and inoffensive as goldfish swimming in a fishbowl"; "[There are] words never failing to bestow on even the haughtiest woman the sadness, the hollow hopes, and the freedom of the whore: You'll be leaving in the morning, won't you?"

Mishima's four-novel cycle uses the decline of the Samurai tradition, with its seven principles of honor, courage, filial piety, loyalty (to the emperor above all), respect for others, justice, and honesty, as a metric to measure the corruption of Japan from 1910 to 1970. Each novel focuses on a particular facet of the degeneration of Japanese society: the luxury enjoyed by the aristocracy prior to the First World War (rule of the effete and contemptible); the political and business élite between the wars—men who have no feeling for the poor and compromise the emperor thanks to their materialism and greed; the post-Second World War loss of confidence in Japan's historical authorities and conventions; and modern Japan, which is simply an imitation of America with its own traditions compromised.

Spring Snow★★ (1969, translated 1972) is about a young man of great physical beauty who is utterly worthless as anything except an ornament. His grandfather was a great Samurai, but the young man represents what the hereditary aristocracy has become circa 1910. Descriptions of art and nature are beautiful (there is a wonderful passage about cherry trees in bloom), the romantic scenes are impassioned, and the depiction of the artificiality of social interaction is even more effective than that in Gogol's *Dead Souls*.

There are some striking passages: "Any sort of serious thought was beyond the Baroness, who was was amazed at the intellectual awakening among Japanese women. She observed it with the same excited curiosity that might have been aroused in her by hens laying eggs of some novel shape—pyramids, for instance"; "his solemn pinch-faced children with their mouths turned down in perpetual obsequious respect"; "He was like a husband so jealous that he insists his wife have the very dreams he has".

Some small talk at a gathering:

The Count: "As to animals, whatever one says … the rodent family has a certain charm about it."

The Baron: "The rodent family? … You have pets of that sort, sir?"

The Count: "No sir, not at all. Too much of an odor. It would be all over the house. … Actually, sir, every charming creature, no matter what sort, seems to have a strong odor."

The Baron: "Yes, indeed, sir. I believe one might say so."

In *Runaway Horses*★ (1969, translated 1973), a group of young men try to revive the Samurai tradition, which dictates the murder of the wicked—in this case the élite who dominated between the wars. They plot to assassinate those who were business leaders during the Great Depression, men who corrupted Japan with their greed and disdain for the poor. Worst of all, the businessmen are the shock troops of Western influences that undermine spirituality, culminating in stripping the emperor of his divine status.

This act of purifying Japan is to be followed by purifying the self through ritual suicide. An honorable death is seen as the only valid goal of life. Their experiences at university did not tempt these young men to embrace different goals. At the end of a boring lecture "There was the same feeling of relief with which one sees a frightfully squawking chicken suddenly breathe its last and become tranquil."

You understand why less than 20,000 men out of Japan's army of six million were captured alive during the Second World War. These Japanese were close relatives of today's Islamic fundamentalists who become suicide bombers. Mishima is posing the same question that now obsesses Islam: How much of what is best in a religious tradition can be salvaged in a modern industrial society?

In *The Temple of Dawn* (1970, translated 1973) a lawyer named Honda emerges as the character who will tie the four volumes together. The book has two halves: first, Buddhism, plus the doctrine of the transmigration of souls from one life to another; second, the desire to spy on a young woman having sexual intercourse. I would recommend it only to those who share these obsessions.

Honda has two "soul-shaking" experiences: a sacred cow looks directly into his eyes; and he discovers the "ultimate waterfall". He believes a girl is the reincarnation of two Japanese youths. He fantasizes about the woman she becomes, seeing "the brilliant soles of her feet", finding a trace of her spittle, and imagining her death. He is deeply convinced that post-war Japan is still going downhill: it has smashed its idols, leaving only a vacuum.

In *The Decay of the Angel* (1971, translated 1974), Honda adopts Toru, a sixteen-year-old boy, whom he suspects is the reincarnation of the girl who was the reincarnation of Honda's boyhood friends. Personal obsessions push aside the analysis of Japan's decline. There are a few asides about how Japan has replicated American shops, with the specter of Coca-Cola looming over all. But the focus is on Honda's expectations about Toru, and his belief that the boy will die at twenty, ideally mourned by a lovely widow offering "a pure crystallization of beauty".

Toru survives, but only after becoming demoralized and blind. Honda, despite his frustrated expectations, finds peace of mind. Buddhism tells him that everything, including

Japan's decline, is an illusion. This is disappointing. What we needed to complete the story of Japan's decline was social analysis, not a purely personal solution. Elegant style is wasted on the beauty of cruelty, the absurdity of love, and the meaninglessness of life.

It is a pity that Mishima's cycle lost its way. Perhaps he had lost interest in the fate of his nation. Indeed, he became obsessed with the significance of his own writing and began to foreshadow that he would commit suicide on the day the four-novel cycle was finished. He did so on November 25, 1970, at the age of forty-five, in accordance with the rites of the Samurai.

SAUDI ARABIA

In 1932 the Saudi clan unified most of the Arabian Peninsula into one nation and they continue to rule it like a tribal fiefdom. Since 1953 the kings have all been half-brothers. The regime has been stable thanks to cooperation between it and the ulamä, powerful religious leaders whose followers take fundamentalist Islam as seriously as Catholics and Protestants took religion at the time of the Reformation. Keeping the masses happy with part of its huge oil wealth has helped. The Saudis support, primarily with money and arms, the Sunni side in the great struggle that is taking place between Sunnis and Shiites all over the Middle East. Prince Bandar bin Sultan, the former head of Saudi intelligence, reportedly once told the head of the British secret service

Sir Richard Dearlove: "The time is not far off in the Middle East, Richard, when it will be literally 'God help the Shia'. More than a billion Sunnis have simply had enough of them."

The Saudi regime is medieval in the sense that shops are closed for prayer five times a day, executions take place in the street, and women are completely subservient. Only in 2014 did they receive permission to drive cars, but with many limitations.

Incredible as it seems, given its rhetoric, the US supports this regime in order to get oil. This is despite the fact that Saudi Arabia is a fierce opponent of Israel and a player in destabilizing the Middle East, and that the Taliban is America's official enemy in Afghanistan. The Taliban owes much to the ulamä of Saudi Arabia: it is largely composed of the children of Afghan refugees educated at Pakistani theological schools whose academic staff received their degrees from Saudi Arabia. The children learn Wahhabi fundamentalism, the Sunni doctrine embraced by Saudi Arabia.

At one time the US supported the Taliban in Afghanistan for tactical reasons, but after 9/11, when the Taliban government refused to give up Osama bin Laden, America decided its members were terrorists. These terrorists have never been eliminated and now may become part of a new coalition government in Afghanistan.

When the Arab Spring hit Bahrain in early 2011, the majority Shiites were asking for relief from the rule of their self-declared Sunni king. Naturally, Saudi Arabia sent 1,500 troops and helped the king suppress the protests with great brutality. The United States averted its gaze. Why not? The king is an ally. Ever since "Operation Iraqi Freedom" began in 2003, Bahrain has hosted the key US military base in the Middle East—that is, Naval Support Activity Bahrain.

Private Saudi money has probably also been used to finance Isis, the self-declared Islamic State of Iraq and Syria. Despite this, Isis now has the government of Saudi Arabia next on its list of targets. This exemplifies a Saudi dilemma: the hothouse religious atmosphere that is at its core breeds youth so fanatical that the government cannot control them. When you educate youths for religious fanaticism, some take Islam so seriously they turn against their own regime and decide they must eliminate even it to purify the nation. Others direct their energies abroad. The Saudi government did not want the Twin Towers' destruction and death of 2,753 in New York, but it surprised no one that fifteen of the nineteen hijackers were Saudi. For more on the radicalisation of youth, read Ayaan Hirsi Ali's *Infidel* (pages 219–221).

Without understanding Saudi Arabia, you cannot understand the holy war that is devastating the Middle East and the utter folly of US policy in the region. Between 1618 and 1648, during the Thirty Years' War, Catholics and Protestants fought over the corpse of Germany and half its population died. At that time, the sultan of Turkey wanted to conquer Europe. However, he was not mad enough to try and send a benevolent and impartial army to tromp all over Germany with the aim of reconciliation and creating stable states. There was plenty of moral "justification" of course: Catholic and Protestant were hanging each other and burning people alive.

The notion that two faiths, seemingly alike, each believe the other preaches a message that will damn souls to hell is not foreign to me. When I taught in Richmond, Kentucky in 1960, there was a Church of Christ and a Christian Church. They were identical in every way except the Christian Church used an organ although the New Testament makes no mention of using a mechanical instrument of music at worship services. For this alone, as far as the Church of Christ was concerned, members of the Christian Church were damned and every convert a soul lost to God. Doctrinal debate was fierce but federal law forbade an actual holy war. Then in 1978 I lived near a community of highly orthodox Jews. They lamented the fact they could no longer kill all apostate Jews: a rabbi in the seventeenth century had told them to hold their fire for the time being.

It is sometimes said that Sunni and Shiite lived in harmony for many generations, the implication being that the contemporary conflict is in some way contrived. There have certainly been times when people wanted to get on with their lives, and made friends and married across the divide, but there was also smoldering resentment. Often one persuasion had to make do with living under a regime dominated by the other and suffered serious discrimination, sometimes as a repressed minority (in Saudi Arabia) but sometimes as a repressed majority (in Syria and Iraq). There is a legacy of historical grudges to be settled. Both politicians and fanatics—the Saudi religious establishment and Isis— find plenty of tinder at hand.

There is a factor that holds out hope: the economic progress and consequent urbanization of the Middle East. The armed militants have their following in mainly conservative rural areas, which feel threatened by the whole modern world. When groups such as Isis impose their own draconian version of sharia law, they tend to alienate Muslims who are becoming modernized, particularly those in cities. Faced with such groups, progressive Sunnis and Shiites may decide the real struggle is less between them and mainly between them both and all those who hate the modern world. However, this assumes economic progress can continue to take place. Constant civil war, sometimes exacerbated by the West, as in Iraq and Afghanistan, erases gains.

Robert Lacey (born 1944)
Inside the Kingdom★ (2009) by this British journalist and author is a penetrating analysis of Saudi society. I owe Lacey a debt for making me see the charm that fundamentalist Islam, and the communal life it fosters, holds for its adherents. A man laments its demise: "When I was a child we lived in one another's houses. … If the neighbors saw me misbehaving they would tell me off, and my parents would say thank you. … Then the money came. Everyone … built themselves villas behind high walls … And suddenly we found we

were separate. We felt somehow empty inside. If we had a wedding to celebrate we didn't [string] lights round the neighbors' houses and yards. We'd hire a ballroom in some modern hotel."

Islamic fundamentalism is based on a literal interpretation of Mohammed's recitations: the Arabic for recitation is "koran". The Koran stresses concern for the poor, a chivalrous attitude toward women (if you ignore the fact they are dependent on the whim of often not chivalrous husbands), and the maxim of an eye-for-an-eye, which was humane at the time, in a world in which vengeance knew few limits.

Whatever the Koran's merits, those who live by its letter, when not killing heretics, are often outstanding for their kindness to one another. When they caution a woman for striding along with indecent haste, they address her as "sister". As Lacey says, Mohammed tried to create a life precisely as God wanted it. When Muslims sense their world is going wrong, some measure themselves against the original template and despise those who have compromised it.

Some Saudis are suspicious of their own Shiite minority. Traditionally, local ordinances forbade the Shiites having cellars for fear they would conduct orgies, whose bastard offspring they would then sanctify as their religious leaders. A pivotal event took place in 1979, when a group of purifying fanatics seeking the overthrow of the Saudi royal family seized the Grand Mosque in Mecca. This was attributed to a society lacking piety, and the regime took a sharp turn towards placating the religious establishment, which demanded strict prohibitions on everyday life and an educational system that taught mainly the Koran. The concept of jihad, holy war, invaded the universities.

Osama bin Laden was a student studying engineering at King Abdulaziz University in Jeddah at the time. He was quiet, shy, soft-spoken, well liked, and an outstanding soccer player. To the end of his life, he refused to drink anything with artificial preservatives. In 2001, when he organized the destruction of the Twin Towers, many in the religious establishment were favorably impressed. A schoolteacher who was critical received the hint that his thinking was "secular", which equaled apostate, which equaled the death penalty. However, the Saudi government condemned the attack and took steps to eliminate potential terrorists. It suspected they would strike at home and they did in 2003, in a series of lethal bombings. One terrorist decapitated an American technician and kept his head in a freezer as a trophy. At Guantánamo Bay in Cuba, fundamentalists found that their Puerto Rican guards also hated Americans; the guards managed to sneak the prisoners special food.

Lacey makes plausible the US–Saudi alliance. Tensions over Israel have been overridden not only by oil but also by Saudi money. The Saudis got arms, against Israeli opposition, by bribing members of Congress. More importantly, they helped the administration by financing the US proxy war in Nicaragua, which Congress had forbidden. The two nations have had a common enemy in Shiite Iran (until of course the US befriended the new Shiite regime of Nouri al-Maliki in Iraq). There has rarely been a problem with arms supply: since 1950 Saudi Arabia has bought or been supplied with almost a hundred billion dollars worth.

The Saudi secret police can be subtle. A woman who advocated women's rights was held for three months in prison in an attempt to make her, by definition, unmarriageable. The police obey Islamic law, beating the soles of a suspect's feet because the Prophet said torture should leave no marks on the body. However, they have instituted a humane approach to try and reform imprisoned terrorists.

As for the press, reporting unwelcome news, even the high rate of traffic accidents in the kingdom, is sedition. Newspapers are, however, free to report on the arrests of witches and fortune tellers. In 2002, after fifteen girls died because "holy ones" would not let them escape from a burning school as they were not suitably dressed, the government took over the schools from the religious authorities. In 2005 Abdullah came to power and made some significant changes. In January 2015 he died and his half-brother, seventy-nine-year-old Salman, took the throne. This king's intentions about reform are unclear. However, in the municipal elections of 2015 women participated for the first time. Twenty-one were elected. There is a campaign to allow women to drive without restrictions, although this is opposed by eighty percent of Saudi women. There are still no national elections or political parties.

The alliance between Saudi Arabia and the United States has always been based on mutual benefit: the Saudis get

US protection; the US gets their oil. Lacey concludes that recent events have killed this. He argues that the United States overthrowing Saddam, a Sunni, in Iraq showed the Saudis that America could not be relied on. The Saudis have replaced an old friend with a new one: they now sell more oil to China than to America. Lacey's conclusion may, though, be premature. In late 2007 the US announced the sale of twenty billion dollars worth of sophisticated arms, mainly to Saudi Arabia and Egypt. It still wants to preserve the Saudi regime—and certainly the repressive Bahrain regime—no matter what liberal rhetoric it preaches.

AFGHANISTAN

The history of Afghanistan since 1700 has involved the attempts of the Pashtuns of the south, about forty-two percent of the population, to dominate the country; the resistance of the Tajiks, Hazaras, and Uzbeks of the north, who collectively make up about forty-five percent, to such domination; and five tries by European nations to meddle in its politics, three by Britain, one by Russia, and most recently one by the US.

In 1978 the communist People's Democratic Party overthrew the regime of President Daoud Khan and began to displace, imprison, and murder thousands of the traditional élite, behavior not unusual enough to alienate the general population. What did alienate them was the party's attempt to give women equality by educating them, liberating them to pursue whatever occupations they wished, appointing them to government posts, and forbidding child marriage. This, along with land reform, provoked outrage and revolt. The US decided to oppose Soviet influence (as if Russia was going to get anything but trouble by meddling with this nation) by recruiting, financing, and arming mujahideen rebels.

In 1979 the USSR was stupid enough to invade Afghanistan to bolster the government. It gave up in 1989, leaving behind between 15,000 of its own dead (another 10,000 were left disabled) and over one million dead Afghans. Six million more had fled to Pakistan and Iran. The fall of the communists was followed by a terrible civil war won by the Taliban (read Pashtuns) in 1996, partly due to support from Pakistan. The Taliban began to enforce a barbaric version of Islamic law.

After the 2001 attack on the Twin Towers in New York and the Pentagon in Washington, D.C., undeterred by the Soviet failure at "nation-building" the US decided to try its hand. It put the northern tribes in control and was amazed when they did not restore women's rights: in rural areas they make disobedient women eat pig excrement. The tribes were corrupt and could not subdue the south. The US excuse for the invasion was to hunt down Osama bin Laden, who was responsible for the 9/11 attacks. Sending an army gave him plenty of warning and he hid in Pakistan (an American ally) for ten years before spies and special forces got him. The distraction of overthrowing the Afghan regime only made that task more difficult.

Khaled Hosseini (born 1965)

Hosseini's first novel *The Kite Runner* (2003) is melodramatic in style and the references to recent Afghan history are episodic. That said, it is readable and describes the privileged position of males in Afghan society.

His second novel, *A Thousand Splendid Suns*★ (2007), is better. The characters are still a bit one-dimensional—the sweet young girl, her true love, the kind father, the mother unhinged by grief—but Hosseini gives an excellent account of what the people of this nation have endured in recent times, including a devastating four-year drought from 1997 to 2000, which killed two million people, disabled one million, and turned three million into refugees. The book's main characters are women, for whom the communist regime was a brief paradise. They, of course, hated the Taliban who took over. There is a moving description of the execution of a woman for killing her brutal husband. The portrayal of the saintly Taliban judge who sentences her to death with love is the best thing in the book. It ends on a note of optimism in April 2003.

The author's latest novel, *And the Mountains Echoed* (2013), does not quite rate a star. The clean prose style and psychological insights are above what most writers achieve but not remarkable. The story centers on Abdullah and Pari, brother and sister separated at the age of three, when Pari was "given away" to start a better life. There are a lot of appealing sections: the fable at the beginning, the drug lord who takes over their ancestral home, a broken promise to help a child victim of violence, and Abdullah and Pari reunited after Abdullah's memory has failed. The context is Afghanistan, but the story is universal in the sense that its logic would be much the same if it were set in another developing nation.

Qais Akbar Omar (born 1982)
A Fort of Nine Towers (2013) is a memoir about the trials of a professional family in Afghanistan and is an easy read. There are some passages about the legacy of atrocities, horrible beyond belief, which divide the Afghan tribes. During the tribal warfare that followed the fall of the communist regime, snipers killed people for sport and shot dogs when people were unavailable; all sides took pleasure in torture. It ends with two periods of relative stability: the bizarre peace enforced by the triumph of the Taliban, and the recent decade during which the American presence forced the northern tribes to give up killing in favor of corruption. An elderly man laments what makes his country's situation worse: "The problem … is where we are located and the neighbors we have. Our stupid politicians let them interfere in our affairs."

None of these books about Afghanistan ends on a note of optimism. This is understandable. The domestic economy is built on sand, ninety-seven percent of it tied to foreign aid or foreign military presence. It is estimated the country can feed only half its people. As of 2011, only twelve percent of women could read. US and NATO troops were dwindling from 400,000 to 9,800. In late 2014 the US set a higher limit of 12,000 on the troops to be left behind. Fewer might lead to economic collapse and probably another murderous civil war. The Pashtuns, who seem to have moderated their religious fanaticism a bit, govern much of the south and may try to take Kabul. The northern tribes are arming themselves under what they call the New National Front.

As usual, foreign troops on Afghan soil have accomplished nothing. No one in the West really cares about the people of Afghanistan except in the sense we would like everyone to be happy and a stable nation would allow US politicians to justify America's intervention. After this fifth Afghan War, the nation will revert to acting out its unhappy history. One thing Afghanistan has been spared is religious conflict. It is three-quarters Hanafī Sunni and the rest Shiite but there is an Islamic council of clerics that works to maintain harmony, successfully so far despite periodic attempts of tribal groups to use religion as a weapon.

IRAN

Iran, formerly Persia, is the core of what was an ancient empire dating from 625 B.C. The Sasanian dynasty attained a high culture and ruled for centuries until Islam overthrew it between AD 633 and 656. The Mongols and Turks then occupied Persia but it won back independence in 1501 under the Safavid dynasty, which embraced Shiite Islam.

Steps toward modernization did not begin until 1905, when there was a revolution driven by demands for a parliament. In 1953, thanks to the United States and Britain, the shah, Mohammad Reza Pahlavi, became absolute ruler. The nation became divided between Shiite religious leaders who hated the shah's program of modernization (which included emancipation of women), Westernized Iranians who wanted democratization, and Marxists wanting power.

In the revolution of 1979 all three of these groups deposed the shah. As the fundamentalists gradually imprisoned and killed Westernized Iranians and Marxists, Grand Ayatollah Ruhollah Khomeini became all-powerful and instituted an Islamic state with all that entailed: rejection of Western cultural influences, and subjecting women to Sharia law, which meant for most a subservient role as wife and mother. Nonetheless, the country's leaders want Iran to master Western technology and become a powerful state. Its size, unity, and technical development make it the state most likely to rival Israel militarily and break that country's monopoly over nuclear weapons in the Middle East.

Thanks to the United States, Iraq has become Shiite-governed, and Shiite Iran is now leading the fight against the Sunni Isis and thus is active in Iraq, Syria and Yemen. This extends Iran's influence across the Middle East up to Israel's border. Israel wants at least an air war against Iran that would devastate the country and keep it weak and underdeveloped. Thanks to Obama, America has normalized relations with Iran, while trying to insure its nuclear facilities are only for peaceful purposes. I suspect Iran will eventually want nuclear weapons so it can "deter" Israel.

A number of books by Iranians or about Iran have been translated into English. Some have been highly praised so I hoped to find writers of distinction. I found many of the authors were women who hated the strictures Sharia law placed on their dress, behavior and ambitions, and understandably wanted the freedoms of Western women. They had usually had trouble with their mothers. Other authors transcended this theme and at least one book, Hedāyat's *The Blind Owl,* has attracted devoted readers for the last sixty years.

Sādegh Hedāyat (1903–1951)

Hedāyat's suicide ended a solitary life made miserable partly through political exile but also because of chronic depression, alcoholism, and drug addiction. He wrote many novelettes and his 1945 book *Hājī Āqā* (The Pilgrim) is considered a novel. However, only one of his works has been translated into English. *The Blind Owl** (1937) has been rightly hailed as the best literary work to emerge from Iran. It gained some currency in the West in 1957 but appeared in a definitive translation only in 2011. It is available online and comes to the equivalent of fifty-three pages, but these are double-length and it reads like a novel of a little over 100 pages.

It is an introspective work, divided into three parts: a fantasy-cum-real encounter between the male author and a woman whose fleeting presence fills him with joy; his life with his wife, called a whore because she slept with everyone but him—the story is not autobiographical as Hedāyat never married; and his preoccupation with death and its consolation of total oblivion.

I normally hate books like this but the style has a vibrancy that is hypnotic. Here are a few examples:

"I was growing inward incessantly; like an animal that hibernates during the wintertime. … The loneliness and the solitude that lurked behind me were like a condensed, thick, eternal night, like one of those nights with a dense, persistent, sticky darkness which waits to pounce on unpopulated cities filled with lustful and vengeful dreams."

"No, I will not call her by name, because she, with that ethereal body, slim and misty, with those two large, wonder-stricken, sparkling eyes behind which my life was gradually and painfully burning and melting away, she no longer belongs to this base, fierce world."

"How could a sensual woman, who needs one man for lust, another for love and still another for torture, fall in love with only one man? … I am certain that she had chosen me for torture, indeed, she could not have made a better choice".

"In fact, I did not need to see [the rabble] to know them; one was enough to represent the rest. They were all like one big mouth leading to a wad of guts, terminating in a sexual organ."

Jalal Al-e-Ahmad (1923–1969)

Al-e-Ahmad approved of Ayatollah Ruhollah Khomeini's rejection of Western culture. *The School Principal* (1958, translated 1974) is his most influential work. The scholar who wrote the introduction to my edition complimented the translator as having done the best job possible. Nonetheless, the English that emerges uses idioms I doubt the author would have chosen so one has to judge it on content rather than style.

The school principal in question has a dark view of his school. It is subject to Western influence, gives the children no sense of connection with the history and culture of their nation, offers a curriculum that is empty, and corruption rules at every level. The book is mainly a rave, without much cognitive content, about the pettiness of the man's job and I cannot recommend it as outstanding. The author, though, has wit and will convince you that many of our own complaints about schools apply universally. On why one wants to become a principal: "I was utterly nauseated with teaching, the blank, gaping faces of children." When the principal looks at a map "the blue of the seas [was] as pale as a dead man's saliva". The school is surrounded by a wall—"a high barrier to prevent education's improbable attempt to escape". A member of the school council looks "like a monkey who, by wearing glasses, was imitating a human being".

Iraj Pezeshkzad (born 1928)

My Uncle Napoleon (1973, translated 1996) is a comic novel set in the 1940s. The most widely read novel in Iran, it generated a popular television series. The leading character is obsessed with British plots against Iran, an obsession shared by Iranians in general until the United States emerged as chief villain. Pezeshkzad is, of course, making fun of him.

I can see how with the right actors it would play well on TV as the humor is mainly slapstick. There is a scene featuring a detective rather like Inspector Clouseau from the Pink Panther series. In 1979 the book and television series were both briefly banned by Iran's religious censors. Perhaps they resented some of the Orthodox Islamists. For example, a character extols the high moral standards of his hometown. His evidence: A man heard that before they'd got married his wife's veil had slipped off in a mosque. He divorced her, but all the people in Ghiasabad blamed him for not killing her. They shunned him and he died of shame.

Betty Mahmoody (born 1945)
Not Without My Daughter (1987) is the true story of an American woman who went to Iran with her husband and daughter for what was supposed to be a few weeks and found herself trapped because she could not leave without her husband's consent. The book underlines the difference between a woman's status in the two nations, and you may want to read it for that reason. The Iranian hostility against America is presented as if it had no justification. *Not Without My Daughter* attracted much publicity and was made into a film, which was criticized because the Iranian characters were seen as stereotyped. They are treated more fairly in the book but it is just a lightweight memoir.

Azar Nafisi (born 1947)

Reading Lolita in Tehran★ (2003) was on *The New York Times* bestseller list for 127 weeks. I've awarded it a star for pedagogical reasons—namely, its account of life under Ayatollah Khomeini and his Revolutionary Guards, who held power from 1979 to 1989. Women were inspected to see if they were virgins, and harassed, jailed, and beaten because of their dress, running when late to class, smiling, and even eating an apple "provocatively". A scholar was killed because he wrote about Iran's pre-Islamic past: for fanatics, Iranian history begins only with the Arabic conquest.

Nafisi has a night out at a theater. The players are not allowed to sing or show any emotion. If the audience begins to move or clap in time to the music, two men leap out from the wings and command them to stop.

During this era Khomeini's theological works were promoted but caused embarrassment. He discussed whether a man who has had sex with a chicken could then eat the chicken. He could not, nor could his family or his immediate neighbors. Starting with those who live two doors away, it became permissible to eat the chicken.

Nafisi describes the lives of young women who discussed forbidden classics of world literature at her home. Being an academic, she feels she must pontificate about the writers themselves: Nabokov, Fitzgerald, Henry James, and Jane Austen. This makes for long excerpts from what reads like an adequate introductory literature course. The style and depiction of characters is reasonable rather than brilliant.

Nafisi's next book, *Things I've Been Silent About* (2008), is a highly personal memoir that adds little of historical interest. In 2014 she published *The Republic of Imagination: America in Three Books*. She extols fiction as a passport not only to knowledge of one's country but to a free mind, a view with which I am much in sympathy.

Nahid Rachlin (born 1961)

After reading *Jumping Over Fire* (2006), I didn't read Rachlin's other novels. In the book a young girl laments her lot in Iran and yearns for America. Although there are no serious flaws, I didn't feel *Jumping Over Fire* deserved the praise it attracted. It is written at the level of a twelve year old. This is tedious even when the main character is twelve but deadly when she is older. The drama of her life revolves around a man she believes is her brother. At first she never doubts he is her brother. Then the two of them come to believe they are not related and have sex. Then they go to America and she is torn between him and another man. Then they pursue successful lives apart—he goes back to Iran—and she finds out he is her half-brother.

Marina Nemat (born 1965)

Prisoner of Tehran (2007) is an unusual memoir because the author is a Christian, and as a teenager spent two years in Tehran's notorious Evin Prison under a death sentence. The account of her life is anguished but unfortunately pedestrian. The sequel, *After Tehran: A Life Reclaimed* (2010) should not have been published. Half of it is lifted from the earlier book. We are told how she got that book into print, and she repeats, over and over, how much she suffered, even after emigrating to Canada.

Nomads without a Country
Jamil Ahmad (1933–2014)
Some four million people still wander the plains of Pakistan, Afghanistan, and Iran with only a sense of tribal identity. Their story is told in a remarkable book, *The Wandering Falcon*★★ (2011), whose spare and moving style is magical. Sadly, Jamil Ahmad, a Pakistani civil servant, did not publish this, his first book, until he was seventy-eight. The stories match the best of Hemingway. Tor Baz is a child orphaned when his parents, a fugitive couple, are hunted down by their tribe. He reappears episodically thereafter to link nine tales. By the last story, he is an adult and reflects that perhaps it is finally time to settle down with a wife. He casually purchases a woman.

The excellence of every tale makes it hard to choose favorites: the stark tragedy of his parents and the fate his mother fled from, a marriage with a man whose taste ran to boys; four rebels doomed by their sense of honor; the crucifixion of these tribes by the modern state; a "mad" mullah; the kidnapping profession; an exile and his guide; a daughter sold; a woman less regarded than her husband's performing bear—she is the one eventually sold to Tor Baz.

The speech of the tribal peoples has a formal dignity that makes the dialogue a treat.

TURKEY

The history of Turkey is atypical of the Islamic Middle East in two respects. First, it was the seat of a great empire, the Ottoman, which from 1453 to 1918 ruled much of the Middle East, the coast of North Africa, and the European Balkans. The empire declined as Europe industrialized and it did not survive the First World War. The Turkish Republic that replaced it has never aspired to its re-creation. Rather it is dominated by a fierce nationalism, which makes it unforgiving toward the aspirations of its Kurdish minority, about twenty percent of the population, for autonomy or independence. They are called "mountain Turks" in an effort to define them out of existence.

Second, Kemal Ataturk, who founded modern Turkey in 1923, loathed Islam, all the way from its religious observances to its traditional dress. He admired the European Enlightenment and his heroes were French and Russian revolutionaries. The secularist faction in Turkey worships him to this day, and for much of modern Turkish history the army, a bastion of secularism, made sure Islamic parties did not govern.

However, in 2002 a government sympathetic to Islam won the election and appears dominant, with the secularists now a minority and the army subject to political control.

In theory, the constitutional court has the power to ban any political party deemed anti-secularist. It still has some independence: in 2008, when the government tried to make it legal for women to choose to wear a headscarf to university, the court struck down the legislation and fined the ruling party.

As virtually every Turkish novel testifies, Turks admire the civilization and power of the West and hate themselves for admiring the civilization and power of the West. They resent that every step they take toward modernization degrades them in their own eyes. Yet modernization is inevitable. Before the end of this century Turkey promises to be as highly developed as France.

Orhan Pamuk (born 1952)

In 2006 Orhan Pamuk won the Nobel Prize in Literature, becoming the first Turk to win a Nobel. I recommend reading Pamuk's 2002 novel *Snow*★ (translated 2004), not only because it lays bare the murderous intensity behind Turkey's divisions, but also because it is a fine novel. Ka is a poet who has lived abroad. He visits Kars, a city near the Russian border, ostensibly as a journalist but actually to try to retrieve a lost love. The city is newsworthy thanks to a series of young women who commit suicide because they cannot (so they claim) wear their headscarves to class. The climax occurs when a woman publicly takes off her scarf onstage. Secularists and Islamists start killing each other and neutrals are considered beyond contempt. Kurds are exterminated. Ka finds himself suspected by all and perceives he is being followed:

"Are you following me for intelligence purposes or for my protection?"

"God only knows, sir. Whichever sounds better to you is fine by me."

I read four novels that also preceded the award of the Nobel. *The White Castle* (1979, translated 1990) is at times interesting but not memorable. It takes place in seventeenth-century Turkey. The local Pasha gives a captive Italian to a Turkish scholar as a slave and collaborator. He is rather casual about the Italian's fate: "You may want to get rid of him, poison him if you like, or if you like free him." Twenty-five years of worrying about the problem of personal identity—master and slave closely resemble one another—unhinges the scholar. After the two give the sultan a weapon that is a failure, anger is directed at the infidel rather than the Turk.

The men then change places: the Turk pretends to be the Italian and goes back to Italy; the Italian pretends to be the Turk and lives quietly away from the sultan's court. The final chapter is ambiguous as to whether all this really happened, and who is still in Turkey writing the story. No points for that from me.

The Black Book (1990, translated 1994) begins with a turgid style—events, people, images, all mixed together—but later it improves. Rüya, the wife of Galip, a lawyer, leaves him. He suspects her half-brother Jelal (called Celâl in some translations) because he has also disappeared. He takes

Jelal's place by writing his newspaper columns. There is an effective scene in which Galip finds that Jelal has collected photos of Rüya for many years, and the ending is moving.

Digressions constitute most of the book. There is advice on how to get to sleep. I enjoyed the images of current life in Istanbul but the decipherments, anonymous caller, and analyses of Jelal, history, films, heroes, and plots for redemption are tedious. The short stories are mixed. The chapter on the story of the prince, if published on its own, would be better than the book. The prince realizes with horror that he intends to rule like a Frenchman, and the significance of the fact that his room has Venetian blinds. The ideal of personal identity is reduced to ad absurdum: the only way to be truly free of all "alien" influences (including Turkish ones) is to be nothing at all.

In *The New Life* (1994, translated 1997), Osman reads a book that captivates people into believing they can have a new life. Unfortunately a Dr Fine has agents who kill everyone who follows and promotes the book. He began his crusade because he sees the book as the epitome of Americanization and thinks (mistakenly) that his son, Mehmet, died after coming under its spell. Mehmet is actually still alive and thinks the book merely confers a peace of mind that cannot be explained.

Osman kills Mehmet for what he sees as a betrayal of the message of the book and out of jealousy. Eventually, Americanization is triumphant and kills off Fine's organization. Osman thinks the book dictates taking bus rides, hoping the bus will crash, thereby killing some and sparing others. The theory is that an angel will then appear to guide you. Osman eventually meets his angel. This summary should be enough for you to assess whether or not you find this plot appealing.

My Name Is Red (1998, translated 2001) is a tour de force spoiled by being a tour de force. Pamuk clearly has a real appreciation and encyclopedic knowledge of the history of the visual arts in Persia. There are about eighty passages in which miniaturists, who decorate books, agonize about the purity of their stylized tradition compared to the European art that uses perspective and depicts recognizable individuals. The casual acceptance of sex between men and boys is informative. The style may be appropriate to the subject but has a stiff dignity that distances the author (and therefore the reader) from his characters.

ISRAEL AND THE WEST BANK

The problem that has dominated much of Israel's literature over the last generation is the fate of the West Bank of the Jordan: whether this conquered territory should be settled by Israelis, the conduct of the soldiers who protect the Jewish settlers living there, the conditions of the Arabs who are still most of its inhabitants (and must be cowed), and the cynicism all this engenders. Setting history aside, I began reading Israel's writers with anticipation. Its people are so literate it seemed a good place to look for contemporary classics.

A.B. Yehoshua (born 1936)

This novelist and playwright is much honored in Israel. *Friendly Fire* (2007, translation 2008) is a competent novel and holds one's gaze. There is an interesting insight at the end of chapter eight: the Jewish obsession with their history sets them apart; they understand themselves so well they find it difficult to understand others. But aside from that I did not detect anything exciting enough to encourage me to read his other books.

Amos Oz (born 1939)

Amos Oz's autobiography *A Tale of Love and Darkness*★ (2003, translated 2004) is indispensable for anyone who wants to understand the passion, blood, sweat, and tears that went into the founding of the state of Israel in 1948. It is very even-handed. A character remarks: "But if they'd beaten us in 1948 ... they wouldn't have left a single Jew alive ... [but] if we take even more from them some day ... that will be a very big sin." This last is, of course, a reference to the West Bank. Oz is strongly opposed to Israel's attempts to absorb that area.

Oz was born into a Jewish neighborhood in Jerusalem in 1939 and went to live on a kibbutz at age fifteen. A kibbutz is a rural commune that combines agriculture with light industry and (at one time) high socialist idealism. He later studied philosophy and literature. There are sections of the autobiography that drag but it gets better as it goes on. It wonderfully describes the fear-filled, idealistic, intellectually and emotionally charged world of his Jewish family and their friends and neighbors.

One neighbor was a Pole with a Russian soul. He was sad about everything: the fate of the Poles, the history of the Jews, a piglet that had been bludgeoned to death, birds enduring winter, the suffering of Christ on the cross, and a lost love of his youth. He took his pistol, fired through the window (wounding a pigeon), shattered a wine bottle, shot himself in the thigh, fired twice at the chandelier, and with his last bullet blew his brains out.

Oz's mother was a romantic, beautiful and intelligent woman, banished from the great cities of culture she admired, married to a librarian who tried heroically to become a scholar of repute. She killed herself at the age of thirty-eight when Oz was not quite thirteen. His mother and father and he as a child are portrayed in a way that breaks the heart. The burden of being the repository of all the frustrated hopes of two highly intellectual Jewish parents is horrifying. At the age of three or four "it was not enough for me to be intelligent, rational, good, sensitive, creative and thoughtful with the dreamy vision of an artist. In addition, I also had to be a seer and a fortune-teller, a kind of family oracle."

I read four of his novels, all highly praised in Israel and America, but found none of them matched the autobiography. His first novel, *Elsewhere, Perhaps* (1966, translated 1973), is about an idealized kibbutz. The style is rather stiff and formal. There are some scenes that ring true, including one between a sixteen-year old girl and her would-be lover. His second novel, *My Michael* (1968, translated 1972), is an advance. A narcissistic woman, totally self-absorbed and with intellectual pretensions, marries a man she half despises. Naturally she finds aging unbearable. She is so dysfunctional that her husband carries, uncomplaining, a huge burden of work and child rearing. Eventually, she finds her husband's lack of maturity intolerable—he can never be more to her than a "thoughtful elder son"—and leaves him. She, of course, is really little more than an infant. That the novel takes place in the woman's mind limits its appeal. Do we want 200 pages of narcissism? But as a study of a kind of person that many of us encounter, it is has value.

As for later works, in *A Perfect Peace* (1982, translated 1985) Oz takes a realist approach to life on a kibbutz. Despite his stylistic skill the prose is often extravagant and some dialogue approaches melodrama. The story shows how those raised in kibbutzim differ from the generation that founded them; if you have a special interest in the kibbutz movement you may want to read it.

The Same Sea (1999, translated 2001) is divided up into lots of little sections that alternate poems with short prose pieces. It is the kind of self-indulgent book you are apt to get from a writer who has been praised too much. Leaden homilies and empty musings (about how life ends in death, for example) follow another. It is about as bad a novel as a good writer could write.

Haim Be'er (born 1945)

Be'er grew up in an Orthodox Jewish family in Jerusalem. His autobiographical novel *The Pure Element of Time*★R (1998, translated 2003) is dense with references to Jewish history and religion and this may alienate some. However, the way in which his grandmother, mother, and father are revealed by slowly peeling back layer after layer is powerful. The mother, as seen by herself and her son, husband, and sister, undergoes a transition from a brilliant rational person to someone half mad and riddled with superstition. The father, called "evil" but really rather good, joins her to make a couple not far from being certifiable. When the father is stricken, the mother surprises us by showing she has total insight into his tragedy.

The mother gives a perceptive analysis of Tolstoy's novella *The Death of Ivan Ilyich* (1886, various translations), a masterpiece. Ivan Ilyich, a junior judge in a provincial Russian city, is consumed by cancer. He wants to be pitied like a sick child and cannot understand that his wife and children see him as too important a personage to be treated like that. Only his servant can respond to his needs, and offers him solace by letting him rest his legs on his shoulders and talking to him unaffectedly. This man, a simple peasant, helps him face the inevitability and incomprehension of the death that awaits us all.

Clearly it was worth reading Be'er's only other novel that has been translated into English. *Feathers* (1979, translated 2004) portrays the foibles of an Orthodox community in

Jerusalem in the 1950s to 1960s. They are as superstitious as medieval peasants and there are some amusing incidents, but I do not think this book would appeal to an international readership unless they were as interested in Jewish culture as I am.

Edna Mazya (born 1949)

Although David Grossman is said to be Israel's best and most influential novelist, I could not believe there was no one better so I read further. Edna Mazya's *Love Burns*★★ (1997, translated 2006) is her first novel. I gave it two stars. The portraits of a young wife engrossed in her first affair but not without guilt, and her older husband, who is utterly unadventurous but becomes embroiled in an absurd melodrama, are utterly convincing. The story of his relationship with his mother is even better: despite being Jewish, his mother once tried to join the Hitler Youth. (She was rebuffed.) Mazya makes stream of consciousness work because it is unpretentious and she actually develops character and plot. No history to be learned here but the book is worth reading for its own sake. Mazya's plays are said to be a treat and I hope to have an opportunity to see one. Let us hope she writes some more novels.

David Grossman (born 1954)

The most controversial act of Israel is its military occupation of the West Bank of Palestine. David Grossman's son Uri was killed on the last day of the 2006 Israeli offensive in

Lebanon. Long before that he had decided the occupation was a mistake.

The Yellow Wind* (1988, translated 1988) contains Grossman's interviews with both Jews and Arabs. The Israeli occupation army is unusual in that it does not rape or steal and some of the soldiers are humane people. But as Northern Ireland and Vietnam proved, no army can act as a police force among a hostile population without being brutalized to some degree. Torture exists, a father's home is demolished because of a son from whom he has been estranged for years, parents are spat on in front of their children, Arabs are often hired only for the most menial jobs, books and poems by Arabs are censored. The "pioneers" who expand the settlements see themselves as rectifying a 2,000-year-old injustice and are oblivious to the fact they are creating a new injustice.

Sadly, Grossman's first novel *The Smile of the Lamb* (1983, translated 1990), about the occupation, is simply dreadful. Characters who spend endless pages baring their souls smother the insights about the occupation. They are so poetic and perceptive, or perhaps not perceptive, or perhaps perceptive in realizing they are not perceptive, and so forth.

You may like this sort of thing better than I do. Here is a sentence selected at random (really): "Lie here in your swaddling flesh, child of the moon, a moment ago you trembled with a passing fear and tried to leap at me and grab the shining toy I took from the turd that was dropped by the iron horse in front of my cave yesterday, where once, I recall, anguish dropped tender babes, or frightened mothers, their bellies swollen with sin, and now they drop these iron toys here, and even you turned to iron when you tried to cut loose the fetters of love I girded around you, so sleep and rest, let me cover you with gossamer quilts, with the silken map unfurled as always to the four corners of the earth, where a likeness of you is dimly visible, and soon the cloth will touch you and the images will kiss each other and you will know no more pain."

Twenty-five years later, Grossman published *To the End of the Land* (2008, translated 2010). This novel is much better, which is to say it is readable if nothing special. The concept is encouraging. A woman's son is at risk as a tank commander. She flees her home: she feels she will be complicit in his death if she is made aware of it, and therefore aims at being unavailable to be informed. She goes on a trek across Israel. She also wants to memorialize her son by telling her companion, a former lover who is the young man's real father, every detail of his life from conception to adulthood. The style makes much tolerable but a hundred pages of this would have been enough. Five hundred and seventy-five are just too much.

Sayed Kashua (born 1975)

I found only one Israeli novelist who is also an Arab, namely Sayed Kashua. His *Let It Be Morning*⋆ (2004, translated 2006) is just a better than average novel, but I gave it a star because it gives an Arab account of what it has been like to live in an Arab village within Israel proper. The advantages of Israeli citizenship—the welfare state and a prosperous economy—have encouraged acceptance of Israeli rule among the villagers. They look down on and exploit the more "primitive" Arabs who are under Israeli occupation on the West Bank. The latter are thoroughly anti-Israel.

At one point, the villagers come to believe they are suspected of harboring Palestinian workers who are in Israel illegally. They are alarmed that the Israeli army has surrounded them. They send the workers out into the no man's land between the village and the army: two are promptly shot (a breakdown in communication this). Don't take the peace settlement announced at the end of the novel seriously. Like all such settlements, it soon failed because the parties had no real common ground.

Ron Leshem (born 1976)
Beaufort (2005, translated 2007) is a stand-alone novel by a journalist that had a powerful impact in Israel. It portrays the psychology of soldiers stationed in Lebanon during the Israeli occupation from 1988 to 2000. These young men could bear the casualties and terrible conditions, but found it devastating to be told by their country it had all been a pointless mistake.

As a war novel, *Beaufort* does not compare with the many classics of the genre. The soldiers talk about sex all the time. There is one good joke. An ant is walking through the woods and comes to a river. She sees an elephant and says,

"Elephant, elephant, be a man and get me across this river."
He does and she says, "Thank you very much, elephant."
The elephant says: "What do you mean 'thank you'? Take
your clothes off."

THE MIDDLE EAST AND BEYOND

William Dalrymple (born 1965)

I have already recommended V.S. Naipaul's travel books.
Those by William Dalrymple are comparable in quality.
*From the Holy Mountain: A Journey Among the Christians
of the Middle East*★ (1997) gives an overview of much of
the Middle East. It contains some stunning insights. Every
ethnic group in every nation has had little real long-term
tolerance of the presence of others, and unpredictable bouts
of ethnocentrism bring slaughter that extends to babes and
household pets. It is little wonder some Israelis doubt their
presence will ever be tolerated.

The Israelis are reluctant to expose themselves to charges
of wanton slaughter, but they are quite capable of giving their
allies an opportunity to express themselves. They gave tacit
approval when the Christian Phalange militia of Lebanon
killed inhabitants of the Sabra and Shatila refugee camps in
1982. Estimates of those who died vary from 600 to more
than 3,000. (The International Red Cross has said 2,400.)

Like many a nation, the Israelis have bombed civilian
neighborhoods—for example in Beirut—with suction and
phosphorus bombs. The latter burn you to death slowly from

the outside; sometimes the corpses reignite at burial. The Israelis do engage in torture but not as horribly as some. The Phalange routinely begin with electricity and rapidly proceed to breaking bones—first the kneecaps, then the arms, then the breastbone—with death within four hours. They even kill other Christians.

Within all groups there are individuals capable of great kindness. When one Palestinian family "voluntarily left the West Bank"—that is, fled in terror—during the 1948 Arab-Israeli War, the father's Jewish employer gave them his van, which had Hebrew writing on it, so they could escape without being bombed.

On the West Bank, the Palestinians are being systematically pressured to leave, if only by being charged higher rents than others to run a shop. Since Christians are a minority everywhere in the Middle East they are slowly being eliminated, even from towns they have inhabited for 2,000 years. Even the Copts, who are ten percent of the population of Egypt, are subject to violence against which they have no redress.

Ironically, the great refuge of Christians has been Assad's Syria. Since Assad's rule was based on a minority Shiite sect he wanted all the support he could get from other groups, mainly Christians and Druze. The privileges granted Christians have made them hated by the Sunni Islam majority, who hope to take over the country. If they tolerate Christians, which doesn't this seem very likely, they will be the only Middle Eastern Islamic state that does.

Reading Dalrymple's tale of ethnic carnage makes you wonder why Western nations think it is noble to send armies and arms to tip the balance here in favor of some ethnic groups over others. It is, of course, because we think we know how to nation-build and turn these countries into modern democracies.

Dalrymple has a sense of humor and extracts some funny anecdotes from both past and present. An ancient monk loved animals as much as Saint Francis did, and not only fed birds but spread flour for ants. A teacher has a vision of one of his pupils in hell, up to his neck in fire: he thanks God every day for sparing his pupil's head. Saint Gregory the Great advises always making the sign of the cross over lettuce because of the demons that hide in the leaves.

Dalrymple wrote an earlier travel book, *In Xanadu: A Quest* (1989), when he was twenty-two. It traces the route of Marco Polo from Jerusalem to China. There are interesting reflections on the history of all the lands he passed through. If you are a travel writing buff you will enjoy it, but it assumes a good deal of knowledge and should not be the starting point for learning the history of these nations.

INDIA

William Dalrymple has also written five histories of India. The *City of Djinns*★ (1993) is an account of Delhi with historical reflections. It reveals the racism, self-righteousness, and brutality of British rule. Dalrymple captures the fascinating diversity of Delhi. (I would have appreciated some background on how the "Street of the Cat Killers" got its name.) It anticipates many of the themes he later developed, and if it awakens a special interest in India you will enjoy the five histories. For an introduction to modern India between the years of 1960 and 1990, remember, too, to read Naipaul's three books listed on page 92.

Paul Scott (1920–1978)

Scott belongs to an earlier generation but it would be remiss to omit his monumental four-volume series on India, *The Raj Quartet*. The first volume, *The Jewel in the Crown* (1966), is about the last years of British rule, set in the midst of the Second World War but with references back to the First World War.

If you want more evidence of why British rule became intolerable you will find it here—not just broken promises but the English people's utter patronizing contempt for people of color. It pervaded everything: who traveled first class on a train (an English person would be accommodated even if it meant canceling an Indian's reservation); who went to the country club; what nurse did menial chores; who progressed in the civil service; who was a crime suspect; and of course who could marry whom. The English were conditioned to such behavior by their class background: they were used to treating one another with contempt. Most of the narrators show much the same temperament, a sort of philosophical detachment, a perception of the larger significance of everything. A rather ordinary young woman says, "The farther away from the equator you get the more sensitive you become to the rhythm of light and dark, the way it expands and contracts and organizes the seasons, so that time itself develops a specific characteristic."

I also read Scott's novel *Staying On*★ (1977), which won the Booker Prize. It pokes gentle fun at a British couple who have remained in India long after independence, and their small circle. There is an Indian servant who makes sure to brew bad coffee whenever there is a guest he dislikes. The final pages, with the husband dead and the widow distraught, are moving. The British woman faces an isolated, barren future, and her only consolation is the posthumous realization that her husband truly loved her. It may not be a great book but it is a satisfying read on a quiet afternoon.

Rohinton Mistry (born 1952)
A Fine Balance★★ (1995) is the best diagnosis of the caste system I have ever read. It also covers the period between independence and the state of emergency, and culminates in the punitive castration of an untouchable who insulted a local landowner. Sadly, even if caste disappeared in India tomorrow, it has inculcated attitudes that poison the country. I refer to the sense that it is simply vile to trouble those on top, particularly if the trouble is caused by their whining inferiors.

The following is a story demonstrating the impunity of the powerful by my friend, the distinguished scholar Ramesh

Thakur: "Ruchika Girhotra was an aspiring fourteen-year-old tennis player in August 1990 when she was sexually molested by the president of the provincial tennis association, senior police officer S.P.S. Rathore. On December 21, 2009 (nineteen years later!) Rathore was convicted of the offence, sentenced to six months imprisonment with a $250 fine, but granted bail pending an appeal. In the meantime, Ruchika was expelled from her school … subjected to vilification and harassment, and committed suicide on December 28, 1993. Family members who pursued her case were repeatedly harassed and abused."

I next read Mistry's first novel and discovered that he can write more than one good book. *Such a Long Journey*★ (1991) describes the friendship that binds three men together. Two die, one while in prison, and the third heads an Indian family clinging to its middle-class status despite poverty. There are poignant passages about the man's father, the hospital wards, the funerals (with prayers by a Parsi priest), the pall-bearers (who are treated as untouchables), and his grieving (salt tears merge with the saltwater of the ocean). It captures the atmosphere in the 1980s when India fought Pakistan over Kashmir. During air raids, two people could hide under the same desk if they were the same sex. The president of Pakistan was described as a crazed syphilitic. Richard Nixon was drawn with rat's eyes and Henry Kissinger as a constipated ox.

Mistry's latest novel *Family Matters*★ (2002) is a hymn to the affection that dignifies a Bombay family. Although the wife is already overworked, and they have no money to spare, and their flat is already too tiny, they care for the wife's father who is dying of Parkinson's disease. Mistry's style rarely catches fire, but he knows how to awaken sympathy and that you are not quite sure how he does it is a measure of his skill.

The glimpses of India are disturbing. When a boy and girl fall in love across caste lines, the village court sentences them to be mutilated and then hung. The boy's father weeps for mercy. He suggests unsuccessfully that his son lose only his ears and nose but be left alive. He is offered the privilege of mutilating the girl, which he refuses. The girl's father is happy to do the job. In a government hospital rats eat a patient's toes and a newborn baby. A peon is lucky enough to rent a room for twelve hours a day, rather than merely eight.

MODERN AUTHORS RANKED

When I began this book I was pessimistic. I felt too many books were being spoiled by the fashions of the day: magic realism; endless streams of consciousness; tedious essays about time, life, art, and love; and a contest to write the world's longest sentence. Magic realism is supposed to have the virtue of abolishing space and time. But when an author literally collapses time—puts an airplane in eighteenth-century century Portugal, for example—much of the charm is gone. I believe great literature can transcend its time without using tricks. Great writers have always used stream of consciousness and interjected essays into their novels, but you have to be very good to be up to the task. Dostoevsky put his views on ethics and religion into the mouths of characters in *The Brothers Karamazov* and Victor Hugo interrupted *Les Misérables* with essays on the battle of Waterloo and monasticism. But these were great essays, not prolonged meditations about time.

You cannot manufacture something interesting to say when you have nothing interesting to say, yet today's novelist is virtually coerced into saying profound things in every chapter. Most are not up to it. Indeed, most novelists at any time would not be up to it.

Novelists who are good dramatists or humorists, or have eyes for capturing a place or time, far outnumber those who are also good philosophers or sociologists or psychologists. After wonderful portrayals of the rural gentry of the day, Gogol ruins the second half of *Dead Souls* with his essays on the reform of Russian agriculture. As Nietzsche said, he proved himself a great stylist but child-brained. Using events to do the talking is often far more powerful than talking. The huge horse that Émile Zola describes in *Germinal,* trapped in the mine from infancy to death, is a far more telling image than an essay on the grievances of the working class.

London Fields by Martin Amis is about as compelling a novel as anyone can write if they think their musings on the modern world are far more interesting than character and plot. The best example of an author spoiling a novel with thoughts is Kevin Powers in *The Yellow Birds.* The moving portrayal of the lot of those who had to fight in Iraq was enough. It need not have been punctuated with passage after passage on whether the protagonist's life or anyone's life or any possible person's life made sense any more. Powers thanks his editors. I suspect they convinced him he had to do this stuff to be a real writer.

Contrast this with the wonderful understatement of Sebastian Faulks in the first part of *A Possible Life.* The post-traumatic stress of a soldier who had to do worse things than any soldier in history is not conveyed by endless streams of consciousness. It is conveyed, with consummate art, by his quixotic search for the loved woman who was tortured into betraying him, and by the total collapse triggered when he cannot locate her. The best art usually occurs when awareness of the artist disappears, and not when someone shouts, "Me, me, me." The current fashion dictates personalizing the novel. Many writers would do well to reveal themselves less and let their dramatic abilities speak for themselves.

Nonetheless, despite all the temptations to spoil novels, the supply of books of high quality has been respectable over the last fifty years. Perhaps this is because far more people are writing them (as distinct from reading them).

I am going to rank according to merit the contemporary authors I have featured, plus a few who wrote a bit earlier, or wrote much earlier and have been translated into English only recently. Since there are only eleven writers at the very top, and only nine of them are novelists, you may wonder why I think today's authors equal the number of great names from 1900 to 1965 whom most of you could list. This is because my judgment is tenuous.

Setting aside historians, there are another nineteen novelists who write very well but of whom I have read only a few books and want to read more before passing judgment. There are another eighteen who are accomplished enough that I would not be surprised if history acclaimed them. There are thirteen novelists who have made a promising start and may eventually compile a list of admired works. Finally, there are of course contemporary novelists I have not read and some of them are bound to be good.

The lists within these categories are alphabetical. Use the index to find the book assessments that support my ranking of an author.

THE VERY BEST

John Banville, Sebastian Barry, William Dalrymple (travel), E.L. Doctorow, Elena Ferrante, Kazuo Ishiguro, Erik Larson (history), Sándor Márai, V.S. Naipaul, Edna O'Brien, and Philip Roth.

Whatever Ishiguro writes from now on, I think his five starred novels render him secure and, as the reader knows, I think his style sublime. However, John Banville, Sebastian Barry, and Sándor Márai rival him for top place, and Erik Larson is a historian blessed with a narrative style I have never seen excelled. Some of the others are such that it seems impertinent to put them below anyone, although Naipaul, in my opinion, ranks a bit higher as a travel writer than as a novelist.

THOSE I WANT TO READ MORE OF

Jalal Al-e-Ahmad, Haim Be'er, John Boyne, Anthony Burgess, Peter Carey, John Charles Chasteen (history), Robert O. Collins and James M. Burns (history), Joan Druett (history), Amos Elon (history), Romain Gary, Alan Hollinghurst, Omar Jalal, Robert Lacey (history), James Lasdun, Mario Vargas Llosa, Federico García Lorca, Hilary Mantel, Larry McMurtry, Qais Akbar Omar, Michael Ondaatje, Charlotte Randall, Donna Tartt, Paul Scott, and Tim Winton.

Every one of these novelists has enough talent for me to want to read more. A few, such as Donna Tartt, are still in mid career and must prove themselves in future books.

In the wings

Julian Barnes, Ian McEwan, Sebastian Faulks, Maurice Gee, Rebecca Goldstein, Sādegh Hedāyat, Patricia Highsmith, Howard Jacobson, Tahar Ben Jelloun, Cormac McCarthy, Naguib Mahfouz, Yukio Mishima, Rohinton Mistry, Toni Morrison, Jane Smiley, Robert Stone, Muriel Spark, and Colm Tóibín.

Thus far at least (and some have finished their careers), I do not see sufficient signs of consistent quality in these authors, despite their having written one, two or even three starred novels. But most are eligible for promotion and I am open to persuasion.

There are also those authors who wrote only one novel (Jamil Ahmad, aged seventy-eight), two (Truman Capote) or three (Roald Dahl) and their quality is very high. It will be interesting to see if these novels become revered as stand-alone classics. After all, Gustave Flaubert wrote only two really great novels, *Madame Bovary* and *Sentimental Education.*

Promising

Eleanor Catton, Junot Díaz, Jonathan Franzen, Ayaan Hirsi Ali (autobiography), Ben Fountain, Sebastian Junger (history), Hannah Kent, Herman Koch, Rian Malan (autobiography), Diego Marani, Hisham Matar, Edna Mazya, Candice Millard (history), Ann Patchett, Tom Rachman, J.K. Rowling, and Hanya Yanagihara.

These authors are beginners or in mid career, and have published either a first book or a few early books that are good enough for us to anticipate the possibility of a distinguished career.

NOT QUITE GOOD ENOUGH

Peter Ackroyd, Martin Amis, A.S. Byatt, Italo Calvino, J.M. Coetzee, Douglas Coupland, Don DeLillo, Umberto Eco, Shūsaku Endō, Ildefonso Falcones, Gillian Flynn, Janet Frame, Julia Franck, Patrick Gale, John Grisham, David Grossman, Russell Hoban, Khaled Hosseini, Arnaldur Indriðason, J.M.G. Le Clézio, Doris Lessing, Jonathan Lethem, Andreï Makine, David Malouf, Gabriel García Márquez, Colum McCann, John McGahern, David Mitchell, Azar Nafisi, Jo Nesbo, Amos Oz, Iraj Pezeshkzad, Chuck Palahniuk, Orhan Pamuk, Marilynne Robinson, José Saramago, Lionel Shriver, Antonio Tabucchi, Barbara Vine, David Foster Wallace, Patrick White, and Carlos Ruiz Zafón.

This is a long list, but I have included it to alert you to novelists sometimes called great but whose output is not always well written. When you look them up in the text I may recommend a few books but warn against reading everything they have published. Some, such as Peter Ackroyd, Martin Amis, A.S. Byatt, and Italo Calvino, made a good start but spoiled their work later on, after unstinting praise led to self-indulgence.

UNPROMISING

Sayed Kashua, Ron Leshem, Betty Mahmoody, Marina

Nemat, Kevin Powers, Nahid Rachlin, Lee Rourke, and A.B. Yehoshua.

These are writers whose first or early novels were acclaimed as promising when they in fact promised little.

AWFUL

Karl Ove Knausgård, Stieg Larsson, and Javier Sierra.

THE BEST BOOKS

Two Stars

Jamil Ahmad	*The Wandering Falcon*
John Banville	*The Untouchable*
	The Newton Letter
Sebastian Barry	*A Long Long Way*
Truman Capote	*In Cold Blood*
E.L. Doctorow	*Ragtime*
Sebastian Faulks	*Birdsong*
Romain Gary	*The Roots of Heaven*
Graham Greene	*The Power and the Glory*
Kazuo Ishiguro	*A Pale View of Hills*
	The Remains of the Day
	When We Were Orphans
James Joyce	*Dubliners*
Erik Larson	*The Devil in the White City*
James Lasdun	*The Horned Man*
D.H. Lawrence	*Sons and Lovers*
Sándor Márai	*Portraits of a Marriage*
Gabriel García Márquez	*In Evil Hour*
Hisham Matar	*Anatomy of a Disappearance*
Edna Mazya	*Love Burns*
Larry McMurtry	*Lonesome Dove*
Yukio Mishima	*Spring Snow*
Rohinton Mistry	*A Fine Balance*

V.S. Naipaul	*The Middle Passage*
	India: A Wounded Civilization
Philip Roth	*American Pastoral*
Marion Starkey	*The Devil in Massachusetts*
Donna Tartt	*The Secret History*
Thornton Wilder	*The Bridge of San Luis Rey*

ONE STAR

Peter Ackroyd	*The Clerkenwell Tales*
	The Lambs of London
	The Fall of Troy
Martin Amis	*Koba the Dread: Laughter and the Twenty Million*
	London Fields
	The Practice and Theory of Bolshevism
John Banville	*The Sea*
	Doctor Copernicus
	Kepler
	Christine Falls
	The Silver Swan
	Vengeance
Julian Barnes	*The Sense of an Ending*
	Flaubert's Parrot
	Arthur and George
Sebastian Barry	*On Canaan's Side*
	The Secret Scripture
	The Whereabouts of Eneas McNulty

Haim Be'er	*The Pure Element of Time*
Tahar Ben Jelloun	*This Blinding Absence of Light*
	Leaving Tangier
John Boyne	*A History of Loneliness*
	Next of Kin
Anthony Burgess	*Time for a Tiger*
	The Enemy in the Blanket
	Beds in the East
	Earthly Powers
A.S. Byatt	*Possession*
Italo Calvino	*The Path to the Spiders' Nests*
Truman Capote	*Breakfast at Tiffany's*
Peter Carey	*Oscar and Lucinda*
	True History of the Kelly Gang
John Charles Chasteen	*Born in Blood and Fire: A Concise History of Latin America*
J.M. Coetzee	*Disgrace*
Robert O. Collins and James M. Burns	*A History of Sub-Saharan Africa*
Douglas Coupland	*All Families are Psychotic*
Roald Dahl	*Boy: Tales of Childhood*
	Going Solo
	My Year
William Dalrymple	*City of Djinns*
	From the Holy Mountain: A Journey Among the Christians of the Middle East
Junot Díaz	*The Brief Wondrous Life of Oscar Wao*

E.L. Doctorow	*Welcome to Hard Times*
	Book of Daniel
	World's Fair
	Billy Bathgate
	Homer and Langley
Joan Druett	*Island of the Lost*
Umberto Eco	*The Name of the Rose*
Amos Elon	*The Pity of It All: A History of the Jews in Germany, 1743–1933*
Shūsaku Endō	*The Sea and Poison*
Sebastian Faulks	*The Fatal Englishman*
	Engleby
	A Week in December
	A Possible Life
Elena Ferrante	*The Days of Abandonment*
	My Brilliant Friend
	The Story of a New Name
	Those Who Leave and Those Who Stay
	The Story of the Lost Child
Gillian Flynn	*Gone Girl*
Ben Fountain	*Billy Lynn's Long Halftime Walk*
Julia Franck	*The Blindness of the Heart*
Jonathan Franzen	*The Corrections*
	Freedom
Maurice Gee	*Plumb*
	Going West
	Live Bodies
Rebecca Goldstein	*The Mind-Body Problem*
	The Proof and Paradox of Kurt Gödel

David Grossman	*The Yellow Wind*
Dashiell Hammett	*The Maltese Falcon*
Sādegh Hedāyat	*The Blind Owl*
Ayaan Hirsi Ali	*Infidel: My Life*
Patricia Highsmith	*The Talented Mr. Ripley*
Alan Hollinghurst	*The Line of Beauty*
Khaled Hosseini	*A Thousand Splendid Suns*
Kazuo Ishiguro	*An Artist of the Floating World*
	Never Let Me Go
Howard Jacobson	*The Finkler Question*
	The Mighty Walzer
Sebastian Junger	*The Perfect Storm*
Sayed Kashua	*Let It Be Morning*
Thomas Kenneally	*Schindler's Ark* (also *Schindler's List*)
Hannah Kent	*Burial Rites*
Herman Koch	*The Dinner*
Robert Lacey	*Inside the Kingdom*
Erik Larson	*In the Garden of Beasts*
	Thunderstruck
D.H. Lawrence	*Lady Chatterley's Lover*
J.M.G. Le Clézio	*Wandering Star*
Doris Lessing	*The Grass is Singing*
	Retreat to Innocence
Jonathan Lethem	*You Don't Love Me Yet*
Federico García Lorca	*The House of Bernarda Alba*
Naguib Mahfouz	*Palace Walk*
	Palace of Desire
	Sugar Street
Rian Malan	*My Traitor's Heart*

David Malouf	*Remembering Babylon*
Hilary Mantel	*Bring Up the Bodies*
Sándor Márai	*Embers*
	Rebels
Gabriel García Márquez	*Love in the Time of Cholera*
Hisham Matar	*In the Country of Men*
Cormac McCarthy	*All the Pretty Horses*
Ian McEwan	*On Chesil Beach*
	Saturday
John McGahern	*The Barracks*
Larry McMurtry	*The Last Picture Show*
Candice Millard	*Destiny of the Republic*
Yukio Mishima	*Confessions of a Mask*
	The Sailor Who Fell from Grace with the Sea
	Runaway Horses
Rohinton Mistry	*Such a Long Journey*
	Family Matters
David Mitchell	*Black Swan Green*
Toni Morrison	*Beloved*
	Sula
	Song of Solomon
	Home
Azar Nafisi	*Reading Lolita in Tehran*
V.S. Naipaul	*The Suffrage of Elvira*
	The Return of Eva Perón, with *The Killings in Trinidad*
	A Bend in the River
	In a Free State

	The Masque of Africa: Glimpses of African Belief
	India: A Million Mutinies Now
	Among the Believers: An Islamic Journey
V.S. Naipaul (cont'd)	*Beyond Belief: Islamic Excursions Among the Converted Peoples*
Edna O'Brien	*House of Splendid Isolation*
	Down by the River
	Wild Decembers
Michael Ondaatje	*In the Skin of a Lion*
	The Cat's Table
Amos Oz	*A Tale of Love and Darkness*
Chuck Palahniuk	*Fight Club*
Orhan Pamuk	*Snow*
Ann Patchett	*Bel Canto*
Kevin Powers	*The Yellow Birds*
Tom Rachman	*The Imperfectionists*
Charlotte Randall	*Dead Sea Fruit*
	The Curative
	The Crocus Hour
Marilynne Robinson	*Gilead*
Joseph Roth	*The Radetzky March*
Philip Roth	*The Anatomy Lesson*
	Operation Shylock: A Confession
	I Married a Communist
	The Plot Against America
	Exit Ghost
	Nemesis

J.K. Rowling	*The Casual Vacancy*
Paul Scott	*Staying On*
Lionel Shriver	*We Need to Talk About Kevin*
Jane Smiley	*A Thousand Acres*
C.P. Snow	*The New Men*
Muriel Spark	*The Prime of Miss Jean Brodie*
	The Mandelbaum Gate
	Loitering with Intent
Robert Stone	*A Hall of Mirrors*
	Dog Soldiers
	A Flag for Sunrise
Antonio Tabucchi	*Pereira Maintains*
Donna Tartt	*The Little Friend*
Colm Tóibín	*Nora Webster*
	Brooklyn
	The Story of the Night
Mario Vargas Llosa	*Aunt Julia and the Scriptwriter*
	The War at the End of the World
	The Feast of the Goat
Barbara Vine	*The Chimney Sweeper's Boy*
	A Dark-Adapted Eye
Tim Winton	*Cloudstreet*
Tom Wolfe	*I Am Charlotte Simmons*
Carlos Ruiz Zafón	*The Prince of Mist*

INDEX OF AUTHORS

Authors are listed alphabetically by surname and books in order of first publication. The editions of books given are usually the most recent US editions in paperback, or in hardback if there is no paperback edition. Many books have been published over the years in a variety of editions, and by different publishers in different territories. The dates in parentheses indicate when the work was first published. Where the book originally appeared first in a language other than English, the date of first translation into English is also given.

The Torchlight List
Around the World in 200 Books
Jim Flynn

One of the best books of the year
— The Sunday Star-Times

A professor for over forty years, Jim Flynn found fewer and fewer of his students had the time or inclination to read for pleasure. However, they were willing to try books he recommended. He was inspired to create this list: books so wonderful to read, and so revealing about times and places, they take the reader beyond day-to-day concerns into a magic realm of knowledge and imagination.

There have been many books about reading. No other has set out such a brilliant road map for discovering history, science, civilization and the human condition. From Arthur Koestler on the universe to Barbara Tuchman on life in the fourteenth century, F. Scott Fitzgerald on American morality, Chimamanda Ngozi Adichie on civil war in Nigeria, and Robert Fisk on Western power plays in the Middle East, this book will inspire you to reread books you love and discover and relish many new ones.

An ambitious yet intimate celebration of the power of literature
— Finlay Macdonald

Flynn's descriptions are like tantalizing movie trailers—short bursts of images that teleport your mind from one side of the Earth to the other
— Psychology Today

AWA PRESS

ISBN 978-0-9582916-9-9
Available from all good bookstores
and online at awapress.com